Simon Green

success

CW00792646

Upper Intermediate
Students' Book

4

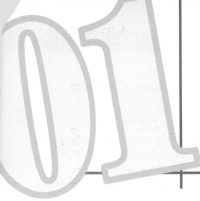

A fresh start

Read, listen and talk about new experiences.
Practise present and past tenses, articles; collocations, phrasal verbs and expressions with *start*.
Focus on reading more efficiently; making formal phone calls.
Write a CV.

GRAMMAR AND LISTENING

1 Look at the photos. How different are the two people? In pairs, talk about them using the adjectives in the box.

appearance: sporty, cute, untidy, slim, plain, sloppy, well-groomed
clothes: professional, casual, smart, trendy, scruffy, unfashionable, elegant
personality: good-natured, serious, ambitious, fun-loving, self-conscious, reserved, outgoing

2 Read about Colin and complete the texts with possible time expressions. Then answer the questions.

1 How has he changed? Give specific examples.
2 Why do you think he decided to make these changes?

ExtremeMakeover
STYLE SECRETS

BEFORE

AFTER

BEFORE

¹_____ May, Colin was studying business administration at college. He was outgoing with a laid-back attitude to life – and a motorbike and clothes to match. He ²_____ dressed casually, with a black leather biker's jacket being the number one item in his wardrobe. He hadn't been to the hairdresser's ³_____ two years, and because of his hectic social life in the house he shared with college friends, he'd stopped playing football and wasn't feeling very fit.

AFTER – SIX MONTHS LATER

Colin's worked for a large company ⁴_____ three months and has changed dramatically both in terms of his appearance and personality. He's bought some smart clothes and is sporting a new hairstyle to go with his new professional look. He doesn't go out very ⁵_____ but he's been working out a lot ⁶_____ he graduated, and the effects are already beginning to show. He ⁷_____ shares a flat with a friend but is thinking of buying his own. He sold his motorbike two months ⁸_____ and bought a small car – but he still loves his biker's jacket.

Work it out

3 Find an example for each meaning of these tenses in the texts about Colin. Which two meanings are there no examples of?

> **Present Simple**
> **1** routines and habits
> **2** permanent situations or facts
> **3** states
>
> **Present Continuous**
> **1** actions in progress now
> **2** temporary actions around now
> **3** change and development
>
> **Past Simple**
> actions completed at a specific time in the past
>
> **Past Continuous**
> **1** actions in progress in the past
> **2** actions in progress when something else happened
>
> **Present Perfect Simple**
> **1** actions and states that began in the past and continue up to now
> **2** actions completed at an unspecified time in the past
>
> **Present Perfect Continuous**
> actions in progress over a period of time up to now
>
> **Past Perfect**
> the earlier of two past actions

4 Look at these sentences. In which can the Present Perfect Continuous replace the Present Perfect? Why?

1 Colin <u>has</u> always <u>wanted</u> to work in business.
2 Colin <u>has worked</u> for a large company for three months.
3 Colin <u>has been</u> with the company for three months.

➤ **Check it out** page 151

5 Match sentences a and b to the sentences above them. Explain your decisions.

1 I <u>was getting up</u> when I heard a crash. ☐
2 I <u>got up</u> when I heard a crash. ☐
  a The noise woke me up.
  b I'd just turned the alarm clock off.

3 We <u>lived</u> in London for five years. ☐
4 We<u>'ve lived</u> in London for five years. ☐
  a But then we left and came to live here.
  b But we're thinking of moving now.

5 She<u>'s seen</u> him twice recently. ☐
6 She<u>'s been seeing</u> him a lot recently. ☐
  a Their relationship is getting serious.
  b Once in a club, and the second time in a shop.

7 The concert <u>started</u> when we arrived. ☐
8 The concert <u>had started</u> when we arrived. ☐
  a So we didn't miss anything.
  b So we missed the first part.

6 Complete the text with the best forms of the verbs in brackets.

It's been the worst day of my life. Everything went wrong from the start. First I woke up late because I [1]_____ (set) my alarm clock for 7p.m. instead of 7a.m. When I ran out of the house, it [2]_____ (rain) hard and I [3]_____ (not have) an umbrella. I finally arrived at the office, very wet and thirty minutes late. My boss [4]_____ (stand) by my desk. 'What [5]_____ (do), Smith? Swimming?' he said. I apologised and sat down. Things went from bad to worse. First I [6]_____ (break) the photocopier and then came back late from lunch because I got lost. 'We [7]_____ (not do) very well, are we, Smith?' said my boss. Then I crashed the office computer system. That was it. My boss [8]_____ (appear) and said: 'You [9]_____ (not make) a very good start, Smith. I [10]_____ (not think) this is the right place for you.' That was the end of my first day in my first job. Back to the Job Centre tomorrow.

7 CD1.2 Listen to two conversations about Colin and answer the questions.

1 Who are the people and what's their relationship to Colin?
2 Who is/isn't impressed by Colin's appearance? Why?
3 Why do they think he has changed?
4 Whose opinion do you agree with more? Why?

8 CD1.3 Listen to a conversation between Colin and his friends, Jack and Dave. Correct five facts in the summary and complete the last sentence.

After Dave had called him, Colin met his two old friends and explained why he'd changed his look. He'd been for a job interview the week before, and later, had heard the three interviewers talking about him in a café. One of the women was criticising his hairstyle. But that wasn't what made him change his appearance. It was because …

9 In groups, discuss the questions.

• Do you think Colin did the right thing? Why?
• What other reasons are there for having a makeover?
• Would you ever change your image? Why?/Why not?
• If so, what would you change?

Life Changing Days

If you want to have a thrilling adventure, explore a new direction or learn new skills with the help of the experts, why not try one of our Life Changing Days?
Go to lifechangingdays.com for more information.

Face Your Fears

A _____ The best way to get over your 'creepy crawly' phobia is to face it! Come to Sandstone Wildlife Park where our experienced trainers can provide the support you need. You don't have to do anything you don't want to, but when you're ready, the keepers help you handle harmless snakes and other friendly reptiles. And if you want a real sense of achievement, you can even hold a tarantula!

There's No Business Like Show Business

B _____ If so, come and learn all about the music business from our expert, Tony Bellamy, who has worked with EMI, MTV and dozens of top musicians. You learn all about the business, from making a demo CD to developing an image and signing a contract. He also gives advice about performing live, music publishing, PR and marketing. And if you already have a demo CD, bring it with you and get his professional opinion.

The 007 Experience

C _____ Our highly-trained ex-MI5 instructors will teach you all the essential 'spying' skills. After a brief introduction to the course, you learn how to fire automatic pistols and rifles. You then try your hand at unarmed combat and escape techniques. After lunch, we show you how to hide surveillance cameras and use listening devices. Finally, you take part in a shoot-out with the other double agents, using high-tech laser guns!

Change Your Image

D _____ Come for a consultation with us, and we promise to give you a fantastic new image. Ladies, are you an Aphrodite or an Athena? Gentlemen, are you a Hercules or an Apollo? Get key advice about clothes that flatter your shape and colours that suit you. We also analyse your face and tell you what hairstyles and accessories to use. We guarantee to give you more confidence – and save you money on future shopping trips, too!

The Chopper Experience

E _____ If so, take our helicopter flight and get hands-on experience of the only flying machine that goes backwards and sideways, as well as forwards! Your pilot is a CAA qualified instructor and the flight counts towards a helicopter pilot's licence. During the flight, you wear headphones so you can talk to your pilot and hear his conversations with air traffic control. Finally you take the controls yourself – but don't worry, your instructor does the take-off and landing!

READING AND LISTENING

1 Which words in the box describe you most closely? In pairs, explain why.

> risk taker   smart dresser   loner   free spirit
> outdoor person   home lover   chatterbox
> daredevil   thrill seeker   partygoer   wimp

2 Look at the layout, headings and photos in the text and answer the questions.

> **1** What kind of text is it, eg an article, an advert, a brochure? Why?
> **2** What do you think it will be about?

3 The sentences below begin each paragraph of the text. In pairs, guess what the paragraphs will be about.

> **1** Have you ever dreamt of winning *Pop Idol* or writing a Top Ten hit?
> **2** Would you like to fly like a bird?
> **3** Do you scream when you see a spider or faint if you see a snake?
> **4** Why not go on a mission and learn what it takes to be a secret agent?
> **5** Do you want to find a new look that's just right for you?

4 Match two of the phrases in the box to each topic sentence in Exercise 3. What more can you say about each paragraph now?

> air traffic control   flatter your shape
> demo CD   phobia   hands-on experience
> creepy crawly   unarmed combat   accessories
> performing live   surveillance cameras

5 **CD ROM** Read the text and complete it with topic sentences from Exercise 3. How much did you guess about each paragraph?

6 Find acronyms 1–3 in the text. What do they stand for? Use the context and match them to a–c. Then check on page 146.

> **1** EMI ☐   **a** a government intelligence agency
> **2** CAA ☐   **b** an aviation association
> **3** MI5 ☐   **c** a recording company

7 Read Train Your Brain and decide how each point helps you to read more efficiently. Match the points to Exercises 2–6.

TRAIN YOUR BRAIN | Reading skills

Reading more efficiently

a Use the layout, headings, etc to identify the text type and predict the content. ☐

b Read the topic sentences and try to predict the main ideas. ☐

c Use the context to cope with cultural references such as acronyms. Guess the general area they refer to, eg the type of company, etc. ☐

PROFILE

Ginny is 21 and _____.
She organises conferences for multinationals like IBM. She's self-assured, sociable and a risk taker. After she left school, she did voluntary work with a UN organisation and then travelled around Africa, doing as many new and exciting things as possible. She now has 'itchy feet' and has started looking for a new challenge.

PROFILE

Hugo's 20 and _____.
Unfortunately he got the sack because he paid more attention to the music than the customers. He's been thinking of going travelling but is very undecided about where to. He likes the outdoor life as long as he doesn't have to sleep under canvas, though nobody knows why. On the whole, he prefers to play his guitar and write songs.

8 Read the profiles. Use the advice in Train Your Brain and follow the instructions in points 1 and 2.

> **1** Finish the topic sentences with your ideas and read them to the class. Decide whose sentence is the best and why.
> **2** Look at the acronyms in blue and guess what they refer to.

9 **CD1.4** Ginny and Hugo each did a *Life Changing Day*. Use their profiles in Exercise 8 and discuss which ones they did. Think about the points below. Then listen and check.

> • their strengths, weaknesses, skills, qualities, problems
> • the courses they would enjoy and/or learn from

10 **CD1.4** Listen again. Are the statements true (T), false (F) or is there no information (NI)?

> **1** Ginny paid for the experience herself. ☐
> **2** It was exactly how she'd imagined it. ☐
> **3** She was very good at handling the controls. ☐
> **4** Hugo went to live in Africa when he was five. ☐
> **5** He clearly remembers how he was traumatised. ☐
> **6** He didn't overcome his fear immediately. ☐

11 In groups, discuss these questions.

> • Which *Life Changing Day* would you like to do? Why?
> • Think of four people you know well. Which experience would you recommend to each friend? Why?

GRAMMAR

1 Look at the title of the quiz and the photos.
In pairs, discuss the questions.

- What do you know about the events shown?
- When and where do you think they happened?

2 **CD1.5** Listen to three people talking about their family
history. Complete the table.

	Patricia	David	James
1 family originally from	Ireland		
2 emigrated to		The USA	
3 date of emigration			
4 reason			
5 life now			

Work it out

3 Look at the <u>underlined</u> phrases in sentences a–g and
answer questions 1–4.

a But we still observe <u>Polish customs</u> at home.
b <u>Life</u> was very hard and over one million
  people left Ireland then.
c More than half of the population live in
  <u>the capital</u>, Buenos Aires.
d Mum was working in <u>a local restaurant</u>.
e <u>The restaurant</u> belonged to her family.
f I am <u>a descendant</u> of an Irish family.
g My grandmother is still <u>the head</u> of the family.

Which article (*a/an*, *the* or zero article – ø) do we use
1 when something is one of many?
2 when we mention something for the first time?
3 in general statements with
  a plural countable nouns?
  b uncountable nouns?
4 when we know which thing or person
  it is because
  a it is mentioned for the second time?
  b it is unique?
  c it refers to something specific?

4 Decide which sentence in each pair is a general
statement and which refers to something specific
and complete them with *the* or ø.

1 a ___ <u>life</u> of an immigrant is often very hard.
  b ___ <u>life</u> in the 21st century is changing fast.
2 a ___ <u>children</u> grow up faster nowadays.
  b ___ <u>children</u> in my street are very noisy.
3 a ___ <u>love</u> makes the world go round.
  b He never lost ___ <u>love</u> he had for his country.

5 **CD1.6** Complete the quiz with *a/an*, *the* or ø and choose
the correct answers. Then listen and check.

the great emigration quiz

Pilgrim Fathers

British emigrate to Australia

**Millions of people throughout history
have migrated from one country or
continent to another and created the
world we know today. How much do
you know about them?**

1 Over forty percent of ___ population of Argentina
are ___ descendants of ___ immigrants from
which country?
a Italy   b Spain   c Portugal

2 British people who emigrated to Australia in the
1950s are called ___ £10 poms. Pom stands
for Prisoner of Her Majesty because the original
eighteenth century immigrants had been
a servants of the Queen.
b transported convicts.
c sent by the Queen.

The Gold Rush

Oktoberfest celebrations in Brazil

3 The Gold Rush in 1849 attracted 100,000 immigrants to ___ state of

a Florida.   b Texas.   c California.

4 The largest Japanese population in ___ world outside Japan lives in which city?

a San Francisco   b São Paulo   c Paris

5 In August 1620, the Pilgrim Fathers sailed from Plymouth, England to ___ coast of North America, where they founded ___ town of

a Boston.   b Plymouth.   c New York.

6 In the eighteenth century, ___ thief who stole ___ bread or ___ apple in England could be transported for life to which country?

a Australia   b Africa   c India

7 In the last few years, ___ immigration to Britain has averaged how many people a year?

a 35,000   b 158,000   c 250,000

8 The second largest Oktoberfest worldwide takes place in Blumenau, ___ small city in the south of Brazil. ___ city was founded by immigrants from which country?

a Hungary   b Greece   c Germany

Work it out

6 Find an example in the quiz for each category in the list below. Which categories use *a/an*, which *the* and which zero article – ø?

1 most place names (cities, countries, continents)
2 superlatives
3 ordinal numbers
4 months, years
5 decades, centuries
6 phrases to show number with month/day/year

➤ **Check it out** page 151

7 Complete the text with *a*, *the* or *ø*.

The first Europeans to settle in [1]___ Australia were [2]___ prisoners from Britain. In [3]___ 1788, the ships of [4]___ First Fleet took around 1,000 convicts to Botany Bay. Twenty percent of them were [5]___ women. More than 162,000 prisoners were transported over the next eighty years. Life in [6]___ new colony was extremely hard for [7]___ convicts but they were not usually put in prison. Instead, they built towns and worked on [8]___ farms to feed [9]___ new nation.
A hundred years later, in [10]___ 1950s and 60s, Britons once again emigrated to Australia, but this time as free men and women. There was a shortage of labour so [11]___ Australian government offered [12]___ migration papers, temporary housing and [13]___ sea passage for the price of £10 [14]___ ticket. Around one million people accepted [15]___ offer, and became '£10 poms'.

Mind the trap!

We don't use an article with nouns like *prison*, *hospital*, *school* when we talk about their **purpose** as an institution.

They were sent **to prison.** (purpose)

He works **in the prison** on the hill. (building)

8 Complete the sentences with *the* or *ø*.

1 They had beautiful flowers in ___ church for their wedding.
2 He's been in ___ hospital for nearly a week.
3 Can I meet you in front of ___ school at four?
4 I went to ___ church every Sunday when I was a child.
5 After I left ___ school, I got a job.
6 She works in ___ hospital near her house.

9 In groups, discuss these questions.

• Why do people give up everything to start a new life in another country?
eg to get rich, for adventure
• Would you like to emigrate one day? If so, where to? Why?

VOCABULARY AND SPEAKING

1 In pairs, finish the sentence in the cartoon. Read your sentence to the class.

"DID HE JUST SAY 'YAHOO'? MAYBE HE CAN START ..."

2 Cross out five nouns that don't collocate with the verb *start*. Which verbs do you use them with?

a computer   a career   an argument
a rumour   a business   a noise   university
a journey   classes   a course   a radio
a fire   a race   a fight   a bicycle   a band
school   a hairdryer   a fashion   work

3 **CD1.7** Listen and complete the sentences using a phrase from Exercise 2 in the Present Perfect.

Rachel has started university.

1 Rachel   4 Tina
2 Jack   5 Mandy
3 They   6 Roger

4 What do the <u>underlined</u> phrasal verbs have in common?

1 We <u>set off</u> early for the airport as we wanted to miss the rush hour.
2 She always <u>bursts into</u> tears at the end of romantic movies.
3 They need to <u>take up</u> some kind of sport to get more exercise.
4 He's <u>set up</u> an online company and is doing very well.
5 I <u>burst out</u> laughing when I saw his new haircut. He looked awful!
6 Once the plane had <u>taken off</u>, she began to relax.

Mind the trap!

Verbs *burst out* and *burst into* mean the same but are followed by different forms.

She **burst into** tears/song/laughter.

She **burst out** laugh**ing**/cry**ing**.

5 Complete the sentences with the correct forms of phrasal verbs from Exercise 4.

1 She _____ crying when she got her exam results.
2 I've been feeling much better since I _____ swimming.
3 They _____ before lunch so they should be there by now.
4 The plane _____ two hours late because of engine trouble.
5 When he started the chorus of his Number One hit, the audience _____ song.
6 They moved to the countryside and _____ home in a caravan!

6 Match the two parts of the sentences and <u>underline</u> the expressions with *start*.

1 I lost my project on the computer ☐
2 He lived in Paris when he was younger ☐
3 Jack and I started off on the wrong foot ☐
4 Let's make a start ☐
5 They emigrated to Canada ☐

a but we're quite good friends now.
b because they wanted to make a fresh start.
c so I had to start from scratch.
d because we've got a lot of work to do.
e so he had a head start in our French classes.

7 Finish the sentences using a suitable expression from Exercise 6.

1 Rob and Jane decided to stop arguing and …
2 He burnt the dinner he'd cooked and had to …
3 They left half an hour before us so they …
4 When I said that he looked like his brother, I knew I'd …
5 We have to finish this job by 5p.m. so why don't we …?

8 In groups, ask and answer the questions.

1 When did you last start an argument with someone?
2 Would you like to start your own business one day? What kind?
3 When did you last take up a new hobby or activity? Why?
4 Have you ever started off on the wrong foot with someone? How?
5 When did you last burst out laughing or crying? Why?

Learn to sail
Enquire here

Contact Bob on 01236 722566

SPEAKING AND LISTENING

1 What skills and qualities do you need to work on a yacht? Think of three more for each column.

skills	qualities
ability to obey orders	fit

2 **CD1.8** Listen and answer the questions.

1 Who are the people?
2 What are they talking about?
3 Is the conversation formal or informal? Why?
4 What skills and qualities are mentioned?
5 What does Ben need to prepare before the interview?

3 **CD1.8** Listen again and complete the *Informal* column with corresponding sentences from the conversation.

SPEAK OUT | Formal phone call

Formal	Informal
Starting a call 1 Hello, this is *Emma* speaking. 2 I wonder if I could speak to *Ben*, please. 3 I'm calling about *the job advertisement*.	_____ _____ _____
Asking for information 4 Would you mind telling me *what the job is*, please? 5 I'd like to know/Could you tell me *what it says*? 6 I was wondering *what qualifications I need*. 7 Would it be possible for you to *tell me what the salary is*, please? 8 Do you think you could *help me*?	_____ _____ _____ _____ _____
Ending a call 9 Thank you very much *for your help*. I really appreciate it. 10 Please call again if you need *any further information*.	_____ _____

4 **CD1.9** Complete the exchanges using Speak Out. Then listen to Ben's conversation and check.

1 A _____ speak to the recruitment manager, please.
  B I'm sorry, I'm afraid he's not in the office at the moment.

2 B But I'm his assistant. Can I help you?
  A I'm not sure. _____ the advertisement for the job on a yacht.

3 B What would you like to know?
  A _____ if you'd received my CV.

4 B First of all, _____ telling me your name, please?
  A No, of course not. It's Ben Harris.

5 B We've written to invite you to an interview on Friday.
  A I'm sorry, I have to work then. _____ to change it?

6 A One last thing. _____ could tell me what the salary is, please?
  B I'm afraid I don't know. Sorry.

7 A _____ help. _____
  B It's a pleasure. Goodbye, Benjamin.

5 Correct the two mistakes in each sentence. Use Speak Out to help you.

1 Could you telling me what time would it be convenient, please?
2 I wonder that you could tell me when does the job start.
3 I like to knowing how much it is.
4 Would you mind to contact me when do you know the interview dates?
5 It would be possible to giving me more information?
6 I was wonder what kind of promotion prospects are there.

6 Work in pairs and roleplay the conversations. Student A, look below. Student B, look at page 149.

Student A
1 You saw an ad for a job with a package holiday company. Phone and ask for the information below.
  • length of contract   • working hours
  • country/location   • interview date

2 You work for a department store and advertised for trainee managers. Answer Student B's questions using the prompts below.
  • interview: July 11th
  • start 3rd August
  • working hours: 9.30–5.30, five days a week
  • training period: six months
  • salary/holidays: £14,000 a year/four weeks

WRITING

1 Ryan is finishing a course in Sports Science and is looking for his first job. How should he do this? Put steps a–f into a logical order.

He should
a research the company and the job as fully as possible ☐
b attend an interview ☐
c find a job that he is qualified for ☐
d write a CV ☐
e look at job advertisements ☐
f send in his CV and a covering letter ☐

2 Match 1–7 with a–g to make phrases commonly used in job advertisements and CVs.

1 highly ☐
2 work flexible ☐
3 good communication ☐
4 a competent ☐
5 a proven ☐
6 practical ☐
7 a sound ☐

a user of
b motivated
c experience of
d hours
e knowledge of
f skills
g ability to

3 Read the job ad and <u>underline</u> key words or phrases that Ryan should consider when he applies for the job. Justify your choices.

HEALTH

Fitness Instructor

Are you highly motivated, fit and outgoing? Have you got a sound knowledge of the principles of exercise? Are you a good communicator who can work flexible hours? Then we want you to join our enthusiastic team.

Fitness For All is looking for an additional instructor with fitness-related qualifications. The work involves using computerised fitness equipment, so IT skills are desirable. The ability to motivate individuals, create personal exercise programmes and work unsupervised with customers is essential.

Does this sound like you? Then send your CV, including details of two referees to:

Serena Timms, Fitness For All, Lakeside Road, Banktown BT2 5MS

fitness for all
HEALTH CLUB

---

4 Cross out three items below which you don't need to include in a CV. Explain why.

- education and qualifications
- interests
- marital status
- employment history
- information about your health
- key skills and achievements
- a personal profile
- name and contact details
- date of birth
- names of referees and their contact details
- expected salary

5 Look at Ryan's CV and number the items from Exercise 4 in the order that they appear in the CV.

6 Put these pieces of information into the correct gaps (1–6) in the CV.

a National Diploma in Sports Science, completion date July 2007
b Established and coordinated college self-defence classes
c Part-time post, from 5 to 15 hours per week
d Worked in reception, dealing with money and answering phone enquiries
e Biology (A)
f Royal Society of Arts Exercise to Music Teachers' Award

7 In pairs, discuss these questions about Ryan's CV.

1 Why did he put the section on education and qualifications before the one on employment?
2 What effect do the following verbs have on Ryan's 'image'?
motivated, established, coordinated, trained, supervised
3 Why does he avoid using 'I', eg *Established and coordinated, Trained,* etc?
4 Are his interests relevant to the job?
5 Why has he chosen Mr Wells and Ms Sween as his referees?
6 How has he made his CV suit the job advertised? Circle key words and phrases that 'match' those you underlined in the advertisement.

Ryan Clarke

15 Moorlands Close,
Banktown, BT2 KLH.
Telephone: 01321 455622
Email: ryanc100@yahoo.co.uk
Date of birth: 21/08/1987

PERSONAL PROFILE:

Enthusiastic and outgoing college leaver with excellent communication skills, practical experience of teaching sport and fitness and a proven ability to work without supervision.

KEY SKILLS AND ACHIEVEMENTS:

- Motivated others to share my passion for sport and fitness
- Competent user of Microsoft Office
- Trained school netball team to reach finals of county championship
- 1_____

EDUCATION AND QUALIFICATIONS:

2005–2007   Banktown Community College
2_____

Subjects studied:
- Core Science
- Supervision and Management
- Diet and Nutrition
- Sports Psychology
- Practical Sports
- Safety and Sports Injuries
- Organisation and Administration
- Human Physiology

Qualifications gained:
- Computer Literacy Certificate Level 3
- 3_____

1998–2005   King George's School, Banktown
GCSEs with grades:
- Physical Education (A)
- 4_____
- Chemistry (B)
- Maths (C)
- English Language (B)
- English Literature (B)
- Art (B)
- French (D)

EMPLOYMENT:

2005 to present. Banktown Swimming Pool. Pool Attendant.
5_____

Supervised swimmers
6_____

Working towards National Swimming Association Swimming Teacher's Award

INTERESTS:

Circuit training, netball, cross-country running

REFEREES:

Mr J Wells
Manager
Banktown Baths
Queen Street
Banktown
BT1 KFJ

Ms L Sween
Course coordinator (Sports Science)
Banktown Community College
Market Street
Banktown
BT2 RLM

---

8 **Read** Train Your Brain. **Are the statements true (T) or false (F)?**

TRAIN YOUR BRAIN | Writing skills

Writing a CV

1 Include contact details, education, qualifications and employment history. ☐
2 Do not write about your personality. ☐
3 If you do not have much work experience, list your education and qualifications first. ☐
4 Make the CV sound personal by using 'I' as much as you can. ☐
5 Make yourself sound positive by using verbs like *motivate, train, establish, coordinate, supervise*. ☐
6 List all your interests, even if they are not relevant to the job. ☐
7 Use friends and family members as referees. ☐
8 Adapt your CV to suit the job that you apply for. ☐

9 **Practise writing a personal profile.**

1 How did Ryan combine these sentences for his personal profile?
I am a college leaver. I am enthusiastic and outgoing. I have excellent communication skills. I have practical experience of teaching sport and fitness. I can work without supervision.
2 Write personal profiles using the sentences in a and b. What jobs do you think the people are applying for?
a I am a school leaver. I am highly motivated and responsible. I have experience of working with young children. I have a working knowledge of Italian.
b I am a graduate. I am hard working and energetic. I have very good administrative skills. I can work under pressure.
3 Write your personal profile.

10 **Write your CV for the job advertised on page 146. Use** Train Your Brain **to help you.**

What do you mean?

Read, listen and talk about communication, how English is changing.
Practise forms to talk about the future; prefixes.
Focus on listening more efficiently; clarification in speaking.
Write a formal letter.

GRAMMAR AND LISTENING

1 In pairs, look at the photo. Where are Sam and Liz? What are they talking about?

2 **CD1.10** Listen to the conversation and complete the sentences.

1 Sam hasn't finished his assignment because …
2 Liz is having problems with her assignment because …
3 Liz wants to move out of the hall of residence because …
4 On Sunday afternoon Sam will probably …
5 Liz reminds Sam about …
6 Professor Evans wants Sam to …

3 **CD1.10** Circle the correct verb forms. Then listen again and check.

a I *'ll look / 'm going to look* at that flat for rent.
b My uncle and aunt *will come / are coming* to lunch on Sunday.
c You *are having / are going to have* a busy weekend.
d I *'ll ring / 'm ringing* you as soon as my aunt and uncle *leave / will leave*.
e Maybe we *'ll have / 're going to have* time to go and look at the flat then.
f The lecture *will start / starts* in ten minutes.
g I think I *'ll give / 'm giving* it a miss.

4 Think Back! **Match sentences a–g in Exercise 3 to meanings 1–7. What verb form do we use to show each of the meanings?**

1 prediction based on some evidence you have now ☐
2 prediction based on opinions or expectations ☐
3 plan or intention for the future ☐
4 future arrangements ☐
5 decision made at the moment of speaking ☐
6 future event which is part of a timetable ☐
7 in a subordinate clause after linkers like *when, as soon as, before, after*; the main clause contains a future form ☐

Work it out

5 **Look at these sentences from the conversation. Which use the Future Continuous and which the Future Perfect? Complete rules 1–3 with the correct tense.**

a By the time we're sixty, more people <u>will be speaking</u> Hinglish than 'standard' English.
b <u>Will</u> you <u>have finished</u> it by then?
c <u>Will</u> you still <u>be working</u> on it at 5.30?
d In 100 years' time half the world's languages <u>will have disappeared</u>.
e They'<u>ll be bringing</u> my little cousin.

1 We use the _____ for actions that will be completed before a specific time in the future.
2 We use the _____ for actions that will be in progress at a specific time in the future. The action will begin before and continue after that time.
3 We also use the _____ for actions that will happen as part of the normal course of events.

➤ **Check it out** pages 151–152

6 **Which pair of sentences has the same meaning? Explain the difference in meaning between the sentences in the other pairs.**

1 a This time tomorrow you'll be taking your driving test.
  b This time tomorrow you'll have taken your driving test.
2 a It's June 20ᵗʰ: by the end of the month we'll have finished our exams.
  b It's June 20ᵗʰ: in ten days' time we'll have finished our exams.
3 a When you get here I'll open my birthday presents.
  b When you get here I'll be opening my birthday presents.
4 a They'll buy the tickets on Saturday.
  b They'll have bought the tickets by Saturday.

7 **Complete the predictions with the Future Continuous or the Future Perfect of the verbs in brackets. Which prediction is the most/least likely, do you think? Why?**

By 2050

1 most language schools _____ (teach) Chinese rather than English.

2 American English _____ (become) more important globally than British English.

3 many English people _____ (forget) how to spell because of computer spell-checkers.

4 English students _____ (use) the language of text messages to write their essays.

5 a minority of English speakers _____ (speak) English as we know it today.

6 'isn't it?' _____ (replace) all other question tags.

8 **Match sentences a and b to the sentences above them. Then explain the use of the future forms in each pair of sentences.**

1 Can you come back at 6.00? ☐
2 Can you wait for five minutes? ☐
  a I'll finish this email, then we can go.
  b I'll have finished all my work by then.

3 Sorry, only staff are allowed in here. ☐
4 I've got to go in and see the doctor now. ☐
  a OK, I'll wait outside.
  b OK, I'll be waiting for you here when you come out.

5 Mum's going to phone at 7.00. ☐
6 Mum'll be phoning later. ☐
  a She always does on Sunday afternoon.
  b She wants to ask us about a birthday present for Jasmine.

7 Phil and Sandra are arriving at 7.30. ☐
8 It's 5.30 and Gabi's plane arrives at 6.00. ☐
  a Is everything ready?
  b You're going to be late.

9 Choose the correct answer. In one case all three choices are possible.

1 One day ___ married.
  a I'm getting   **b** I'll get   **c** I get

2 ___ Jane and Simon at Beluga Bar tomorrow. Do you want to come?
  a I'll meet   **b** I'll have met   **c** I'm meeting

3 Clarissa's failed all her exams! What ___?
  a is she going to do   **c** does she do
  b is she doing

4 This time tomorrow, we'll have handed in our assignments and ___ in the park.
  a we'll be relaxing   **c** we'll relax
  b we're relaxing

5 Dad says ___ smoking in two months' time.
  a he's going to give up   **c** he'll be giving up
  b he'll have given up

6 Goodbye! ___ about you every day until you come back.
  a I think   **c** I'll be thinking
  b I'll have thought

10 In groups, ask and answer questions about your future, using the prompts and the best future forms. What do all of you have in common?

1 Do/anything special/next weekend?
2 How many hours/spend studying/by the end of the week?
3 What/do/as soon as/finish/exams/this year?
4 What/do/this time next year?
5 get/married/by the time/you/twenty-five?
6 Where/live/in five years' time?
7 What/achieve/by the time/you/thirty?

11 In pairs, think about your country and make five predictions about one of these topics. Then share them with other students.

music   a famous person/family   fashion
the media   the environment   politics

LISTENING

1 You are going to listen to two conversations. Look at the photos, pictures and quotes and discuss the questions.

- What is the topic of the conversations, do you think?
- What different opinions might people have about this topic?

2 CD1.11 Listen to the first part of each conversation and answer the questions.

1 Where are the people and what are they doing? (What 'clues' can you hear in the background? What words do the speakers use that help you?)
2 What is the relationship between the speakers?

3 CD1.12 In which conversation do you think you will hear these opinions? Mark them 1, 2 or B (both) and justify your choice. Then listen and check.

1 Standards of English are falling in the UK. ☐
2 A lot of schools in the UK are not teaching grammar nowadays. ☐
3 It's more important to communicate your ideas than to spell and punctuate perfectly. ☐
4 English is alive. It's natural for it to change. ☐
5 It's more important for written English to be correct than spoken English. ☐
6 It's acceptable for writers to use 'incorrect' English in their books. ☐

4 CD1.12 What do you think 1–8 refer to? Listen again and choose from the list. Use the context to help you.

a place   a newspaper   a measurement
a book   an exam   a TV programme
a writer   a TV channel   a shop   an artist

1 the Guardian ___	5 Leith ___
2 IQ ___	6 Taggart ___
3 Boots ___	7 Richmal Crompton ___
4 'A' level ___	8 Just William ___

18

2

i dont care if
u cant spell I
still luv u

Options

Back

Is our language in decline?

3

JUST WILLIAM

White rat from China, ladies an' gentlemen, pink an' blue striped. All rats is pink and blue striped in China. This is the only genwin China rat in England – brought over from China special last week jus' for the show. It lives on China bread an' butter brought over special, too.

19

5 Complete Train Your Brain. Look back at Exercises 1–4 to help you.

TRAIN YOUR BRAIN | Listening skills

Listening more efficiently

1 Try to _____ the topic of the conversation by using any visual clues.
2 Use _____ noise and key _____ to help you work out where the _____ is taking place and what the _____ are doing.
3 Decide what the _____ between the speakers is.
4 Once you know what the context is, try to _____ what the speakers might say.
5 Use the _____ to help you guess what any cultural references mean.

6 CD1.13 Listen to another conversation and answer the questions.

1 Where are the speakers and what are they doing?
2 What is the relationship between them?
3 How do they feel about what they see on the website?
4 What do they decide to do?
5 What do you think these names refer to? (Listen again if necessary.)
  a the States   **d** Vicky Pollard
  b the West Country **e** Little Britain
  c Venue

7 In groups, discuss these questions.

• What do people in your country think about standards of grammar, punctuation and spelling?
• What do you think about the effect of email and text messaging on your language?
• Has your language changed a lot through the centuries? In what way?

"SO WHERE WAS YOU WHEN YOU MET HIM, THEN?"

"WELL, I WERE JUST STOOD AT THE BUS STOP, AND HE WERE STOOD BEHIND ME IN THE QUEUE."

4

READING

1 Work in pairs. Take turns to close your eyes while doing the task. Then answer the question below.

- Agree on a city you'd both like to visit. (Student A close your eyes.)
- Agree on a film you'd both like to see. (Student B close your eyes.)

Is it easier or harder to listen with your eyes closed? Why?

2 Some experts say that 93% of a first impression is based on nonverbal rather than verbal communication. What is included in *nonverbal communication*? Make a list.

3 Look at the photos in the article. What message does the body language give in each case?

4 **CD ROM** Read the article and match the photos to the paragraphs. Do you agree with everything the article says?

5 Are the statements true (T) or false (F), according to the article? Correct the false ones.

1 You need to keep eye contact for at least seventy percent of the time if you want to show interest in a person. ☐
2 You can look nervous if you are not breathing properly. ☐
3 Nodding your head shows authority. ☐
4 You should keep your arms out of sight in order to look confident. ☐
5 If you want to make a good impression, don't cross your arms or legs. ☐
6 When you shake hands, you shouldn't hold your palms up or down. ☐
7 It is better to stand too near someone than too far away. ☐
8 To communicate successfully, you should listen more than you talk. ☐

Actions speak louder than words

Do you realise that your body language is telling people a whole range of things that you may not be conscious of? In this introduction to her series on nonverbal communication, Rebecca Cripps gives us ten top tips for interpreting and using the unspoken code.

1 D **Eye contact** is one of the most important aspects of body language, especially with people we've just met: it shows respect and interest in what they have to say. In the UK people tend to keep eye contact around sixty to seventy percent of the time. Any more than this and you can be too intense, any less and you signal a lack of interest in the person or their conversation.

2 ☐ **Posture** is the next thing to master: get your posture right and you'll automatically start feeling better. Next time you notice you're feeling a bit depressed, take a look at how you're standing or sitting. Chances are you'll be slouched over with your shoulders hanging down and inwards. This flattens the chest and prevents good breathing, which in turn can make you feel and look nervous or uncomfortable.

3 A **Head position** is a great one to play around with. When you want to be authoritative and what you're saying to be taken seriously, keep your head straight both horizontally and vertically. Conversely, when you want to be friendly and in a receptive, listening mode, tilt your head just a little to one side or other.

4 ⬚ **Arms** give away clues as to how open and receptive we are to everyone we interact with, so keep your arms out to the side of your body or behind your back. This shows you are not scared to take on whatever comes your way. In general terms the more outgoing you are as a person, the more you tend to use big arm movements. The quieter you are, the less you move your arms away from your body. So try to strike a natural balance. When you want to come across in the best possible light, crossing the arms is a no no. Obviously if someone says something that really annoys you, then by all means show your disapproval by crossing them!

5 ⬚ **Legs** are the furthest limbs from the brain, consequently they're the hardest bits of our bodies to control consciously. They tend to move around a lot more than normal when we are nervous or being deceptive. So it's best to keep them as still as possible in most situations. Be careful too in the way you cross your legs. Do you cross at the knees, ankles or bring one leg up to rest on the knee of the other? Just be aware that the last position mentioned is known as the 'Figure Four' and is generally perceived as the most defensive leg cross.

6 ⬚ **Angle of the body** in relation to others gives an indication of our attitude towards them. We lean towards people we find attractive and interesting and away from those we don't, it's that simple!

7 ⬚ **Hand gestures** are so numerous it's hard to give a brief guide but here goes. Holding your palms slightly up and outwards is seen as open and friendly. Gestures with the palms down are generally seen as dominant and possibly aggressive. This palm up, palm down distinction is very important when it comes to shaking hands and we suggest you always offer a handshake upright and vertical, to convey equality.

8 ⬚ **Distance from others** is crucial if you want to give the right signals. Stand too close and you'll be seen as pushy. Stand too far away and you'll appear unfriendly. Neither are what we want, so observe in a group situation how close the other people are to each other. If you move closer to someone and they back away, you've probably overstepped the mark and are just a bit too much in their personal space.

9 *G* **Ears** play a vital role in communication with others, even though most people can't move them much, if at all. However, you've got two ears and only one mouth, so try to use them in that order. If you listen twice as much as you talk, you come across as a good communicator who knows how to strike up a balanced conversation without being 'me me me' or the wallflower.

10 ⬚ **Mouth movements** can give away all sorts of clues. We purse our lips and sometimes twist them to the side when we're thinking. We might also use this movement to hold back an angry comment. Then of course we smile: people smile for all sorts of reasons, only one of which is to signal happiness. But more of that next week.

6 Vocabulary Complete gaps 1–8 with adjectives and nouns from the text. Then complete the verb column.

verb	noun	adjective
_____	1 _____	respected respectful
____✗____	authority	2 _____
_____	3 _____	disapproving
_____	deception	4 _____
_____	defence	5 _____
_____	6 _____	indicative
_____	domination	7 _____
_____	push	8 _____

7 Vocabulary Complete the sentences with the correct words from Exercise 6.

1 We find it very difficult to talk to Andy: he always _____ the conversation.
2 It's true that Hayley *looks* innocent, but appearances can be _____ .
3 I have the greatest _____ for Tim, but I don't always agree with his ideas.
4 There's no need to be so _____ : I only asked when you'll be ready!
5 My grandmother always _____ of the clothes I wear.
6 Pat's reaction yesterday was _____ of his emotional state of mind.
7 You have to be quite _____ to work in the sales department.
8 I don't think Martin is confident enough to be in a position of _____ .

8 Vocabulary Use the phrases in the box to make collocations with phrasal verbs from the article. Then look at page 146 and follow the instructions.

a clue a conversation in a good light
responsibility a secret a comment
a friendship extra work a sneeze
as a good communicator

1 give away _____ _____
2 take on _____ _____
3 come across _____ _____
4 strike up _____ _____
5 hold back _____ _____

9 Find sentences 1 and 2 in the article and complete the gaps. What kind of pattern can you see? Then finish sentences 3–6 with your own ideas.

1 The _____ outgoing you are as a person, the _____ you tend to use big arm movements.
2 The _____ you are, the _____ you move your arms away from your body.
3 The older you get, …
4 The more you travel, …
5 The more chocolate and biscuits you eat, …
6 The richer people are, …

10 In groups, discuss these questions.

1 The article says, 'people smile for all sorts of reasons'. Why do people smile, apart from when they're happy? Think of three other reasons.
2 Look at the examples of nonverbal communication in the box. Which do you think are
 • conscious/unconscious?
 • the most/least important?
 • influenced by a person's culture?

hair (length, colour, style), clothes and accessories, voice, touch, facial expression, hand gestures (as shown in the photos)

3 How could an understanding of nonverbal communication be useful
 • at school or work?
 • with family and friends?

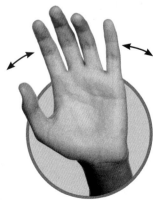

❶ 'The great enemy of clear language is insincerity.' George Orwell

❷ 'The kindest word in all the world is the unkind word, unsaid.' UNKNOWN

❸ 'Language is the most imperfect and expensive means yet discovered for communicating thought.' *William James*

❹ 'Silence is often misinterpreted but never misquoted.' Unknown

❺ 'Once a word has been allowed to escape, it cannot be recalled.' HORACE

❻ 'Foolishness always results when the tongue outraces the brain.' *Unknown*

VOCABULARY

1 The quotes above are about language and communication. In pairs, answer the questions.

- What do they mean?
- Which one do you like best? Why?

2 Look at the underlined prefixes in quotes 1–3.

1 What effect do the prefixes have on the meaning of the word?
2 Use them to make the opposites of these words:
__mature   __dependent   __healthy
3 What prefixes are used to make the opposites of these words?
__legal   __responsible   __honest

3 Look at the underlined prefixes in quotes 4–6.

1 Match the prefixes to their meanings:
again __   in the wrong way __
better/more __
2 What do the prefixes at the beginning of these words mean?
anti-government   underpaid
overcooked   nonverbal   ex-wife
3 Complete the words with the prefixes from point 2.
__sleep   __-President   __-social
__value   __alcoholic

4 Complete Train Your Brain with the examples from Exercises 2 and 3.

TRAIN YOUR BRAIN | Prefixes

Prefixes can form the opposite of the word. Give one more example for each.
1 *un*friendly, _____   **4** *in*efficient, _____
2 *im*possible, _____   **5** *ir*rational, _____
3 *il*logical, _____   **6** *dis*satisfied, _____

Prefixes can change the meaning of the word in other ways. Complete with examples or the meaning.

examples	meaning
1 *mis*understand, *mis*spell, *mis*hear	_____
2 *re*write, *re*take, *re*marry	_____
3 _____ , _____	too much
4 _____ , _____	too little
5 _____ , _____	without, not
6 *out*number, *out*play, *out*sell	_____
7 _____ , _____	former
8 _____ , _____	against

5 Rewrite these sentences using a word with a prefix so that the meaning stays the same.

1 Sorry, I think you didn't hear me correctly: I said *Vine Street*.
2 It's against the law to drive without a seatbelt.
3 I hate vegetables which have been cooked for too long.
4 I'll have to wait until autumn to take my exams again.
5 Who's that with the boy who used to be my boyfriend?
6 Could I have a drink that hasn't got any alcohol in it, please?
7 Manchester United deserved to win: they played much better than Liverpool.
8 This bar is open to people who are not residents.

6 Complete the gaps in these questions with a suitable prefix. Then, in pairs, ask and answer the questions. Which of your partner's answers surprised you? Tell the class.

1 Which do you find more difficult: __mature people or __friendly people?
2 Do you prefer to read fiction or __-fiction?
3 What __healthy food or drink do you find __possible to give up?
4 When was the last time you __slept?
5 Do you think it is __-social to smoke in public?
6 Do you think it's worse to be __worked or __paid?
7 What English words do you often __spell?
8 In your family, do the males __number the females, or vice versa?

SPEAKING AND LISTENING

1 [CD1.14] Marta is studying English at a school in London. Listen to three conversations and answer the questions.

1 Who is she talking to? Match the conversations 1–3 to the people.
  a an English friend ___
  b her landlady ___
  c her English teacher ___

2 In which conversation does she find out the meaning of:
  a toad-in-the-hole ___
  b to rattle someone's cage ___
  c a 'mock' ___

2 [CD1.14] Complete Speak Out with headings a–d. Then listen again and tick the phrases that you hear. Which are neutral? Which are more informal?

a Checking that you have understood
b Asking for clarification
c Checking that somebody understands
d Explaining what you mean

SPEAK OUT | Clarification

1 _____
I don't know what you mean by … ☐
Could you go over that again? ☐
Sorry, I'm not with you. ☐
Sorry, you've lost me there. ☐
I don't understand what you are getting at. ☐

2 _____
If I understand you correctly, … ☐
So are you saying … ? ☐
So in other words, … ☐

3 _____
What I meant was … ☐
Yes, that's exactly what I meant. ☐
No, that wasn't quite what I meant. ☐

4 _____
Are you with me? ☐
Do you see what I mean? ☐
Do you get what I'm saying? ☐

---

3 [CD1.15] Listen to some phrases from Speak Out and repeat them.

4 Complete these exchanges with suitable phrases. In some cases there is more than one possibility. Who are the speakers in each case?

1 **A** So in other words, you haven't done your homework.
  B No, _____ I haven't finished it yet.
2 **A** I just can't sleep for more than an hour or two and I'm so tired all day. I really need something to help me sleep.
  B _____ you want some sleeping tablets?
  A _____ .
3 **A** OK, first you need to close all the applications and shut down the computer, then you need to reinstall all the software.
  B _____ ?
  A Sure. First, close all the applications.
  _____ ?
  B Yes, OK I've got that. Then I …
4 **A** I really should go home now, or my name'll be mud.
  B _____ ?
  A Oh, I mean I'll be very unpopular – I'm late!

5 Work in pairs and roleplay the conversations. Student A, look below and at page 147. Student B, look at page 149.

Student A
Roleplay the situations with Student B. First, think about what you are going to say.

1 You want to buy two tickets for *Romeo and Juliet* next Friday. Phone Student B, who works at the theatre box office, and ask what tickets are available. Ask him/her for clarification when necessary.
2 You work in a video library. Answer Student B's questions, using the following information: When joining, people must provide some ID and proof of address. Members can borrow up to five DVDs at one time. Overdue DVDs will each incur a fine of 50p a day. Membership can be terminated at the discretion of the library staff.

"NO, SIR. THAT WASN'T QUITE WHAT I MEANT WHEN I SAID TAKE A SEAT."

WRITING

1 **Work in pairs. Then compare and discuss your lists.**

Student A, how often do you use these ways of communicating? Number them 1–8.
Student B, how easy are these ways of communicating to use? Number them 1–8.

- letters ☐
- emails ☐
- blogs ☐
- faxes ☐
- chat rooms ☐
- mobile phone calls ☐
- calls from a land line ☐
- text messages ☐

2 **Read the letter and answer the questions.**

1 What has Dominic Carter done?
2 Why does he need to contact Jeremy Barker?
3 Is the style of the letter formal or informal? Why?

3 **Some of the words and phrases in the letter are too informal. Replace them with the more formal equivalents from the box.**

was unobtainable   on a number of occasions
assume   was returned to me   discuss
provided us with   I regret   was incomplete
resolve this issue   obtained   contact
at your earliest convenience   I have no doubt
as soon as possible   deliver it
according to company policy

4 Think Back! **Write** *Do* **or** *Don't* **in front of these statements about formal letters.**

1 ____ use contractions.
2 ____ include the address of the person you are writing to.
3 ____ use abbreviations, eg *etc, asap, eg*.
4 ____ use *Yours sincerely* or *Yours faithfully*.

5 **Read the information and follow the instructions.**

An English person recently came to your school to give a talk (*what was the talk about?*). He/She left a personal possession (*what is it?*) at the school (*where exactly?*). You want to return the possession (*how will you return it?*) but you have had difficulty contacting the person (*how have you tried to contact him/her?*). You have a possible address for the person, but you're not sure if it's correct (*why?*).

Write a letter to the person.
- Thank them for coming to give the talk.
- Explain the situation.
- Ask them to contact you.

Quizzical

MG Publications
44 Gray Square
Manchester MC2
www.quizzical.co.uk
Tel: 0161 454545

Mr Dominic Carter
18 Springfield Road
Bristol BS4 2EQ

June 25th 2007

Dear Mr Carter

I am writing to congratulate you on winning the first prize in our 'Word Wizard' competition. My company says I need to confirm your address and arrange for the prize to be sent by registered post, or for a courier to drop it off. I have therefore tried to telephone you loads of times to talk about this, but the number you gave us on the entry form didn't work. I also sent an email to the hotmail address which I got from the entry form, but it bounced back, so I reckon the address had something missing.

I'm sure that you would like to sort this out asap, and I'm really sorry about the delay which has been caused. I would therefore be grateful if you could get in touch with me on the above telephone number as soon as you can.

Yours sincerely

Jeremy Barker

Jeremy Barker
Senior Administrator

VOCABULARY AND GRAMMAR

1 Match 1–5 with a–e and 1–7 with a–g to make compound nouns and collocations.

1 surveillance ☐ a skills
2 communication ☐ b language
3 thrill ☐ c experience
4 hands-on ☐ d seeker
5 body ☐ e camera

1 flatter ☐ a one's head
2 tilt ☐ b responsibility
3 give away ☐ c one's lips
4 hold back ☐ d a comment
5 start off ☐ e one's shape
6 purse ☐ f a clue
7 take on ☐ g on the wrong foot

2 Complete the sentences. Make new words from the words in capital letters.

1 This argument is completely
_____ . It makes no sense. LOGIC
2 Blogs are beginning to _____
newspapers nowadays. NUMBER
3 In many countries education is
not valued and teaching is one of
the most _____ jobs. PAY
4 You can _____ the exam as many
times as you like until you pass it. TAKE
5 Is _____ the norm in political
life, or am I just a pessimist? DECEIVE
6 If we don't voice our _____ ,
nothing will change. APPROVE
7 Jill's behaviour is an _____
of her feelings of frustration. INDICATE
8 I know children can be taught to
be _____ and cooperative
without the need for punishment. RESPECT

3 Complete the second sentence so that it has a similar meaning to the first sentence using the word given. You must use between two and five words including the word given.

1 The exam started before we arrived at school.
ALREADY
When we arrived at school _____ started.
2 The last time I saw her was fifteen years ago.
FOR
I _____ fifteen years.
3 When I left school, I decided to start a business.
UP
I _____ own business when I left school.
4 This work will be over by eight o'clock at the latest.
FINISHED
We _____ this work by eight o'clock.
5 I'll write to you the moment I arrive.
SOON
I'll write to you _____ arrive.
6 My plane to Rome leaves at 7p.m. and arrives at 8.30p.m.
BE
At 7.30p.m. _____ to Rome.

4 Decide where articles (*a*, *an* or *the*) have been omitted and add them in. The number of articles is given in brackets.

1 My flatmate Eduardo has two siblings: brother and sister. His brother is working in local library, and his sister is training to be accountant in capital, Madrid. (5)
2 George W. Bush is fifteenth president in history of USA to win second term. American president can hold office for two terms. (5)
3 Ozone layer (sitting about 15–30 kilometres above Earth) screens out sun's damaging ultraviolet radiation. (3)
4 We went to hospital to listen to lecture on cancer prevention and control. Talk by one of doctors, Ian Jones, was very informative. (4)

5 Complete the text with the correct forms of the verbs in brackets.

Almost everyone I spoke to [1]_____ (have) an amusing anecdote involving misinterpreted nonverbal communication. One of them [2]_____ (come) from Arsena Ianeva-Lockney – a native Bulgarian who [3]_____ (work) as a German teacher for quite a long time now. In fact, by the end of this year, she [4]_____ (be) in the teaching profession for ten years. Although she is a language teacher, Arsena [5]_____ (experience) numerous misunderstandings herself. During one of her first stays in Germany, she [6]_____ (share) a flat with a German girl. One day her roommate [7]_____ (offer) her some chocolate. 'Ja,' said Arsena, at which point the roommate promptly [8]_____ (remove) the chocolate from the table. Arsena later [9]_____ (realise) that she [10]_____ (use) body language which, she now [11]_____ (believe), may be unique to Bulgarians and Greeks. Arsena's roommate [12]_____ (respond) to the nonverbal cue instead of the verbal one.

Realising the importance of nonverbal communication, Arsena [13]_____ (decide) to address this issue. Currently, she [14]_____ (prepare) a series of workshops on the dangers of *not* learning the body language of another culture. She [15]_____ (hope) that she [16]_____ (draw) attention to this often ignored aspect of communication and that all language teachers [17]_____ (teach) body language in their courses. It is estimated that about thirty percent of German teachers from Sofia [18]_____ (attend) Arsena's training by July. Hopefully, this time next year most of them [19]_____ (implement) her ideas in their own classrooms.

PRONUNCIATION

1 CD1.16 Look at the sentence and listen to the sentence stress and intonation in polite requests. Then listen to four more formal requests and repeat them.

Could you tell me what the job involves, please?

LISTENING SKILLS

1   CD1.17 Peter (P), Carol (C), Beth (B) and Matt (M) were interviewed about *Pop Idol*. Listen and match them to questions 1–5.

   1 Who has changed his/her mind about appearing on *Pop Idol*? ☐
   2 Who is very critical of *Pop Idol* judges? ☐
   3 Who implies he/she would suffer from stage fright? ☐
   4 Who has mixed feelings about the programme? ☐
   5 Who points out a weakness of the programme but accepts it? ☐

READING SKILLS

1   Read the review. Are the statements true (T), false (F) or is there no information (NI)?

   1 The anecdote at the beginning shows how the improper use of a comma can change the meaning of a sentence. ☐
   2 The reviewer doesn't consider the occasional misuse of punctuation a serious problem. ☐
   3 Truss's book is likely to remain the bestselling title for more than two months. ☐
   4 One of the sources of the book author's knowledge about punctuation errors is her friendship with editors of well-known newspapers. ☐
   5 Most examples provided by Lynne Truss in her book concern the improper usage of the apostrophe. ☐
   6 The book is intended as a guide to correct punctuation for non-native speakers of English. ☐

SPEAKING SKILLS

1   What can you say in these situations? Use the words or phrases in brackets.

   1 You want to check that someone you're talking to understands you. (with)
   2 You call a travel agency for some information about holidays in Greece. (mind)
   3 You have no idea what your friend is talking about. (lost)
   4 You want somebody to send you some more information by email. (possible)
   5 Somebody used the word 'assertiveness'. You are not sure if you understand it. (mean)

2   Choose **one** of the topics and prepare a three-minute presentation.

   1 'They always say time changes things, but you actually have to change them yourself.' (*Andy Warhol*) Do you agree? Justify your opinion.
   2 Research suggests that nonverbal communication is more important in understanding human behaviour than words alone. Have you experienced communication problems in your own or a foreign language? What is the best way to overcome them?

A runaway No1 bestseller about ... punctuation? Believe it! And when you read this delightfully instructive gem, you'll see why!

Eats, Shoots & Leaves
The Zero Tolerance Approach to Punctuation
!
LYNNE TRUSS

Eats, Shoots & Leaves
by Lynne Truss

A panda walks into a café. He orders a sandwich, eats it, then draws a gun and fires two shots in the air. 'Why?' asks the confused waiter, as the panda makes towards the exit. The panda produces a badly punctuated wildlife manual and tosses it over his shoulder. 'I'm a panda,' he says, at the door. 'Look it up.' The waiter turns to the relevant entry and, sure enough, finds an explanation. 'Panda. Large black and white bear-like mammal, native to China. Eats, shoots and leaves*.'

Punctuation is an endangered species. We see signs every day advertising 'Banana's' or reading 'Video's sold here.' Competition rules remind us: 'The judges decision is final.' What could be the harm in sloppy usage from time to time? Well, consider how the absence of a single comma can turn a reasonable request ('No dogs, please') into prejudice against an entire species ('No dogs please'); or how a simple colon, combined with a comma, can upset the relationship between the genders: 'A woman without her man is nothing' becomes 'A woman: without her, man is nothing.'

To the rescue comes Lynne Truss, who uses her urbane, witty, and learned voice to advocate for the proper use of punctuation in *Eats, Shoots & Leaves: The Zero Tolerance Approach to Punctuation*. Truss has won the devotion of hundreds of thousands of readers, who have made her book the publishing story of the year: a No 1 bestseller not only in her native England, but in America too – where it has topped the *New York Times* list for eight straight weeks (and counting)!

Eats, Shoots & Leaves is a narrative history of punctuation from earlier days, when writers fought over the proper way to punctuate, to today, when sloppy emails and text messaging have become the norm. The book is full of bizarre true stories even copy editors haven't heard before: From the invention of the question mark in the time of Charlemagne, to George Orwell's avoidance of the semicolon, to *New Yorker* editors' having gentlemanly disagreements over the proper placement of a comma, to errors in punctuation in current film titles and on neighbourhood signs, Lynne Truss reveals them all. A few horrors that she has unearthed (involving the poor apostrophe alone) include:

● Lands' End (mail-order company that roundly denies anything is wrong with its name)
● Prudential – were here to help you
● Cyclist's Only (his only what?)

In Lynne Truss's words, 'If I did not believe that everyone is capable of understanding where an apostrophe goes, I would not be writing this book. There are already excellent punctuation guides on the market. The trouble with most of them is that they are read principally by keen foreigners.' This lively history of punctuation makes a powerful case for the preservation of a system of printing conventions that should not be ignored.

**shoots:* new parts that grow on an existing plant; *leaves:* plural of leaf

Bridging the gap

Read, listen and talk about issues that divide and bring people together.
Practise forms to talk about present and past habits; verb *'d prefer* and *'d rather*; antonyms.
Focus on agreeing and disagreeing with opinions.
Write a letter using linkers to organise ideas.

Family picnic.
July 18th

Joe and Molly

Sophie, Emily, Mark and Ben

Rachel and Pietro

A 'I didn't really like her last boyfriend – he was very unreliable and they were forever breaking up and getting back together again. Anyway, the new one seems much nicer, but sometimes it's difficult to tell because he doesn't speak much English. He tries his best, but then he'll get frustrated and break into Italian, and Molly and I get very confused!'

B 'Of course, now that she's a teenager, she's much more difficult to deal with. She used to spend time at home with the family – we'd watch TV and eat takeaway pizza together on a Saturday night. But now she wants to be independent, and she and Mark are always arguing about the clothes she wears and what time she gets home. For example, he tells her to be home by nine, but she'll turn up at ten and act as if nothing's wrong.'

C 'She's great fun and I adore her, but I think she's a bit out of touch. She's constantly telling Ben that he spends too much time on the computer and that at his age she was fit and healthy because she played outside all day. Then when she comes into my room for a chat, she'll start telling me how all teenagers today are irresponsible, and that in her day she used to go on peace marches and campaign to ban the bomb. I mean, I do care about world peace, but I think she forgets that I'm only thirteen.'

D 'It's not a problem at all now that we're older, but when I was seventeen she was only six, and I used to feel more like a father than an older brother. I often had to look after her when Mum and Dad went out, which really cramped my style! Also, she never understood the concept of 'privacy' – she was always going into my room and taking things without asking – I'd find books and CDs under her bed that she'd 'borrowed' from me.'

GRAMMAR AND VOCABULARY

1 The Williams were interviewed for a TV programme *British families today*. Read the extracts and look at the family tree. Who's talking in each case, and who are they talking about?

2 Read the extracts again and answer the questions.

Who's talking about
1 a generation gap? ☐☐
2 a language barrier? ☐
3 an age difference? ☐
4 a relationship that has changed? ☐☐

Work it out

3 The table contains various forms that can be used to express present and past habits. Complete it with examples from the texts.

habits in the present	habits in the past
Present Continuous 1 _____	Past Continuous 2 _____
will 3 _____	would 4 _____
	used to 5 _____

4 Match the sentences from Exercise 3 to the rules 1–3. Then find one more example for each rule in the texts.

1 past states and repeated past actions __
2 behaviour which is typical or characteristic of the person
  a in the present __   b in the past __
3 habits that are repeated more than usual and that the speaker finds annoying or unexpected
  a in the present __   b in the past __

5 Look at sentences a and b and complete rules 1–3 with *used to* or *would*.

a I <u>used to feel</u> more like a father than an older brother.
b She <u>used to spend</u> time with the family – we<u>'d watch</u> TV and eat takeaway pizza together on a Saturday night.

1 We can introduce a new topic with _____ and we do not need to specify the time.
2 We do NOT use _____ to describe a past state.
3 We use _____ when the topic has been established and we usually specify the time.

Mind the trap!

We can always use the Present and the Past Simple to talk about habits. We use the forms in the table to emphasise the repetitive or 'typical' nature of the activity.

He'll often get frustrated (He often gets …)
We'd watch TV and eat … (We watched TV …)
They are always arguing (They always argue)

➤ **Check it out** page 152

6 Cross out the verb forms which are NOT possible. In some cases both are possible.

When my sister was a teenager there [1]*'d be / used to be* a lock on our house phone to stop her making calls on it. Now she has her own phone and her bills must be enormous: she [2]*'s talking / 'll talk* on it for hours. She [3]*'d work / used to work* as a hotel receptionist, and she [4]*'d tell / used to tell* us funny stories about the hotel guests. Then one afternoon she [5]*used to come / came* home early because she had lost her job. Apparently, she [6]*was always chatting / she'd chat* on the phone instead of doing her work.

7 CD1.18 Does Rachel agree with her brother Mark's description of their relationship? Complete the gaps with suitable verbs. Then listen and check.

❝I've just read Mark's interview, and I can't believe what he said about his social life: I mean, all the girls used to [1]_____ sorry for him because he had to look after me, and they [2]_____ constantly _____ round to the house to help him! And as for taking his books and CDs without asking – well, he wouldn't [3]_____ them to me because he said I was too young to look after them, so I'd [4]_____ them and hide them under the bed. I used to [5]_____ the way he treated me like a child, especially in front of his friends. It's true that we get on better nowadays, but he's still as bossy as he used to [6]_____ , especially when it comes to boyfriends: he [7]_____ forever _____ me what to do! It's ironic, because one thing he doesn't mention is that he often [8]_____ me for advice about how to deal with Sophie. He'll [9]_____ me when Emily's out and tell me all about the latest argument.❞

8 Vocabulary Complete points 1–7 with verbs and phrases from the box to make habits. Then answer the questions.

> take drum leave talk fiddle with
> lose spend ages

1 _____ dirty dishes in the sink, the top off the toothpaste
2 _____ in the bathroom, on the phone
3 _____ to yourself, behind someone's back
4 _____ things without asking, people for granted
5 _____ things, your temper
6 _____ your hair, your jewellery
7 _____ your fingers on the table

- Do you have any of these habits?
- Which do you find annoying/rude/unpleasant/endearing?
- What other habits like this can you think of?

9 Look back at the habits in Exercise 8. Tell your partner about people you know who have or used to have any of them.

A My brother's really disgusting – he'll clean his teeth and leave the top off the toothpaste.
B Yes, I know, my sister used to do that too – I'm glad she's left home!

A My mum's always forgetting where she's put her glasses – I think it's quite endearing.
B Do you? That kind of thing annoys me.

10 Work in pairs. Student A, look at page 147. Student B, look at page 149.

11 In groups, discuss these questions.

- How have you changed in the last five years?
- How have your relationships with other members of your family changed?
- Think of a generation gap, an age difference or a language barrier in your family, or a family you know. What effect (positive or negative) does it have on the family?

A man's job? Not any more!

SPEAKING AND LISTENING

1 In pairs, look at the photos and captions. Discuss these questions.

- What aspects of modern life do the photos show?
- Do you agree with the captions? Why?/Why not?

2 CD1.19 Listen to two conversations and answer the questions.

1 Which topics from the photos do the speakers talk about?
2 What opinions do they have?
3 Do they agree with each other?
4 Who do you agree with and why?

3 Match 1–6 with a–f. Then put the sentences in the correct places in Speak Out.

1 You're absolutely ☐ a of that.
2 I have to admit ☐ b are you?
3 Neither ☐ c right!
4 You're not serious, ☐ d am I.
5 I'd never thought ☐ e agree with that.
6 I don't entirely ☐ f you've got a point there.

SPEAK OUT | Agreeing and disagreeing

Strong agreement

You're telling me! 1 _____ Spot on!/Exactly!/ Absolutely!	That's exactly what I think. So do I./Me too./ 2 _____

Mild agreement

3 _____ You *may/could* be right. Yes, I suppose so.	That's a valid point. True, 4 _____

Strong disagreement

Great? I think it's *ridiculous!* 5 _____ That's not the point!	*Come on/Frankly,* *that's rubbish!* So? What's wrong with that?

Mild disagreement

6 _____ I wouldn't say that. I'm not totally convinced.	I hear what you're saying but … To be honest, I don't think that's true.

Fashion conscious or fashion victim?

Over 50s – act your age!

4 CD1.20 **Use** Speak Out **to complete the conversations. Listen and check. Then practise them in pairs.**

1 A I can't stand that new boy in our class. He's such a wimp!
   B Yes, that's _____ I _____ !
     What a loser!
2 A I think TV soaps are a waste of time.
   B I _____ that. Millions of people are addicted to them!
3 A Tom and Jane are planning to get married. They're only eighteen!
   B So? _____ ?
4 A They should serve vegetarian food in the school canteen.
   B That's a good point. I _____ that.
5 A My dad's not very confident about this new government.
   B _____ I! They're hopeless.
6 A Don't you think they should abolish school uniforms?
   B _____ me! I hate them.

5 CD1.21 **Before you listen to a radio discussion, read the sentences and think what could complete the gaps. Then listen and complete them with one word in each gap.**

According to Janet, women could make better [_____1] and scientists than men.

Marian was [_____2] when a female plumber arrived to fix her [_____3] .

Alan agrees that men aren't very good at [_____4] up when they've finished a job.

Janet believes that women are [_____5] good at doing traditionally male jobs as men.

She says women get paid [_____6] for jobs like plumbing than when they work in a factory or a [_____7] .

6 CD1.21 **Who says what? Listen again and write J for Janet, M for Marian and A for Alan next to the sentences. Whose opinion do you agree with most? Why?**

1 Women should not be excluded from traditionally male jobs. ☐
2 Unlike most male plumbers, females charge reasonable prices. ☐
3 Not all women would enjoy doing traditionally male jobs. ☐
4 People need to get used to the idea of women doing traditionally male jobs. ☐
5 Women would have more freedom if they earned more money. ☐
6 Looking after the home and family is a big enough job. ☐

7 **Work in pairs and prepare your arguments for or against the statements below. Then discuss the statements with another pair using language from** Speak Out.

• Schools should encourage girls to study science and engineering more.
• Parents should not bring their children up to be stereotyped boys and girls.
• Historically, men were the hunters and women the homemakers. It should stay like that.

31

READING AND VOCABULARY

1   **In pairs, discuss these questions.**

   1 What kind of people do you find 'difficult' to
     deal with? Why?
   2 Why might the types of people in the box be
     difficult to deal with? What personality traits
     might they have? Use the pictures in the
     article to help you.

   Types: wet blanket, know-it-all, space cadet,
               loose cannon, bossy-boots, cry baby
   Traits: negative, knowledgeable, pushy,
              conceited, moody, critical,
              out of touch, infantile, unpredictable

2   **CD ROM Read the article and check your answers to
   Exercise 1.**

3   **Read again and choose the correct answer.**

   1 The know-it-all and the bossy-boots both
     a tell people what to do.
     b want to be in control.
     c use knowledge to manipulate others.
     d enjoy an argument.

   2 There are two different ways of dealing with
     a the loose cannon and the wet blanket.
     b the bossy-boots and the space cadet.
     c the cry baby and the wet blanket.
     d the know-it-all and the loose cannon.

   3 The bossy-boots and the cry baby
     a are very confident.
     b manipulate people in different ways.
     c always get their own way.
     d are easy to ignore.

   4 The loose cannon and the space cadet are
     difficult to deal with because
     a you are not sure what they are going to do
       next.
     b they both cause problems for other people.
     c people react very negatively to them.
     d they are both forgetful.

   5 The space cadet is different from the other
     types because
     a they are aware of other people's feelings.
     b they are unreliable.
     c they are unpredictable.
     d there is a positive side to their personality.

4   **Vocabulary Match 1–8 to a–h to make phrases from
   the article.**

1 get your ☐	**a** at face value
2 stand up ☐	**b** over someone
3 take something ☐	**c** own way
4 be on different ☐	**d** and rave
5 have something ☐	**e** to someone
6 rant ☐	**f** world of your own
7 be in a ☐	**g** wavelengths
8 walk all ☐	**h** down to a fine art

5   **Replace the <u>underlined</u> phrases with phrases from
   Exercise 4. Make necessary changes.**

   1 We can't work on this project together: we
     <u>have completely different ideas and opinions</u>.
   2 My sister's very spoilt: she always <u>does what
     she wants</u>.
   3 What was Sam <u>complaining angrily</u> about
     earlier? We could hear him in the next room!
   4 If you don't <u>refuse to accept unfair treatment
     from</u> Jon, he'll just get worse.
   5 Vicky <u>makes Tom do what she wants</u>, but he
     doesn't seem to mind.
   6 Don't <u>accept that</u> all the gossip <u>is exactly as it
     appears to be</u>.
   7 Haley<u>'s very skilled at</u> small talk.
   8 It's no use trying to talk to Lily: she <u>doesn't
     notice what's happening around her</u> at the
     moment.

6   **CD1.22 Listen to a conversation. Are the statements
   true (T) or false (F)?**

   1 A slob is someone who wants to look 'cool'. ☐
   2 Jill's flatmate is very good at doing nothing. ☐
   3 A bore is someone who talks too much
     about other people. ☐
   4 Lisa doesn't think her new flatmate
     is a bore. ☐
   5 Busybodies do not intend to hurt other
     people's feelings. ☐
   6 Gina's neighbour is probably bored. ☐

7   **Work in pairs. Write some advice for dealing with
   the three personality types from Exercise 6 (a slob,
   a bore and a busybody). Then exchange ideas with
   other pairs.**

dealing with
difficult people

> *I try to get along with John, but we seem to be on different wavelengths.*
>
> *The atmosphere always seems to be tense when Michelle's in the room.*

Sound familiar? Unfortunately, some people are more difficult to get on with than others. Let's have a look at six 'difficult' personality types, and offer some advice on how to deal with them.

THE KNOW-IT-ALL

The first on the list is 'the know-it-all'. Know-it-alls see themselves as experts on everything. They appear knowledgeable and will speak confidently about almost any subject, often making other people feel stupid ₁₀ or inferior. This personality type is conceited and competitive, and is likely to react to others' ideas or arguments angrily or dismissively.

First of all, don't take their ₁₅ behaviour personally: it affects most people that they come into contact with. Know-it-alls are driven by a need to control and they use their knowledge as a ₂₀ 'shield' to protect themselves from uncertainty. So in order to cope with this type, you need to get them to consider your ideas without directly questioning their ₂₅ expertise. This means that you need to be well-prepared and diplomatic.

THE CRY BABY

Next is 'the cry baby'. As the name ₃₀ suggests, the cry baby behaves like a child when they don't get their own way. They use moodiness ₃₅ to manipulate other people. They'll go away and sulk, giving you the 'silent' treatment, or they'll complain and even start to rant and rave about ₄₀ how nobody listens to them or takes them seriously, etc. This infantile and inappropriate behaviour can be very annoying.

You need to find out why the cry ₄₅ baby acts like they do. If they are selfishly looking for attention, your best policy is simply to ignore them. However, if their behaviour stems from a real lack ₅₀ of confidence, they need support and encouragement.

THE BOSSY-BOOTS

Next on the unwanted list is 'the bossy-boots'. This type of person is ₅₅ always telling other people what to do. They have a very strong personality and will walk all over you if you let them. They are ₆₀ so used to doing things their way that they have pushiness down to a fine art. A lot of the time you'll find yourself doing what they want, just for a quiet life. ₆₅

Don't try to beat a bossy-boots at their own game: there's no point in telling them what to do. Your first task is to learn to say 'No'. This will be difficult initially, ₇₀ but after you've said it once, it'll get much easier. The trick is to remain calm and polite: this way you'll be able to stand up to them without being drawn into a fight ₇₅ or an argument.

THE LOOSE CANNON

The next type we'll look at is 'the loose cannon'. Like a cannon which is not tied down and rolls around on the deck of ₈₀ a ship, this personality type is unpredictable and can cause problems.

A loose cannon tends to act ₈₅ impulsively without thinking about the consequences. Understandably, people feel anxious around them because they appear to be out of control and unapproachable. ₉₀

A loose cannon needs to be made aware that their behaviour is irresponsible, and of the effect their actions have on other people. You can do this, not by reacting ₉₅ negatively at the time of an incident, but by waiting until you are both calm later and quietly describing what happened.

THE WET BLANKET

Most people have come ₁₀₀ across the next type, 'the wet blanket', at some time in their lives. Wet blankets are negative and critical. They don't ₁₀₅ seem able to see the positive in any situation and always think that the worst will happen. Their attitude makes them appear insensitive and ₁₁₀ spoils things for other people.

You have two options with the wet blanket. You can try to show them the positive where they see the negative. Or you can take ₁₁₅ what they say at face value, so for example, when you invite them to a picnic at the weekend and they say it'll probably rain, you simply reply: 'OK, so you don't want to ₁₂₀ come, then?'

THE SPACE CADET

The last type is 'the space cadet'. This kind of person is intriguing because ₁₂₅ they seem to be in a world of their own and are out of touch with reality. They have difficulty paying attention or ₁₃₀ remembering things, and sometimes behave strangely, which can make other people feel uncertain.

This type can be frustrating, but ₁₃₅ they are not likely to provoke very negative reactions. Try instead to make the best of their uniqueness, and don't put them in a position where you need to rely on them ₁₄₀ for anything.

VOCABULARY

1 **Think Back!** Use a prefix to make these adjectives opposite. Then check in the text on page 33.

1 __certain   4 __sensitive
2 __appropriate   5 __approachable
3 __predictable   6 __responsible

2 **CD1.23** Find the opposites of the underlined adjectives in the box. Then listen, check and mark the stress on each adjective.

> knowledgeable superior tense reassuring mature dull conceited critical incompatible adventurous

1 Have a bath and you'll feel more underlined(relaxed).
2 Steve's a great musician but he's very modest about his abilities.
3 I'm really ignorant about politics. You'll have to ask someone else.
4 Tom's comment really made me feel inferior.
5 The teacher said some really complimentary things about our project.
6 The week before exams is a worrying time for everybody.
7 Harvey told us some intriguing stories about his visit to China.
8 Although their personalities are different, Phil and Amy are very well-matched.
9 I really can't forgive Sylvia for her infantile behaviour: she's nearly nineteen.
10 I'm quite cautious about trying new food in a restaurant.

"YOUR LOBSTER SURPRISE, MADAM."

3 Work in pairs. Student A, look below. Student B, look at page 149.

Student A
On a piece of paper, write down the name of:
• a famous couple who are incompatible,
• a politician who pretends to be knowledgeable,
• an actor who always takes predictable roles.
Close your book. Show the names to Student B and explain why you wrote them.

4 **CD1.24** Listen to the first line of each conversation and in 1–5 below circle the correct adjectives to make logical responses.

1 Did you? I thought some of the things he said were really *appropriate / inappropriate*.
2 Do you think so? I think he's quite *knowledgeable / ignorant*.
3 Have you? I find him really *approachable / unapproachable*.
4 Actually, I think he's quite *infantile / mature* for his age.
5 Huh! I think it's quite *predictable / unpredictable*: rain, rain and more rain!

5 Complete the gaps with a suitable opposite to show that the speakers agree. Then act out the conversations to the class.

A Jackie looked very tense today, didn't she?
B Well, she certainly didn't look ¹_____ .

A That programme about the future of mankind was quite worrying, I thought.
B Mm, it wasn't exactly ²_____ .

A Mr Palmer's critical of everything we do.
B I know, he's certainly not very ³_____ .

A Geri's always so cautious in her choice of clothes.
B That's true, she's not very ⁴_____ at all.

A I'm surprised Kim and Greg are still together – they're so incompatible.
B I know, they're not exactly ⁵_____ , are they?

A That new boy in our class is so conceited!
B I agree, he isn't what you'd call ⁶_____ , is he?

6 Act out similar conversations to those in Exercise 5, using pairs of opposites from Exercises 1 and 2.

34

GRAMMAR

A Yes, **I'd rather eat** a hundred cheese and tomato pizzas, too.

B **I'd rather we tried** something different this time.

So **you'd rather we didn't go** to my mother's for lunch then?

C

D **I'd rather not marry** you, Ted. My Feng Shui would be incompatible with your job.

1 Work in pairs. Look at the cartoons. Which do you think is the most amusing? Why?

2 Match these thoughts to the other character in each cartoon. Are they similar or different to each other?

1 She'd prefer to marry someone who's more like her.
2 I'd prefer not to eat leaves all the time.
3 I'd prefer us to go to a cricket match!
4 She'd prefer us not to have fish and chips again.

Work it out

3 Look at the <u>underlined</u> phrases in the cartoons and Exercise 2 and circle the correct answers in rules 1 and 2.

1 *'d* in *'d rather* and *'d prefer* replaces *had / would*.
2 *'d rather* and *'d prefer* have *the same / a different* meaning.

4 Look at sentences a–d and match them to questions 1 and 2.

a He'd prefer us to go to a cricket match.
b He'd prefer to go to a cricket match.
c He'd rather we went to a cricket match.
d He'd rather go to a cricket match.

Which two sentences say
1 what the subject wants to do? ☐☐
2 what the subject wants someone else to do? ☐☐

5 Complete the table with the correct forms of the verb *go*.

would prefer	would rather
+ She'd prefer [1]_____ .	+ She'd rather [5]_____ .
− She'd prefer [2]_____ .	− She'd rather [6]_____ .
+ She'd prefer us [3]_____ .	+ She'd rather we [7]____ .
− She'd prefer me [4]_____ .	− She'd rather I [8]_____ .

➤ **Check it out** page 152

6 Rewrite the sentences so that the meaning stays the same.

1 He'd prefer to watch sport on Sundays.
   He'd rather watch sport on Sundays.
2 I'd rather we didn't go shopping again.
3 I'd prefer you not to smoke in the house.
4 We'd rather not eat meat – we're vegetarians.
5 They'd prefer not to drive at night.
6 I'd rather we stayed at home tonight.

7 Write responses to the questions using different forms of *'d rather* or *'d prefer* each time. Then ask and answer the questions in pairs.

A *Shall we leave at seven?*
B *No, I'd rather we left at eight.*

1 Do you feel like having a pizza tonight?
2 Shall we watch that new DVD now?
3 How about going for a picnic tomorrow?
4 Do you think I should tell them the news?
5 Would you like to cook the dinner?
6 Do you mind if I listen to some music?

8 **CD1.25** Song Look at the song on page 146. Listen and complete the words. Then, in pairs, write one more verse that fits the theme.

WRITING

1 **Look at the photos and discuss the questions.**

- Which party is in power in your country? Is it left wing, right wing or centre?
- Do people in your country have strong feelings and opinions about politics?
- Does politics play in important role in your family? Can it be a source of arguments? In what way?

2 **Read 'Last week's question'. What's her problem? What advice could you give her?**

3 **Read Reply 1 and choose the summary a–c that best describes the writer's opinion.**

   a Conflict in relationships is not common and is easy to resolve.
   b 'Confused Opposite' should think seriously about continuing her relationship.
   c It is better to agree with everything your partner says.

Conservatives

The Conservative Party

The Labour Party

If you value it, vote for it.

A free and fair NHS or Tory charges for hospital operations. Vote **Labour**

A campaign worker

---

www1.q_and_a.com   search

bookmarks   teenstuff   news   entertainment

Your Questions, Your Answers

We received hundreds of letters in reply to last week's question, which raised the issue of relationships that are threatened by differences. In this week's *Your Questions, Your Answers*, read and decide for yourselves: Can relationships between opposites really work?

LAST WEEK'S QUESTION

My boyfriend of six months is a committed Conservative, and is really excited about the coming election. I was eighteen last year so this is the first time I can vote – and I want to vote Labour. But every time I mention it, he either laughs and says, 'You can't be serious!' or loses his temper and walks out. He actually put a *Vote Labour – if you dare!* sticker on his car yesterday! I'm so angry I feel like breaking up, but for some reason I'm still crazy about him. What do I do?
Confused Opposite

REPLY 1

Dear Confused Opposite,
First of all, I really sympathise with you – politics do seem to have this effect on people! At the same time, there's the saying 'opposit[e] attract'. But even though there are some good arguments for this, on the whole, it's more than most of us can deal with! While it can be exciting to be with someone who's completely different to us, it doesn't seem to last very long. The excitement soon turns to conflict. Moreover, the time comes in every relationship when peop[le] disagree on an important issue. Presumably, you're scared he'll break up with you if you don't agree with him. Unfortunately, there are no easy answers to this. I think the only way to deal with it is to face it. You just have to say what you think and let him do the sam[e]. Nevertheless, remember that you don't have to give anyone an explanation about who you vote for – we all have the right to choo[se]. Therefore, there are times when it's easier just not to discuss politi[cs]. Since this seems to be your problem, perhaps it's also your solutio[n]. However, if you decide to do this, you're also choosing to hide you[r] feelings and opinions. More importantly, you're not allowing yourse[lf] to be the real you. I think it's time to ask yourself, 'Is this really the kind of relationship I want to be in?'
A well-wisher

4 Study the highlighted linking words and phrases in Reply 1. Then write them in the correct category in Train Your Brain.

TRAIN YOUR BRAIN | Writing skills

Organising your ideas in a text

- **Order your points:** first/firstly/ ¹_____/to begin with, secondly, finally
- **Make a general point:** ²_____ , generally speaking, generally, in general
- **Add or emphasise a point:** ³_____ , furthermore, in addition, besides, in fact
- **Introduce a contrasting clause:** ⁴_____ , ⁵_____ , in spite of this
- **Join two contrasting clauses:** ⁶_____ , ⁷_____ , although, though, but
- **Introduce a result:** ⁸_____ , as a result, consequently, so
- **Give a reason:** ⁹_____ , as, because
- **Express your attitude/viewpoint:** ¹⁰_____ , ¹¹_____ , ¹²_____ , personally, apparently

5 Read Reply 2 and cross out any linking words or phrases that are not acceptable. Sometimes both choices are correct.

REPLY 2

Dear Confused Opposite,
¹ *To begin with / Firstly*, let me reassure you. Relationships between opposites are extremely common, even political opposites! ² *Personally / Apparently*, it's the diversity of difference that creates the attraction. ³ *In fact / Besides*, learning to deal with differences has helped break many taboos in recent years. Western societies are more multicultural and people travel more. ⁴ *Consequently / In spite of this*, attitudes have begun to change and become more tolerant.
⁵ *Nevertheless / Though*, it's also true that a relationship of opposites is never easy! ⁶ *Therefore / Furthermore*, you have to ask yourself if you and your Conservative have the ability to make yours work! ⁷ *Even though / Since* you're opposites, it can work if you have the ability to compromise. ⁸ *Finally / Presumably*, remember that part of what makes your 'significant other' attractive is that they have their own mind and opinions, ⁹ *so / in general* see this as a good thing and not a bad thing. Learning to deal with differences is what helps a relationship grow. Good luck!

Opinionated

6 Read the two replies again and discuss the questions in pairs.

1 Do the writers agree with each other? Explain why/why not.
2 What opinion does each of them have?
3 Do you agree with either of them? Why?/ Why not?

7 Join the ideas using the linking words in brackets. You may need two sentences for some answers.

1 I know that opposites have lots of problems/ they are much more fun (while)
   While I know that opposites have lots of problems, they are much more fun.
2 my parents vote for different parties/they never argue about politics (in spite of this)
3 I knew the Green Party wouldn't win/I voted for them (nevertheless)
4 you respect their values/it's difficult to disobey your parents (since)
5 you still have the right to choose/society is changing (although)
6 the older generation finds it hard to accept new ideas/it takes time for attitudes to change (generally speaking, so)
7 the Prime Minister wasn't very popular/none of his ministers supported him (as, presumably)

8 Read the letter from 'Mixed Up'. What's his problem?

I've been going out with my Brazilian girlfriend, Gloria, for six months but I'm afraid to tell my parents. They want me to go out with someone from my own country. I think they're scared I'll get married and live abroad, and they'll never see me again. What can I do?
Mixed Up

9 Write a reply to 'Mixed Up' advising him what to do. Use the ideas below and linking words from Train Your Brain.

- talk to your parents/show them you are serious about Gloria
- explain your feelings/ask them to try to accept her
- tell them you understand their opinion/want them to understand yours
- introduce Gloria to your parents/give them the chance to get to know her

Aren't we amazing?

Read, listen and talk about amazing people, geniuses and intelligence.
Practise narrative tenses with the Past Perfect Continuous, participle clauses; suffixes.
Focus on presentation skills: keeping your audience involved.
Write a memorable story.

GRAMMAR AND READING

1 Look at the photos, the title and the headings.
In pairs, predict what each text might be about.

2 Read the texts and check your predictions.
What is so special about these people?

3 Read the texts again. Are the statements true (T),
false (F) or is there no information (NI)?

1 Hilary Lister was the first disabled
woman to sail from England to France. ☐
2 She'd never done any sailing until two
years before the crossing. ☐
3 Lightning struck Roy Sullivan for the
third time in 1970. ☐
4 By 1973, he'd survived five lightning strikes. ☐
5 Mozart wrote his earliest symphonies
when he was four. ☐
6 Beethoven was twice the age of
Mozart when he died. ☐

4 **Think Back!** Write the names of the tenses and add
three more examples of each from the texts.

Tense	Examples
1 _____	sailed, set, _____ _____
2 _____	was driving, _____ _____
3 _____	had helped, _____ _____

5 Replace the verb with the two other tenses from
Exercise 4. How does the meaning change?

• When Mozart was six, he *composed* his
earliest symphonies.
• When Mozart was six, he _____ his earliest
symphonies.
• When Mozart was six, he _____ his earliest
symphonies.

Amazing People

I n this week's edition of *Amazing People*,
we have decided to include some less well-
known celebrities. They may not be world
famous or household names, but as we often
say, there's more than one way to be special!

Disabled sailor crosses Channel

On August 23rd 2005, a British woman who can
only move her head, eyes and mouth, sailed across
the English Channel and into the record books.
Completing her journey in just over six hours, Hilary
Lister set a record for the world's longest solo sail
by a disabled person. Using only her breathing to
navigate her boat, she reached Calais to a hero's
welcome. Having arrived in France, Mrs Lister said,
'I'm just thrilled', and attributed her success to
the people who'd helped her. When she made her
crossing, she'd been paralysed for four years. And
she'd been sailing for only two. Having lived an
active life before her illness, she took up sailing to
boost her confidence.

Lightning never strikes twice?

Roy Sullivan, a forest ranger from Virginia, was
struck by lightning seven times in his thirty-six-year
career. The first strike was in 1942. He wasn't hit
again until twenty-seven years later, driving his truck.
The following year, another bolt of lightning burnt his
shoulder, while his hair caught fire in a fourth strike
in 1972. A year later, Sullivan was driving around
the park when a bolt came out of a small cloud,
knocking off his shoe. 'I actually saw the lightning
coming straight for me,' he said. Lightning struck
for the sixth time in 1976. But it was the final strike
in 1977, while he was fishing, that put him in the
Guinness Book of World Records. Two of his Ranger
hats, burnt by lightning, are now in Guinness Exhibit
Halls – proof that lightning does strike in the same
place twice.

Child prodigy

Wolfgang Amadeus Mozart showed musical gifts at a very early age, and was already composing his first works when he was four. Born in Salzburg in 1756, he was one of the greatest musical geniuses in history. By the age of six, he'd played before the Austrian empress and had begun to write his earliest symphonies. A year later, he was playing to audiences in London and Paris, astonishing them with his brilliance. He worked all over Europe during the next seventeen years, finally settling in Vienna. He lived just a little over half of Beethoven's life span but was amazingly prolific. He died in 1791, aged only thirty-five, having composed over 600 works, including great operas like *The Magic Flute*. Just before his death, he'd been composing the *Requiem*, one of his most famous works.

Work it out

6 Look at sentences a and b and answer questions 1 and 2.

a Before his death, he'd been composing the *Requiem*. (Past Perfect Continuous)
b Before his death, he'd composed 600 works. (Past Perfect)

1 Which form shows a completed action?
2 Which form shows an action that was not completed?

7 Match sentences a and b to sentences 1 and 2. How does the form change the meaning in sentences 1 and 2?

1 When I got home, I saw that he'd been painting the kitchen. ☐
2 When I got home, I saw that he'd painted the kitchen. ☐

a It looked really fantastic and the colour was great.
b There were cans of paint and brushes all over the place.

➤ Check it out pages 152–153

8 Complete the sentences with the correct forms of the Past Perfect Continuous of the phrases from the box.

rain for a week   train for months
not work hard enough   not listen carefully
wait for an hour

1 He lost his job because he …
2 The town was flooded because it …
3 They were furious when she arrived because they …
4 I didn't understand what to do because I …
5 We won the match because we …

9 Complete the sentences with the verbs in brackets in the Past Perfect or the Past Perfect Continuous.

1 By the time he was twenty-five, he _____ (earn) his first million.
2 She _____ (live) in the town for ten years before she met him.
3 After they _____ (finish) dinner, they went out.
4 When I went to pay the bill, I realised that I _____ (leave) my wallet at home.
5 Just before the accident, he _____ (drive) at 150 mph.
6 At the time of the wedding, they _____ (go out) together for six years.
7 We _____ (play) football in the same club for ages before we became friends.
8 I _____ (already/give up) waiting when he phoned.

10 Complete each sentence with the Past Simple, the Past Continuous, the Past Perfect and the Past Perfect Continuous. Compare your sentences and discuss why you used each tense.

1 When I looked at my watch, I realised that …
2 Tom was upset because …

39

Work it out

11 What do the underlined participles mean? Circle the correct forms in italics. Then match them to the rules a and b.

1 Mozart worked all over Europe, finally <u>settling</u> in Vienna.
and finally settled / and had finally settled
2 He wasn't hit again until twenty-seven years later, <u>driving</u> his truck.
while he was driving / while he is driving
3 <u>Having arrived</u> in France, she said, 'I'm just thrilled!'
After she had arrived / Because she had arrived

Which participle do we use
a when two actions happen at the same time, or one after the other?
b to show the earlier of two actions?

12 Find other examples of participle clauses in the texts on pages 38–39.

> ### Mind the trap!
> The participle and main clause must have the SAME subject.
>
> Driving through the park, he was struck by a bolt of lightning.
> NOT ~~Driving through the park, a bolt of lightning struck him.~~

➤ **Check it out** page 153

13 Complete the sentences with the correct participle from the box.

having finished   turning off   having studied   playing
having been   driving

1 _____ to the dentist, he felt much better.
2 _____ the light, she left the room.
3 _____ for two weeks, they felt prepared for the exam.
4 I hurt my ankle _____ tennis.
5 _____ to work, we saw an accident.
6 _____ lunch, they decided to go out.

14 Rewrite the underlined parts using participle clauses. Do NOT change the meaning of the original.

1 <u>She walked into the room and</u> introduced herself.
2 <u>He'd forgotten to switch on his alarm clock so</u> he overslept.
3 Our team played very well <u>and scored five goals</u>.
4 <u>When we'd finished our homework</u>, we watched a DVD.

15 Complete the text with the correct forms of the verbs in brackets.

The Rainmaker
In December 1915, Lake Morena was nearly empty and everybody in San Diego ¹_____ (pray) for rain. In desperation, the city council ²_____ (contact) Charles Hatfield, the Rainmaker. Hatfield ³_____ (agree) to fill the lake for $10,000. On January 1 1916, he started work, ⁴_____ (use) his secret rain-making chemicals. By January 5, the rain ⁵_____ (start). By January 20, it ⁶_____ (rain) non-stop for two weeks. On January 26, the level of the lake ⁷_____ (rise) by two feet per hour when suddenly it ⁸_____ (stop) – just five inches from the top. ⁹_____ (kept) his promise, Hatfield ¹⁰_____ (want) his money. But the city council ¹¹_____ (refuse) to pay, ¹²_____ (say) that the rain was an 'act of God'. Hatfield ¹³_____ (only/make) a verbal agreement, and ¹⁴_____ (not sign) a contract. He never ¹⁵_____ (receive) a penny.

16 In groups, tell each other about an amazing person you know and what makes them amazing.

Virginia Woolf

Mahatma Gandhi

Sigmund Freud

Bob Marle

Albert Einstein

LISTENING AND VOCABULARY

1 Complete the word web with the words and phrases in the box. Use a dictionary to help you.

brainy   brainwave   brainwash
brainbox   be the brains behind   brainless
pick someone's brains   brain dead
use your brain   brainstorm

Verbs
1 _____
2 _____

Nouns
1 _____
2 _____

Adjectives
1 _____
2 _____
3 _____

Idioms
1 _____
2 _____
3 _____

2 Complete the sentences with the correct expressions from Exercise 1.

1 Let's get together and _____ ideas for our next project.
2 My brother's the _____ one, but I'm better-looking!
3 If you keep watching TV all the time, you'll end up being _____ .
4 Bob Geldof _____ Live Aid and Live8.
5 I've just had a _____ ! Let's go to Prague for the weekend!
6 Advertisements _____ us into buying things we don't need.
7 Dad, I can't do my homework. Can I _____?
8 You just went through a red light, Dan! That was a _____ thing to do.
9 Martin's the _____ of the class. He always gets top marks.
10 You had to _____ to do this exercise!

3 How would you describe a genius? Write your definition and compare ideas in small groups.

4 In pairs, look at the photos and answer the questions.

1 What do you know about these people?
2 What was extraordinary about them?
3 Which of them was a genius, do you think? Why?
4 Who would you consider to be a 'twenty-first-century genius'? Why?

5 CD1.26 Below there are four types of genius. In pairs, discuss who/what they might be like. Then listen to Part 1 of a radio programme and check.

the master   the maker   the introspector
the influencer

6 CD1.26 Listen to Part 1 again and choose the correct answer.

1 Dr Gardner thinks
   a academic work is the most important.
   b everybody has different strengths.
   c exams make people brain dead.
   d we are all intelligent in one way.

2 Mozart was a 'master' because he
   a was a genius.
   b created a new kind of music.
   c wasn't like Freud.
   d was brilliant at what he did.

3 Freud was a 'maker' because he
   a was a musician.
   b created many new things.
   c developed a completely new field.
   d was a psychoanalyst.

4 Virginia Woolf
   a wrote about introspective people.
   b was very self-conscious.
   c was like Mrs Dalloway.
   d worked on understanding people.

5 Gandhi
   a tried to influence Nelson Mandela.
   b wasn't interested in other people.
   c changed the way people thought.
   d didn't affect people in India.

7 CD1.27 Before you listen to Part 2 of the programme, decide if the statements are true (T) or false (F), and why. Then listen and check.

1 A genius is made by ambition, luck and the time they live in. ☐
2 When Einstein was born, physicists were confident about their subject. ☐
3 Einstein was able to think in terms of both space and music. ☐
4 In general, people usually want to learn from their problems. ☐
5 Extraordinary people spend a lot of time reflecting. ☐
6 It doesn't take them long to work out the answers to problems. ☐

8 Look back at Exercises 3 and 4. In groups, discuss the questions.

- How similar/different was your definition of a genius to Dr Gardner's?
- What can you add to your answers in Exercise 4, using the information from the radio programme?

Quiz

What are my multiple intelligences?

¹_____ intelligence
You relate to and understand other people – strong in salespeople, politicians and teachers.

²_____ intelligence
You use words and language – something lawyers, writers and comedians are good at.

³_____ intelligence
You appreciate and produce music – strong in singers, composers and musicians.

$\frac{x}{y} = 12$

⁴_____ intelligence
You use reason, logic and numbers – often found with doctors, accountants and scientists.

⁵_____ intelligence
You control body movements and handle objects skilfully – something found in athletes, dancers, actors and builders.

⁶_____ intelligence
You think in pictures – something artists, designers and architects are particularly good at.

Do our quiz and find out your strongest intelligence.

Put a tick (✔) next to any statements which are true for you. Then work out your score on page 146.

1 I have no trouble reading maps and navigating. ☐
2 People often seek me out to ask for advice. ☐
3 I remember things best by seeing them. ☐
4 I am often asked to explain the meaning of the words I use. ☐
5 There is a powerful link between music and my moods. ☐
6 I have a good sense of balance and coordination. ☐
7 I like to work with calculators and computers. ☐
8 I find it easy to say what I think in an argument or a debate. ☐
9 I work best in an organised work area. ☐
10 I understand how different colours work well together. ☐
11 I get restless if I have to sit still for long. ☐
12 I have a strong preference for group activities rather than ones I do alone. ☐
13 I often use gestures and other body language to express myself. ☐

14 I can often be heard humming, whistling or singing when I'm in the shower. ☐
15 I feel comfortable when dealing with words. ☐
16 I need to categorise and group things in order to see their relevance. ☐
17 I often see patterns and relationships between numbers faster than other people. ☐
18 A rhyme is an effective way of helping me remember something. ☐
19 Having a good social life is important to my happiness. ☐
20 I find it irritating when someone says something illogical. ☐
21 I often touch things because I am curious to know how they feel. ☐
22 I like to have background music when I'm working. ☐
23 I'm quite an artistic person. ☐
24 I enjoy taking the lead and being responsible for other people. ☐

VOCABULARY

1 Match the types of intelligence in the box to the definitions above the quiz.

linguistic bodily-kinaesthetic interpersonal
logical-mathematical musical visual-spatial

2 Which intelligences do you think are your strongest/ weakest and why?

3 Do the quiz. Then answer the questions and compare your answers with a partner.

- Were you right about your intelligences?
- Which intelligence would you like to develop more? Why?

4 Look at the <u>underlined</u> suffixes in the quiz and complete Train Your Brain. Which suffix is used to make nouns *and* adjectives?

TRAIN YOUR BRAIN | Suffixes

Suffixes to form nouns

verb +	-ment [1]	_____
	-ion [2]	_____
	-ing [3]	_____
	-ence/-ance [4]	_____ , [5] _____
adjective +	-ness [6]	_____
	-ity [7]	_____
noun +	-ship [8]	_____

Suffixes to form adjectives

noun +	-ful [9]	_____
	-less [10]	_____
	-al [11]	_____
	-ic [12]	_____
	-y [13]	_____
	-ive [14]	_____
	-able/-ible [15]	_____ , [16] _____
verb +	-ing [17]	_____
	-ed/-d [18]	_____
	-ent/-ant [19]	_____ , [20] _____

5 Complete the words with the correct suffixes. Which type of intelligence does each of these sentences refer to?

1 I enjoy the most thrill___ rides at the fun fair.
2 I like to take part in debates or discuss___ .
3 Music plays a signific___ role in my life.
4 I can multiply measure___ in my head easily.
5 I'd rather draw a diagram than give someone verb___ instruct___ .
6 I make frequent refer___ to things that I've heard or read.
7 I find music that is out of tune very annoy___ .
8 I am sensit___ to other peoples' feel___ .
9 I play at least one sport or do a physic___ activ___ regularly.
10 I have a good sense of direct___ .
11 I find new scientif___ develop___ interest___ .
12 I have several close person___ friends.

6 Complete the sentences with the correct forms of the words in capital letters.

1 Geri's very _____ of my dancing – I'm completely _____ !
                    TOLERATE, COORDINATE
2 I think _____ tests are absolutely _____ – I never agree with the answers!
                    PERSONAL, USE
3 I'm feeling very _____ and I'd like to join a gym, but the _____ fees are very expensive.   HEALTH, MEMBER
4 What is the secret of a really _____ _____ ?   SUCCESS, RELATION
5 My grandmother had an _____ _____ to read peoples' minds.   AMAZE, ABLE
6 I hope you've got a _____ _____ : this is the third time you've been late this week.
                    CONVINCE, EXPLAIN
7 Phil had some very _____ _____ for how to solve our space problems.
                    SENSE, SUGGEST
8 Please be _____ about my ideas. Your opinion is extremely _____ to me.
                    TRUTH, VALUE
9 I admire Alex's _____ , but I don't think she's _____ enough to be a designer yet.
                    CREATE, CONSIST
10 We went to a _____ _____ at the Opera House on Saturday.   WONDER, PERFORM

7 Finish the sentences to make them true for *you*. Then read them to your partner and respond to his/ her sentences.

1 I haven't got much patience with ...
2 I'm quite optimistic about ...
3 It's more important to be confident than ... because ...
4 I never feel very energetic ...
5 There are a lot of similarities between me and ...
6 I sometimes have arguments with ... about ...
7 I find ... very irritating because ...
8 I have a very good relationship with ... at the moment.

A I haven't got much patience with small children.
B Really? Why not?

FACTFILE

F!

Real name [1] _____ Sumner

Stage name and how he got it [2] _____

Born Newcastle, in [3] _____

Most famous song [4] _____

Royalties from this song [5]$_____ a week

Ex-member of [6] _____

Former profession [7] _____

Name of autobiography [8] _____

Started The Rainforest Foundation in [9] _____

In 2004, Queen Elizabeth made him a [10] _____

44

SPEAKING AND LISTENING

1 **CD1.28** Look at the photos and listen to the music. In pairs, discuss the questions.

- What's the name of the song? Who wrote it?
- What do you know about this person? What is he famous for?

2 **CD1.29** Listen to the presentation and complete the Factfile. The information in the Factfile is NOT in the same order as in the recording.

3 What language does the speaker use at each stage of the presentation? Match sentences a–f to the three stages.

1 Introduction ▢▢
2 The main content ▢▢
3 Conclusion ▢▢

a Let me just finish by saying …
b As for his background, …
c I'm sure the writer of this song needs no introduction.
d There's so much more I could tell you …
e The reason I've chosen him is …
f The most amazing thing about him is …

4 **CD1.29** Listen again and number the sentences in Speak Out in the order you hear them.

SPEAK OUT | Presentation skills

Keeping your audience involved

a Maybe you're wondering *why/what* … ▢
b What do we already know about …? ▢
c Why do you think *he's been so successful*? ▢
d And were you aware that …? ▢
e *Did/Do* you know …? ▢
f I hope you'll learn a few things about … ▢
g You *might/might not* know that … ▢
h What you probably *don't/didn't* know is that … ▢
i I'm sure you'll agree that … ▢
j You *will/won't/might* be surprised to hear that … ▢

---

5 **CD1.30** Complete this extract from another presentation about Sting with language from Speak Out. Then listen and check.

And what do we ¹_____ about his family life? He's been married twice, and has six children and seven homes. He's also very keen on yoga and practises daily. Maybe ²_____ . He says that it helps him relax as well as keep fit. So you ³_____ to hear that he did a yoga position on TV! You ⁴_____ also know that he introduced Madonna to her husband, Guy Ritchie. But what you probably ⁵_____ that he's acted in several films too. And were ⁶_____ he also writes movie soundtracks and has won nearly fifty music awards? He also won a humanitarian award in 2004. I'm ⁷_____ agree that he deserved it.

6 Work in small groups. Choose one of the people and prepare a presentation using Speak Out. Give your presentations to the class and choose the best one.

PROFILE EMINEM

Real name Marshall Mathers

Stage name Eminem. Sounds like M&M, his initials and the brand name of famous US sweets.

Profession rap singer and musician. Also a talented record producer; starred in the film *8 Mile* in 2001, loosely based on his life.

Background Born 17 October 1973 in St. Joseph, Missouri. Poor childhood spent there and in Detroit, the birthplace of rap. Married high-school sweetheart, Kim, in 1998. Divorced in 2000 but remarried in 2006. They have one child.

Career Started performing raps when he was 14. Was discovered and supported by Dr Dre. Became famous in 1999 with release of *Slim Shady* CD. Some criticised its graphic violence; others praised its surreal humour. In 2000, *Marshall Mathers* was fastest-selling CD in rap history.

Other albums *The Eminem Show* (2002), *Encore* (2004) and *Curtain Call* (2005).

Achievements Has won many Grammy and other music awards, including a 2003 Oscar for Best Song *Lose Yourself* in *8 Mile*. First white rapper to make a big impact on rap scene.

PROFILE ANNIE LENNOX

Real name Annie Lennox

Profession singer, songwriter, talented artist. Did all the artwork for her CD *Bare*.

Background: Born 25 December 1954 in Aberdeen, Scotland. Attended school for the exceptionally intelligent and studied the flute at the Royal Academy of Music. Left in 1974 before her final exams. Married and divorced twice, she has two daughters, Lola and Tali. Often wears wigs as a disguise. Supports many charities including Oxfam and played at the Live8 concert in 2005.

Career From 1976, played with Dave Stewart in The Tourists band and formed the Eurythmics in 1980. Their first album in a long line of classics, *Sweet Dreams*, was released in 1983 and stayed in the charts for 60 weeks. Went solo in 1990 and had equally successful career with CDs *Diva* (1992), *Medusa* (1995) and *Bare* (2003). Wrote *I've Got a Life* with Dave Stewart for Eurythmics *Ultimate Collection* CD in 2005.

Achievements Has won numerous awards including 1996 Grammy for Best Female Pop Vocalist and 2004 Oscar for Best Song *Into the West* from the film, *Lord of the Rings*.

READING AND WRITING

1 Look at the pictures round story A and find a teapot, a spout, a toadstool and a stem. Do NOT read the story yet!

2 Read story A and story B. Which do you find more memorable? Why?

3 Which three of sentences 1–6 are NOT true about story A? Make them true.

1 It contains vivid 'pictures' to help the memory.
2 The events in the story are quite ordinary.
3 Most of the events could happen in any order.
4 There is a 'turning point', when something happens to change the direction of the story and make it interesting.
5 There is a variety of past tenses and some participle clauses.
6 There are very few adjectives and adverbs.

4 Look at the story about Jill again and follow the instructions.

1 Underline the verbs and phrases used instead of the following: *walk quickly, find, look at carefully, want very much, think about, open, move quickly, go carefully.*
2 Circle the adjectives which mean *very big, very small, very loud.*
3 Underline the adverbs used to describe Jill's feelings as she:
   a slipped through the door,
   b picked her way down the staircase.
4 Think of other words to replace the underlined words.
   She was <u>amazed</u> to find a window in the stem.
   To her <u>horror</u>, Jill thought she could smell burning.
5 Circle the time phrases which mean *a short time later, suddenly, at that moment.*

5 Read Train Your Brain and complete the gaps.

TRAIN YOUR BRAIN | Writing skills

Making your stories more memorable

1 Use a variety of tenses and some _____ clauses.
2 Make sure your story has a _____ point.
3 Use 'dramatic' verbs, eg _____ instead of *find*.
4 Use extreme adjectives, eg _____ .
5 Use adverbs to show how people are feeling, eg _____ .
6 Use adjectives and noun phrases to describe feelings, eg I was *surprised/_____/amused/horrified* to *see/hear/find* ...
   To my _____/*amazement/amusement/horror* ...
7 Use a variety of time phrases, eg *suddenly/all of a _____ , after a little while/a _____ later, just _____ /at that moment.*

Story A

Jill was hurrying through the woods to her aunt's house. It was her aunt's fiftieth birthday and Jill had a present for her: a brand new china teapot. Jill had wrapped it as best she could, but the spout was sticking out of the paper, and it looked rather odd.

After a little while, Jill came across a huge toadstool on the path, which was blocking her way. Inspecting the toadstool – which was taller than she was – she was amazed to find a window in the stem. 'Is there a door anywhere?' she wondered. She walked slowly all round the toadstool, but couldn't see any way in.

Jill longed to have a look inside this curious toadstool, and she sat down under a nearby tree, pondering what to do. She leaned her head against the tree trunk and all of a sudden, a hidden door in the stem of the toadstool sprang open. She must have discovered a secret mechanism. Excitedly, Jill slipped through the door.

Inside, the toadstool was even bigger than it had looked from the outside. There was a spiral staircase at Jill's feet leading into the ground, and she held on to the bright blue railing as she picked her way nervously downwards. Suddenly, the stairs came to an end in front of a tiny door. Just then, deafening rock music started to play on the other side of the door, and, to her horror, Jill thought she could smell burning ...

6 Complete the sentences with adverbs from the box to show how the people are feeling.

anxiously   excitedly   nervously   reluctantly   frantically

1 It was time for Jim's driving test to begin. _____ , he started the car.
2 Diana searched the house _____ , but her handbag was nowhere to be seen.
3 Sam waited _____ in the hospital corridor. Then he saw the doctor coming towards him.
4 Carrie's parcel from her uncle in America had finally arrived. _____ , she untied the string and pulled off the paper.
5 It was a beautiful summer's day. _____ , Jodie sat down to write her essay.

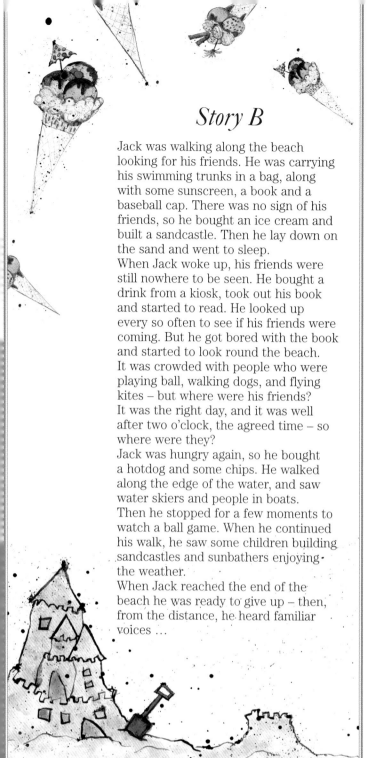

Story B

Jack was walking along the beach looking for his friends. He was carrying his swimming trunks in a bag, along with some sunscreen, a book and a baseball cap. There was no sign of his friends, so he bought an ice cream and built a sandcastle. Then he lay down on the sand and went to sleep.
When Jack woke up, his friends were still nowhere to be seen. He bought a drink from a kiosk, took out his book and started to read. He looked up every so often to see if his friends were coming. But he got bored with the book and started to look round the beach. It was crowded with people who were playing ball, walking dogs, and flying kites – but where were his friends? It was the right day, and it was well after two o'clock, the agreed time – so where were they?
Jack was hungry again, so he bought a hotdog and some chips. He walked along the edge of the water, and saw water skiers and people in boats. Then he stopped for a few moments to watch a ball game. When he continued his walk, he saw some children building sandcastles and sunbathers enjoying the weather.
When Jack reached the end of the beach he was ready to give up – then, from the distance, he heard familiar voices …

7 Choose a suitable noun or adjective from the box and complete the sentences.

amazement/amazed   dismay/dismayed
horror/horrified   relief/relieved
surprise/surprised

1 We were _____ to hear that Jack had moved to South America: he always said he loved Ireland.
2 To her _____ , Sandy found Bob, her kitten, hiding in the wardrobe.
3 Rick was _____ to see a huge spider walking across the bed.
4 Barbara was _____ to find that a balloon had landed in the back garden.
5 To our _____ , it started to pour with rain just as we were unpacking the picnic things.

8 What common verbs can those in each of the following groups replace?

1 wander, stroll, stumble, limp
2 exclaim, cry, yell, call out
3 ponder, wonder, work out, consider
4 spring open, slam shut, fly open, swing shut

9 Read the story and put the words and phrases from the box into the gaps.

reluctantly   just then   anxiously
to her aunt's amazement
she was dismayed to see that

Maggie Banes looked ¹_____ at her watch – as she had done every few minutes for the last three hours. ²_____ it was nearly eight o'clock. 'Where on earth is Jill?' she thought. 'It isn't like her to be so late.' ³_____ , she picked up the plate of sandwiches she'd made for tea and went to the kitchen. ⁴_____ the door opened and Jill walked into the house. She looked tired. 'What a relief! Are you OK?' said Maggie loudly. 'Yes, I'm fine, Auntie,' replied Jill. 'I'm so sorry I'm late, but something strange happened on the way here.' ⁵_____ , Jill explained that, in her hurry to get through the woods, she had tripped and knocked herself unconscious. When she woke up, she realised she was lost. 'I walked around for ages until I found the right path. Then I ran all the way here!'

10 Look at the story in Exercise 9 again and use the verbs and adjectives in the box to replace the more neutral ones in the text.

exhausted   wandered   flew open   bizarre
wondered   cried   stumbled

11 You are going to rewrite the story about Jack to make it more memorable. First, think about the questions below. Then plan and write the story (200–250 words).

- What did Jack have in his bag and why? What were he and his friends planning to do at the beach?
- Where could the turning point of the story be? Think about how long Jack was asleep/ what happened while he was asleep/what happened when he woke up.
- Why were Jack's friends not at the beach when he arrived? Had Jack made a mistake about the time or place? Or had something happened to his friends on their way?

12 Write your own memorable story, beginning with the sentence below.

It started like any other day.

VOCABULARY AND GRAMMAR

1 Circle the correct words or phrases.

1 Being the *reassuring / cautious / modest* type, I read the email again before sending it off.
2 Tom and Meg fight constantly – they are completely *inferior / infantile / incompatible*.
3 It's rude to *fiddle / drum / stand* your fingers even if you're impatient or annoyed.
4 We need someone really smart. He or she doesn't have to *be a brainbox / have a brainwave / pick his brains* though.
5 I know I should *get / talk / stand* up to that girl, but whenever the opportunity arises I can't say anything.
6 He suffered from polio as a child, and as a result, he *stumbles / limps / wanders*.

2 Complete the sentences. Make new words from the words in capital letters.

1 Despite its attractive features, this car has been criticised for its _____ performance.   PREDICT
2 Visit our website to find out about _____ requirements.   MEMBER
3 When applying for the job, give the _____ number of the job ad.   REFER
4 _____ behaviour won't be tolerated.   APPROPRIATE
5 The government failed to provide an _____ for what had happened.   EXPLAIN
6 I understand your comment but I can't see its _____ to our topic.   RELEVANT
7 Frankly, your arguments don't sound very _____ .   CONVINCE

3 Complete the text with one word in each gap.

In my primary school, I ¹_____ to have a lot of friends but one of them, Paul, was very special. He was knowledgeable and witty but a bit of a ²_____ baby at times and always sulking when he didn't get his ³_____ way. I accepted this because most of the time we had a great time together. We ⁴_____ talk to each other every day about everything. My parents complained that I ⁵_____ ages on the phone but they approved of Paul, too. Then suddenly, and for no apparent reason, everything changed – first he started to ⁶_____ me for granted and then didn't have time for me. One day I found out that he ⁷_____ been talking behind my ⁸_____ for a long time. ⁹_____ learnt that, I had no choice but to stop being his friend. When I think of it now, ten years later, I think we were simply on different ¹⁰_____ from the start.

4 Read the diary extract and choose the correct answers, a–d.

> 23/5/06
> I met my old school friend, Anne Gaynor, today. I listened ¹____ amazement as she told me what she ²____ since we left school. I remember she was always very ³____ about politics and I remember she ⁴____ very good at languages but I couldn't believe it when she told me she was working in Brussels for the EU. I must seem very ⁵____ to her. Oh well! Not ⁶____ at all interested in such things, I didn't really understand what she said she was doing. I told her I'd prefer ⁷____ about her personal life!

1 a in   b at   c on   d from
2 a was doing   b did   c used to do
   d had been doing
3 a knows   b knowing   c knowledgeable
   d knew
4 a used to be   b is   c has been   d would be
5 a moody   b dull   c pushy   d unpredictable
6 a be   b to be   c being   d been
7 a hearing   b heard   c to hear   d I heard

5 Use the words in capital letters and rewrite the sentences so that they mean the same as the original ones.

1 Don't throw litter in the street.   RATHER
_____

2 She is in the habit of chattering continually.   WILL
_____

3 After I had completed my degree, I enrolled on a sailing course.   HAVING
_____

4 Steph's uncle always told her off whenever he was in a bad mood.   WOULD
_____

5 I don't want to go on holiday with my brother.   PREFER
_____

6 When we were younger, my sister had a terrible habit of reading my diary.   FOREVER
_____

PRONUNCIATION

1 CD1.31 Listen and circle what you hear. Does the person sound annoyed when they use the full form of *will/would*, or the contracted form?

1 *He'll / He will* talk to himself for ages without realising it.
2 *She'll / She will* interrupt me when I'm speaking.
3 *He'd / He would* phone at all hours of the day and night.
4 *She'd / She would* leave all her dirty dishes in the sink.

2 CD1.31 Listen again and repeat the sentences.

READING SKILLS

1 Complete the article with seven of the sentences a–i. There are two extra sentences.

Generation gap: you don't understand

Times have changed and you often just don't seem to keep up. So here are some useful tips for parents/carers/adults from eighteen-year-old Jess – read them carefully and don't make the same mistakes again.

• You don't understand 'non-uniform' days. We may have 700 items of clothing in our wardrobes but none is suitable for the look we want. Fashion is always changing. ¹___ And as for trainers – don't get me started. We can't have the cheap ones that 'look' like well-known brands. They must be the real thing. Everybody now wears designer labels. ²___

• Just give us a break, please … Even if we have been with our friends all day, we'll always phone them again and again on their mobiles. It makes perfect sense. ³___ Lines of communication are always open between best mates.

• Sometimes we don't want to talk and just need time to ourselves but this doesn't mean that you're a bad parent. Give us some space and we'll come back to you when we're ready. ⁴___

• You don't realise that the mood swings and arguments we have are down to the pressure we come under at school and from friends. With exams starting from Year 9, when we're just fourteen, the pressure starts to build up and it seems that life is all about doing well in the SATs and later in GCSEs.

• And here is a good one! It is NOT funny to tell our friends stories about us in our nappies. It's humiliating. ⁵___ So don't keep on embarrassing us and just drop it.

• It seems that language has changed too … When we say boyfriend/girlfriend sometimes we just mean a boy or girl that is a friend. ⁶___ It's perfectly normal to have a lot of friends of the opposite sex. Wasn't it like that in your day?

• And don't worry, we don't expect you to change. There are some things adults will never understand about teenagers. ⁷___ And we won't try to turn you into Supermum and Superdad. And let's keep it that way, OK?

a No need to make wedding plans or worry that you'll have to push a pram around soon.

b Surely, you wouldn't like us to stick out and be the butt of everybody's jokes.

c It's annoying to be told you're a young adult and then to be treated like a child when you give your opinion.

d What we did when we were babies has nothing to do with what we are like now.

e What's more, new clothes feel good and are always a talking point when you first wear them.

f So don't bother trying to impose your views on us.

g Today the most important topics of conversation are new relationships and clothes.

h After all, everyone has the right to privacy, so don't we deserve it too?

i Exciting things may have happened and they have to be discussed immediately.

SPEAKING SKILLS

1 Respond to the following statements. Write a <u>different</u> answer for each opinion.

1 Middle-aged people nowadays are more youthful in appearance and attitudes.
You mildly agree: _____
_____
You strongly disagree: _____
_____

2 I think everybody is a genius in one way or another.
You strongly agree: _____
_____
You mildly disagree: _____
_____

3 Men and women will never be equal.
You strongly agree: _____
_____
You strongly disagree: _____
_____

2 Choose <u>one</u> of the topics and prepare a three-minute presentation. Use all the necessary phrases to keep the audience involved.

1 'The younger generation knows best.' Do you agree? Justify your opinion.

2 Some people believe that intelligence has more to do with a person's potential than with their abilities. Do you agree with this and how, in your opinion, can this potential be brought out?

Is it good for us?

Read, listen and talk about health, diets, addictions.
Practise gerunds and infinitives, verbs with gerund *or* infinitive; phrasal verbs.
Focus on questions about visual material: avoiding silences.
Write an advice leaflet.

Aspirin® 500mg
16 tablets

1 If you eat after 8p.m., you'll put on weight.
2 Oranges provide the best source of vitamin C.
3 People with red hair are better at dealing with pain than blonds or brunettes.
4 It is dangerous to wake a sleepwalker.
5 You'll probably feel more tired after a lie-in.
6 Taking aspirin reduces your chances of having a heart attack.
7 Wearing high heels damages your knees and back.

GRAMMAR AND READING

1 Discuss these questions in pairs.

1 How could the things in the photos be good/bad for you?
2 Which of the statements 1–7 are facts, and which are myths, do you think?

2 Read 'Myths and Facts' and check your answers to Exercise 1. How many did you get right?

Work it out

3 Read the rules about the use of gerunds and infinitives and find an example of each in extracts a–f below.

1 We use an infinitive:
   • after certain verbs ___ ,
   • after adjectives ___ ,
   • to explain the purpose of an action ___ .
2 We use a gerund:
   • after certain verbs ___ ,
   • after prepositions ___ ,
   • as the subject of a sentence ___ .

a It is dangerous <u>to wake</u> a sleepwalker.
b <u>Sleeping</u> more than usual disrupts your sleep cycle.
c … and so you tend <u>to feel</u> tired.
d Compared with <u>walking</u> barefoot, high heels …
e Some redheads dye their hair <u>to avoid</u> jokes about 'carrot tops'.
f If you fancy <u>having</u> a snack before bedtime …

Myths and FACTS

IT IS what and how much you eat and how much exercise you do that makes you lose or gain weight, not the time of day. If you fancy having a snack before bedtime, avoid eating in front of the television: you're <u>likely to get</u> distracted and overeat.

STUDIES have shown that oranges give you 50 milligrams of vitamin C for every 100 grams you eat. Apparently, parsley gives you 100 milligrams per 100 grams, but have you ever attempted to eat 100 grams of parsley? Anyway, next time you <u>feel like taking</u> a dose of vitamin C, eat some red peppers – they give you 170 milligrams per 100 grams!

SOME redheads dye their hair to avoid jokes about 'carrot tops'. But scientists have found that the 'red hair gene' gives a kind of 'built-in anaesthetic'. Who knows? Perhaps <u>being</u> tougher than the rest gave famous redheads like Cleopatra an extra advantage.

WAKING a sleepwalker is difficult, but not dangerous. Most doctors <u>suggest leading</u> the person gently back to bed, if possible – they may not let you touch them! Some sleepwalkers manage to eat, get dressed, drive a car, and in some extreme cases, commit murder. So, if you think they risk hurting themselves and/or others, wake them up.

IF YOU'RE used to having eight hours' sleep a night, having a lie-in can confuse your internal body clock. Sleeping more than usual disrupts your sleep cycle, and so you tend to feel tired. Consider setting your alarm for the same time every day. This involves sacrificing your lie-in at the weekend, but your body clock won't get confused.

DOCTORS have encouraged us to take it as a simple headache cure for many years, but in the past decade research has shown that aspirin can reduce the risk of heart attacks. It has been used <u>to treat</u> blindness in scientific trials, with some success, and even to protect against certain types of cancer.

COMPARED with walking barefoot, high heels increase the pressure on the inside of the knee by 26 percent. They also push the centre of the body forwards, which forces the spine to bend backwards, to compensate. This can lead to back problems. Many women are aware of these dangers, but still <u>refuse to give up</u> their high heels!

---

4 Match the <u>underlined</u> phrases in 'Myths and Facts' to the rules in Exercise 3, according to the use of the gerund or infinitive.

5 What are these verbs followed by? Put them in the correct column. Then check in 'Myths and Facts'.

encourage   make   avoid   let   force   risk
attempt   involve   manage   consider

+ infinitive with *to*	+ infinitive without *to*	+ gerund

6 Match sentences 1–3 to definitions a–c.

1 <u>I'm used to</u> having eight hours' sleep a night. ☐
2 <u>I'm getting used to</u> having six hours' sleep a night. ☐
3 I <u>used to have</u> a lie-in every Saturday. ☐

a a situation which is becoming more familiar
b past habit
c a situation which is familiar

➤ **Check it out** page 153

7 Complete the gaps with the correct forms of *be used to* or *get used to* and the verbs in brackets.

1 I fell over because I _____ (not wear) high heels.
2 He _____ (not speak) in public, so he was very nervous.
3 It was difficult at first but we _____ (live) in the country.
4 He _____ (go) to bed earlier, that's why he's so tired.
5 I'll never _____ (have) short hair: I hope it grows quickly!
6 When we were in China we found it difficult to _____ (eat) with chopsticks.

8 Complete the text with the correct forms of the verbs in brackets. Which tips would be the easiest/most difficult to follow? Why?

DO YOU GET HAYFEVER? HERE ARE SOME TIPS TO HELP YOU ¹_____ (SURVIVE) THE SUMMER:

- Avoid ²_____ (go) outside when the pollen count is high.
- Wear sunglasses ³_____ (prevent) the pollen from ⁴_____ (get) into your eyes.
- Don't smoke and don't let other people ⁵_____ (smoke) in your house: ⁶_____ (breathe) in smoke irritates your nose and eyes.
- Keep pets out of the house: they are likely ⁷_____ (bring) in pollen on their fur.
- Some people find it useful ⁸_____ (take) homeopathic remedies.
- People with severe cases can get long-term protection by ⁹_____ (have) an anti-allergy injection.

9 Rewrite the sentences so that they mean the same, using the words in capital letters.

1 They don't allow us to use dictionaries in the exam.   LET
_____

2 It's good exercise to go for a walk every day.   GOING
_____

3 Emily saved up £300 so that she could buy a leather jacket.   TO
_____

4 I think I might sell my computer.   CONSIDERING
_____

5 Let's not go to that club: older people usually go there.   TEND
_____

6 The things Pat said forced me to change my mind.   MADE
_____

7 Take a taxi to the airport or it's possible that you'll miss the plane.   RISK
_____

8 I don't want to do any homework tonight.   FEEL LIKE
_____

10 Why are pets good for us? Complete the text with the gerund or infinitive form of a suitable verb.

It's official: ¹_____ a pet is good for you. Studies have shown that pets are good for us in a number of ways. Firstly, ²_____ an animal lowers your blood pressure and makes you ³_____ more relaxed. One study even found that simply ⁴_____ fish in an aquarium made people less anxious. That's why many doctors and dentists decide ⁵_____ an aquarium in their waiting rooms. Next, it can be very therapeutic ⁶_____ to your pet. Although your pet won't give you any solutions for your problems, the act of ⁷_____ your concerns with a good listener may help you ⁸_____ your own solutions. And pets are great listeners. Finally, if you have a dog for a pet, you can expect ⁹_____ for a walk every day, which is good exercise. Even people who can't stand ¹⁰_____ to the gym don't usually mind ¹¹_____ their furry companion for a gentle stroll in the park!

'Do you think it's true that having a pet lowers your blood pressure?'

11 Complete the sentences to make them true for *you*. Read them to a partner. What do you have in common?

1 I find it difficult …
2 I'm looking forward to … soon.
3 I usually avoid eating … because …
4 …ing makes me nervous.
5 My parents have always encouraged me …
6 I'll never get used to …
7 …ing helps me to relax.
8 I've always dreamt about …

Gory burger posters target young

Not all burgers are good burgers. What's on your plate? Visit bhf.org.uk

David Evans Health Editor

POSTERS OF burger rolls filled with bones and fat have appeared across the UK to shock children into improving their diets and help fight obesity. It is estimated that a quarter of young people will be overweight by 2020.

The British Heart Foundation's campaign follows a survey which showed that 36% of eight to fourteen-year-olds did not know the main ingredient of chips was potato. Nearly one in ten of the children questioned thought chips were made of oil, while others suggested eggs, apples and flour.

Percentage of overweight people in the UK

(bar chart, Percentages on y-axis 0–50, years 1985 and 2005 on x-axis)

'Healthy options' offered by burger and pizza chains still full of fat and salt, study finds

SPEAKING AND LISTENING

1 Look at the pictures and graph, and read the article and headline. What issues are represented in this material? Discuss in pairs.

2 **CD2.1** Listen to Marco answering four questions about the material. Which was his best answer, do you think? Why?

3 **CD2.1** Listen again and complete Marco's answers. How do the missing words and phrases help Marco to answer the questions? Which section of Speak Out do they belong to?

1 _____ _____ , how could someone think that chips were made of apples?
2 We're all becoming – _____ _____ _____ ? – 'couch potatoes'!
3 Um, _____ , a diet with the right number of calories – I think _____ 2,000.
4 I know you should eat _____ _____ fruit and vegetables, to get enough vitamins and, and _____ _____ _____ .
5 I've heard that it's good to drink _____ _____ eight glasses of water a day, too.
6 But also the burger and pizza companies should, _____ _____ , be more honest.
7 They should write it clearly on the menu, or _____ _____ _____ .
8 It's _____ _____ _____ the machine the dog's walking on in this cartoon.

SPEAK OUT | Avoiding silences

Vague language: when you can't remember or don't know a word or an amount

What's it called?
(a) kind of/sort of …
… and that sort of thing/and so on
… or someone/something like that
around (fifty)/a couple of …

Fillers: when you need a moment to think
Um …   Like …   I don't know …

4 **CD2.2** Listen and match the answers you hear a–e to questions 1–5.

1 What's 'fast food'? ☐
2 Where can you buy natural remedies? ☐
3 What's an exercise bike? ☐
4 How many calories are there in a banana? ☐
5 What do you call people who don't eat meat, fish or dairy products? ☐

5 **CD2.3** Listen and repeat some phrases from Exercise 4.

6 Work in pairs. Look at page 146 and follow the instructions.

READING AND LISTENING

1 Which of the following can you see in the pictures?

a coffee addict   a compulsive gambler
a workaholic   a shopaholic

2 In pairs, look at the 'everyday' activities in the box and discuss the questions.

watching TV   working   exercising   dieting
eating chocolate   surfing the Internet
cleaning   playing computer games

1 Which would it be possible/impossible for *you* to get addicted to?
2 When and why do everyday activities sometimes become addictive?
3 How would an addiction to one of these activities affect your life?
4 What other everyday activities could become addictive?

3 Work in two groups and follow the instructions.

- Group 1, read texts A and B on page 55. Group 2, read texts C and D on page 56. Complete the table about the two people in your texts.
- Find a partner from the other group and exchange your information.

	Abby	Ben	Rob	Sam
Addiction				
How it began				
Treatment				
Still addicted?				

4 Work together and match the people from the four texts with the questions. Whose addiction:

1 cost them a lot of money? ___ ___
2 made them ill? ___
3 has had some positive effects on their life? ___ ___
4 was caused by problems in a relationship? ___
5 ruined their social life? ___
6 affected their relationship with their family? ___ ___
7 caused them to lose their job? ___ ___
8 started because they moved to a new place? ___ ___

Text A Abby

'I was becoming more and more isolated'

I had never been particularly sporty at school, but in my twenties I started doing sports as a way of meeting people because I'd recently moved to a new town. I took up tennis, squash, aerobics and badminton as hobbies but as I got involved with the clubs and teams, exercise became a central part of my life and I became increasingly determined to keep fit. The three hours a day I was doing soon doubled and I started to become totally obsessed with exercise. I wouldn't miss a day at the gym. It wasn't really about my body any more – I just had to do my workout and get my fix. At the height of my addiction, I was exercising for up to eight hours a day, starting with two hours on my exercise bike before work. I would walk for an hour at lunchtime and then head off for a two-hour run after work,

followed by a three-hour session at the gym. I would spend my holidays at health farms and even get out my exercise bike on Christmas Day. My dress size plummeted from 14 to 8, and my weight slipped to seven stone. Instead of using sport to enhance my social life, I was becoming more and more isolated and was not getting anything out of the exercise at all.

The regime started to take its toll, and I was admitted to hospital with severe cramps and high blood pressure. I can now manage my exercise addiction, thanks to my psychiatrist, who helps me keep on track. I'm still all for people getting fit, but I think more should be known about exercise addiction. It's a slippery slope, and like all other addictions, it can be taken to extremes.

Text B Ben

'It makes you want to remember every interesting detail of your day'

It started as a way of keeping in touch with family and friends when I moved away from home to university, but once I started, it was inevitable that I would get hooked. I've been keeping my own personal diary ever since I was a kid, and since the Internet has become an essential part of my existence, it was only a matter of time before I got bitten by the bug.

To say that blogging is addictive is an understatement. It makes you want to remember every interesting detail of your day and makes you appreciate the simplest of things. I'll often find myself making notes wherever I am – scribbling a few words on a paper serviette in a café, even dictating a few thoughts into my phone while I'm standing at the bus stop – just to make sure that I won't forget the topics I want to write about when I get the chance.

Also, it has exercised my mind into finding something extraordinary in a seemingly ordinary day or event, like an argument I've overheard, or a newspaper headline I've noticed. The more subscribers I have to my blog, the more 'pressure' I feel to write something worth their time: something thought-provoking, something entertaining or informative.

I look forward to going online to update my blog and see how many hits I've had. As well as family and friends, I get visits from strangers from all over the world. It's overwhelming when I get messages from these people telling me that they enjoy the things I write, and I actually think it's strengthened my family ties – they have much more insight into my life now than when I was living at home!

---

5 Vocabulary **Look at the highlighted words and phrases in the texts and match them to the meanings. Then explain them to your partner.**

Texts A and B
1 have a negative effect on
2 unavoidable
3 do something beyond normal limits
4 having a powerful effect emotionally
5 improve
6 develop a strong interest in something

Texts C and D
1 short periods of intensive spending
2 addicted to
3 stop doing something that is bad for you
4 important but not easily noticed
5 spend carelessly
6 borrow a lot of money that you will have to pay back

6 Complete the gaps with some of the highlighted words and phrases from texts A–D.

1 I got _____ chewing gum when I was 12: it helps me to think.
2 All the stress at work has _____ _____ on Simon's health.
3 Everyone's kindness while Clare was in hospital was really _____ .
4 As soon as she got paid, Sue went on a _____ to cheer herself up.
5 They said at the shop that the new software has been _____ , but I can't see any difference.
6 A lot of smokers nowadays are using nicotine patches to help them _____ the _____ .
7 I don't think there's anything wrong with plastic surgery, but some people nowadays _____ it to _____ .
8 I can't believe that Ned _____ his first pay cheque on clothes and CDs.

55

Text C Rob
'I realise now that I was looking for reassurance'

Nowadays I never spend more than £10 a week on texts, which is the goal I set with my counsellor when I started treatment. When things were really out of control I was sending around 700 texts a week, and in one year I squandered £4,500 on text messaging. That was during a period of real insecurity in my relationship with my girlfriend, and it was kind of comforting to get texts from her: I realise now that I was looking for reassurance, constantly needing to know where she was and what she was up to. It's certainly been much easier since she and I went our separate ways. Apparently it isn't unusual for people with an addiction to have underlying problems at work or with a relationship.

I was referred to a counselling service after my boss discovered my problem: I had accidentally sent a text which was intended for my girlfriend to one of my colleagues, and then hit the 'resend' button eight times when I didn't get a reply! My boss started keeping an eye on me and took note whenever I reached for my mobile to send or read a message; then he demanded an explanation for all the time I was spending not doing my job. I decided to resign rather than face disciplinary procedures.

My counsellor says I'm the first case of text message addiction he's treated in ten years of working in the field, but he also thinks there are a good few people out there who don't realise they have a problem. That may well be true, it's certainly easy to get hooked on texting: no sooner have you sent one message, then another comes straight back, kind of like a game of ping-pong.

---

7 CD2.4 Listen to four people talking about addictions. Which of the four questions in Exercise 2 on page 54 is each person answering?

A ___   B ___   C ___   D ___

8 CD2.4 Listen again. Match speakers A–D to statements 1–7.

1 __ thinks addiction can have a negative impact on your personality.
2 __ feels sorry for people with addictive personalities.
3 __ has a relative who went on a trip to get over the death of her husband.
4 __ says that people repeat pleasurable activities because the initial feeling doesn't last.
5 __ doesn't want to admit that he/she has workaholic tendencies.
6 __ thinks that personality is one of the most influential factors in addiction.
7 __ thinks your social life will suffer if you do too many activities on your own.

9 In pairs, answer the questions.

• Which of the four addictions in the texts A–D do you think is the most difficult to deal with? Why?
• Do you know anyone who's addicted to an everyday activity? What is it and what effect does it have on his/her life?

Text D Sam
'I am now successfully rebuilding my life'

By the time I went into the Priory Clinic to be treated for shopping addiction, I had run up a debt of £28,000. From quite a young age, I had to have 'nice' things because they made me feel good. At the age of sixteen I started a part-time job as a waitress and I loved earning my own money to buy whatever I fancied … and when my wages had gone, I borrowed money from my brother.

When I left school at eighteen, I started working in the retail industry. I opened several bank accounts and collected numerous store and credit cards. I often ended up buying things on my shopping trips that I didn't even want or ever use, just because of the 'high' I got from making the purchases. My addiction caused a lot of problems at home since my parents didn't understand what was going on, and I refused to talk about it – I felt too guilty and ashamed, and usually kept all my posessions out of sight. In the end I left home but I just couldn't make ends meet – I was spending my money on useless things and didn't have enough to cover the rent and bills. I had to move back in with my parents and I tried to curb my spending. But I still couldn't kick the habit. Eventually, I got professional help when I lost my job because I was out of the office shopping all day long. Counselling helped me to discover what triggered my shopping sprees, and to set myself weekly goals to change my behaviour. I am now successfully rebuilding my life and I'm slowly repaying my debts. I am finally aware of who I am and I actually like myself now.

GRAMMAR AND LISTENING

1 **CD2.5** What is the situation in the picture? What are the women saying? Listen to Part 1 of the conversation and check.

2 **CD2.6** Listen to Part 2 and answer the questions.

1 What are the 'rules' of Rosie's diet?
2 What does Beth think of the diets Rosie has done?

3 **CD2.7** Listen to Part 3. Why does Rosie insist on clearing up after the meal?

4 **CD2.8** Circle the best forms in these sentences from the conversation. Then listen again and check.

1 I even remembered *to get / getting* your favourite cheesecake.
2 I forgot *to tell / telling* you.
3 I haven't stopped *to eat / eating* cheesecake.
4 They went out hunting all day and only stopped *to eat / eating* one big meal in the evening.
5 And it even sounds as if you like *to do / doing* it.
6 I've been trying *to lose / losing* weight for ages.
7 I'll never forget *to go / going* shopping with you when you were on that Beverly Hills diet.
8 Do you remember *to say / saying* that you wouldn't do any more of these fad diets?
9 I always like *to clear / clearing* up straight after a meal.
10 Have you tried *to turn / turning* it on?

Work it out

5 Look at Exercise 4 again and complete the gaps in these rules with *gerund* or *infinitive*.

remember
+ ^{1}_____: remember something, then do it
+ ^{2}_____: do something and remember it later

forget
+ ^{3}_____: forget about something, so you don't do it
+ ^{4}_____: do something and (don't) forget it later

try
+ ^{5}_____: do something and see what happens
+ ^{6}_____: make an effort to do something difficult

stop
+ ^{7}_____: no longer do something
+ ^{8}_____: stop something in order to do something else

like
+ ^{9}_____: do something because it's a good idea
+ ^{10}_____: enjoy something

➤ **Check it out** pages 153–154

6 Complete the gaps with the correct forms of the verbs in brackets.

1 I stopped _____ (drink) coffee because I read it was bad for you.
2 I'm so sorry I'm late, I forgot _____ (set) my alarm and I overslept.
3 I know the match doesn't start until 4p.m., but we like _____ (arrive) early to get a seat.
4 I tried _____ (do) an Internet search to find the CDs you wanted, but no luck.
5 I don't think I'll ever forget _____ (arrive) two hours late for our first date!
6 Why is that window open? I definitely remember _____ (close) it before we left.
7 It's after midnight! Why on earth didn't you stop _____ (ask for) directions?
8 Can you remember _____ (feed) the cat while we're away? We don't want him to die!

7 Work in pairs. Student A, follow the instructions below. Student B, follow the instructions on page 149.

Student A: Think of:
• something you should stop doing and something you should try to do if you want to lose weight.
• two things you should remember to do before you go on holiday.
• something you try not to do and something you like doing in English lessons.
• something you like to do and something you'll never forget doing before an important exam.
Tell your partner the two things, but not the situation. Can they guess the situation?

A You should stop eating biscuits.
B if you want to lose weight?
A Yes!

57

10 reasons …

NOT to Go on a Diet

1 You don't have to <u>part with</u> lots of money for expensive diet products.

2 It won't matter if you don't go to the gym and <u>work out</u> every day.

3 You don't need to <u>pick at</u> your food and pretend not to be hungry.

4 You can <u>cheer</u> yourself <u>up</u> with a bar of chocolate whenever you get depressed.

5 You can <u>do away with</u> all the scales and tape measures in the house.

6 You don't need to <u>turn</u> dinner invitations <u>down</u>.

7 You won't get upset if you don't <u>stick to</u> the diet.

8 You won't feel guilty if you buy lots of your favourite food and <u>pig out</u>.

9 Your initial enthusiasm for the diet will soon <u>wear off</u>.

10 Someone will <u>come up with</u> a new and better diet than the one you're on.

VOCABULARY

1 Read the extract above. Which do you think are the three most convincing reasons NOT to diet? Why?

2 Match the phrasal verbs in the extract to the meanings a–j.

a do exercise	**f** eat a small amount
b eat a lot of food	**g** think of (an idea)
c make happier	**h** refuse
d keep doing	**i** give unwillingly
e remove, get rid of	**j** lose strength

3 Which sentence 1–4 is not correct? Why?

1 I turned down the invitation.
2 I turned it down.
3 I turned down it.
4 I turned the invitation down.

4 Complete Train Your Brain with phrasal verbs from the extract.

> ### TRAIN YOUR BRAIN | Phrasal verbs
>
> There are four types of phrasal verb:
> **1 verb + particle (no object)**
> eg *work out*, _____ , _____
>
> **2 verb + particle + object (separable)**
> eg *turn down*, _____
> We can put the direct object before or after the particle, unless it is a pronoun – in which case it must come before the particle.
>
> **3 verb + particle + object (not separable)**
> eg *part with*, _____ , _____
> We always put the direct object after the particle.
>
> **4 verb + two particles + direct object**
> eg *do away with*, _____
> We always put the direct object after the second particle.
>
> NB A good English dictionary shows you whether a phrasal verb is separable or not.

5 **Think Back! What types of phrasal verb are the following?**

a take up ___	**d** come across ___
b set off ___	**e** stand up to ___
c set up ___	**f** take on ___

6 **Choose the correct answer.**

1 I'm glad I saw that film, it really
   a cheered up.   **c** cheered up me.
   b cheered me up.
2 Why are you ___ your lunch? Aren't you hungry?
   a pigging out   **b** parting with   **c** picking at
3 Now you've made the decision, you must
   a stick it.   **b** stick it to.   **c** stick to it.
4 You'll have to ___ a better excuse than that.
   a come up with   **c** do away with
   b come across
5 Have you got any aspirin? The anaesthetic is
   a wearing it off.   **c** wearing off my mouth.
   b wearing off.
6 When Lucy left the company, we all had to ___ extra work.
   a turn down   **b** take on   **c** take up
7 Don't let your brother boss you around:
   a stand up to him!   **c** stand to him up!
   b stand up him to!
8 I've had this bike for years: I don't want to
   a part with.   **b** part it with.   **c** part with it.

7 **Put the words in the correct order to make questions and choose four to ask your partner.**

1 out you How work do often
2 would hate possession with you What part to
3 you why last out When did pig and
4 you home up Where to like set would
5 set late When off did last you
6 music people do you turn How tell your down often to
7 would your do What to house away like with you in
8 party down to would an turn Why invitation a you

WRITING

1 How stressful would you find the following situations? Number them from 1–6 (1 – not stressful, 6 – very stressful). Then compare your answers with a partner.

- studying the night before an important exam
- meeting your boyfriend's/girlfriend's parents for the first time
- organising a surprise eighteenth birthday party for your best friend
- giving a speech in front of the whole school
- babysitting three children under the age of six
- getting stuck in traffic on the way to the station or the airport

2 Read the advice leaflet about stress and choose the best headings for paragraphs A–D. There are two extra headings.

1 What causes stress?
2 When should you get professional help for stress?
3 What can you do to reduce stress?
4 Why should you learn to cope with stress?
5 What is stress?
6 What are the symptoms of stress?

3 Complete each gap in the leaflet with one suitable word. What information and advice did you not know about before?

4 Work in pairs. You are going to write an advice leaflet called 'Improving your Social Life'.

1 Discuss and make notes about the following:
   - reasons why people may not have a good social life
   - the effect that not having a good social life can have
   - ways of improving your social life (where to go, what to do/avoid doing, how to behave, what to say/what not to say, etc)
2 Look back at the leaflet about stress and underline any useful phrases for giving advice.
3 Write your leaflet, organising the information into paragraphs with headings.
4 Read other students' leaflets. What was the best advice?

YOUR HEALTH AND WELL-BEING
COPING WITH STRESS

A _____
Stress can affect anyone at any time. It is the body's response to a situation which is challenging or threatening. This response can be helpful at times: positive stress [1]_____ you to meet deadlines or survive physical danger [2]_____ producing motivation and energy. However, when you are under intense pressure, you may experience the symptoms of negative stress.

B _____
Apart from a major trauma like an accident or the death of someone close, not many events are stressful in themselves. Stress arises when you see a situation as threatening or [3]_____ to deal with, or when you have very high expectations. For example, organising a surprise party may [4]_____ you feel anxious because you don't want anything to go wrong, whereas others may enjoy planning it and [5]_____ it secret.

C _____
People who suffer from stress often complain of headaches, sweaty hands or 'butterflies' in the stomach. Lack of sleep, [6]_____ tired and bad-tempered, and not [7]_____ able to concentrate are also common symptoms.

D _____
First, work [8]_____ what is causing it. Knowing what causes stress for you can help you to cope with it better. Here are some strategies [9]_____ coping:
○ Don't take on more than you know you can do: learn to turn [10]_____ some of the requests people make.
○ Take regular breaks: go for a walk, [11]_____ out at the gym, listen to music.
○ Eat a balanced diet and avoid [12]_____ alcohol and smoking.
○ Share your thoughts and fears with friends and family members: this may be difficult at first if you are not used to [13]_____ about your feelings, but studies have shown that socially active people are better [14]_____ dealing with stress.
○ [15]_____ to find humour or absurdity in stressful situations. Laughing reduces stress.

Secret worlds

Read, listen and talk about books and reading, secret agents and societies.
Practise modal and other related verbs; ways of looking, phrasal verbs and expressions with *look* and
Focus on generalising in speaking; ellipsis and referencing in reading.
Write a book review.

GRAMMAR AND READING

1 In pairs, read the statements and tick the ones you think are true. Give reasons.

A good secret agent
- <u>must</u> be an excellent driver.
- <u>doesn't have to</u> be glamorous.
- <u>can</u> swim underwater for extended periods.
- <u>mustn't</u> tell anyone what his/her job is.
- <u>needs to</u> be extremely courageous.
- <u>can</u> carry a gun at all times.
- <u>ought to</u> be an expert dancer.

2 Look at the photos and discuss the questions.

1 How do we use these animals to help us?
2 What other animals do we use? How?
3 Could animals be used as secret agents? How?

3 Read the article. What can animals do, according to the article?

The Secret World of Animals

THERE IS a long history of animals being used to defend and protect us – from Hannibal's elephants to guide dogs for the blind. But nowadays there's a whole new dimension to what animals can do – including spying missions!

A Codename: Mr Codfish

The US Navy started using trained sea lions to protect their ports in 2000. They can see and hear extremely well underwater, and are able to detect enemy swimmers and sea mines. Traditionally, human divers <u>have had to</u> do this job but now they <u>don't need to</u>, as sea lions can stay underwater for much longer periods. They have been so successful that the Navy <u>might</u> start using other marine animals for this work.

B Codename: Goldwing

Pigeons were extensively used as messengers in the two World Wars and were so important that

By Tom Martin

UK citizens <u>couldn't</u> shoot them. They had two crucial qualities: they <u>were able to</u> find their way home from anywhere and <u>could</u> fly at great speed. On one famous occasion in 1918, a heroic French pigeon called *Cher Ami* saved 194 soldiers, and won a medal for bravery! Another equally heroic pigeon <u>had to</u> wear a camera around its neck and was supposed to take photos. Unfortunately he <u>couldn't</u> fly very far with it, but still succeeded in returning on foot two days later!

C Codename: Squeak-squeak-bang-bang

A Belgian research group has trained rats to find landmines in ex-war zones like Mozambique. Rats can do the job very well because of their excellent sense of smell. They <u>have to</u> run around a specified area and are supposed to stop and scratch the ground when they smell explosives. More than 50 people a day are killed or injured by landmines but rats <u>have been able to</u> reduce this risk. On

one occasion, they managed to find nine mines in one day, and are sure to get better at it in future.

D However, not everybody is happy about all this. One animal rights supporter said, 'Why has such cruelty to animals been allowed in this country? Ordinary people <u>can't</u> treat animals badly but scientists <u>are allowed to</u>. There's so much technology these days, they <u>needn't</u> use sea lions! Missions like this <u>can</u> be very dangerous, and the animals could die. In fact, they might! But nobody will ever tell us. Animals <u>shouldn't</u> suffer like this. They <u>should</u> be free!'

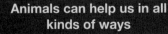
Animals can help us in all kinds of ways

4 Think Back! Look at the <u>underlined</u> verb forms in Exercise 1 and in the article, and write them in the correct places in the table.

obligation/necessity	duty and advice
must	ought to
no obligation/necessity	**ability or lack of ability**
prohibition	**permission**
possibility/probability	

5 In pairs, discuss which three answers are possible in the sentences. How does the meaning change?

1 I ___ do that now. I'll do it tomorrow.
  a needn't   **c** might
  b can't   **d** don't need to

2 You ___ borrow my car because you don't have a licence.
  a won't be able to   **c** mustn't
  b don't have to   **d** can't

3 He ___ speak English until we came to London.
  a didn't need to   **c** wasn't able to
  b couldn't   **d** needn't

4 You ___ arrive on time next Monday or you'll get the sack.
  a must   **c** can't
  b will have to   **d** need to

5 There ___ be life on other planets.
  a can   **c** could
  b might   **d** might not

6 If we finish work early tonight, we ___ go for a meal.
  a could   **c** might
  b can't   **d** can

Work it out

6 Compare these sentences with their equivalents in the article. Then put the <u>underlined</u> phrases in the correct places in the table in Exercise 4.

1 They <u>are supposed to</u> be free. (para. D)
2 They <u>are obliged to</u> run around a specified area. (para. C)
3 Ordinary people can't treat animals badly but scientists <u>are permitted to</u>. (para. D)
4 He <u>managed to</u> return on foot two days later. (para. B)
5 They <u>are bound to</u> get better at it in future. (para. C)
6 They were so important that UK citizens <u>were forbidden to</u> shoot them. (para. B)
7 Another pigeon <u>was required to</u> wear a camera around its neck. (para. B)
8 The Navy <u>is likely to</u> start using other marine animals for this work. (para. A)

➤ Check it out page 154

7 CD2.9 Replace each underlined word or phrase with one from the box to make the phone call more natural. Then listen and check.

General work

WANTED

Dolphin trainer!

Discretion essential.
Phone 985382741

must	are supposed to	might	could you
it can be	do I need	mustn't	bound to
I should	allowed	have to

A [1]Is it necessary to have any specific qualifications?

B Well, you [2]are required to be an experienced dolphin trainer.

A And what would I [3]be obliged to do in the job?

B You [4]are expected to use the Navy training programme.

A Oh, so is that why [5]it's a good idea to be discreet, then?

B Yes, you're not [6]permitted to tell anyone about your work. And you [7]are forbidden to talk to journalists.

A I see. So is the work dangerous?

B [8]Possibly, yes. But for the dolphins more than the trainers.

A Oh! I see. I suppose it's [9]sure to be a challenging job at times.

B It [10]is likely to be, yes. [11]Is it possible for you to come for an interview?

Would you like to do this job? Why?/Why not?

Mind the trap!

To describe the completion of a specific action in the past, we use *be able to*, NOT *could*, in affirmative sentences. In negative sentences both *be able to* and *could* are possible.

He **wasn't able to/couldn't** fly very far but he **was able to** (NOT ~~could~~) get back on foot.

---

8 Complete the sentences with *could, couldn't* or the correct forms of *be able to*. Sometimes more than one form is possible.

1 I tried to phone him but I _____ get through.
2 We _____ finish our project work on time yesterday.
3 I got lost on the way but I _____ get there in the end.
4 She _____ ride a bike since she was four.
5 Pigeons _____ deliver messages easily during the war.
6 We _____ find any bread but we _____ get the milk.

9 Rewrite the sentences so that they mean the same, using the words in capital letters.

1 It isn't necessary to keep this a secret from everybody.   HAVE
2 Why do I have to show my passport?   REQUIRED
3 She has the potential to be a great female secret agent.   COULD
4 Despite the terrible snowstorm, he managed to reach the summit.   SUCCEEDED
5 It's wrong for scientists to experiment on animals.   SHOULDN'T
6 The England football team has a good chance of winning the World Cup.   MIGHT
7 Winters are often bitterly cold here.   CAN
8 You should switch off your mobile phone in class.   SUPPOSED

10 Complete the sentences to make them true for *you*. Then, read your sentences to your partner who should respond appropriately.

1 I was able to …
2 My friends aren't allowed to …
3 I haven't managed to …
4 I'm bound to …
5 I won't have to …
6 Students in my school aren't supposed to …
7 We're forbidden to …

A I was able to write when I was four.
B Really? I couldn't write until I was seven!

11 Look at the cartoon and discuss the questions. Share your ideas with the class.

• What is ironic about the cartoon?
• Do you think it's cruel to train and experiment on animals? Why?/Why not?

Daily News July 14

Secrets revealed?

SPEAKING AND LISTENING

1 In pairs, look at the photos and the headline and discuss the questions.

- What secret societies or fraternities do you know of?
- Why do people create or join them?
- Would you like to belong to one? What kind, and why?

2 CD2.10 Listen to the introduction to a current affairs programme. What is it going to be about? How do we know?

3 Before you listen to Part 2, use your dictionary to check the meaning of the words and phrases in the box.

a sorority   to pledge   rituals   handshakes
initiation rites   to bond

4 CD2.11 Listen to Part 2 and complete each gap with only one word.

Famous public figures often [_____|1]
to secret societies.
In the USA, Gamma Phi Beta is a famous university sorority, a special society for [_____|2] .
The names of such societies often contain [_____|3] letters.
Only members know the secret rituals, like [_____|4] , songs and handshakes.
New members are invited to join fraternities during '[_____|5] Week'.
A minimum grade average is one type of [_____|6] for fraternity membership.
Six US [_____|7] formerly belonged to a fraternity at Yale.

5 CD2.12 Listen to the last part of the programme and answer the questions.

1 When and why did secret societies first begin?
2 Why do students join these fraternities? Which do you most agree with and why?

6 CD2.13 You will hear a presentation on the Cambridge Apostles. First read Speak Out and complete sentences 1–8 with one word in each gap. Then listen and check.

SPEAK OUT | Generalising

It is *said/ believed/ thought* that …
It is *generally/ widely* agreed that …
They tend to …/It tends to …
People/ They have a tendency to …
There's a common belief that …
It is *usually/ often* the case that …
Broadly/ Generally speaking, …
On the whole, /In general, /As a rule, …
In their view, …/ Apparently, …

1 The society is, broadly _____ , a debating club.
2 But now it _____ to be called the Cambridge Apostles.
3 It is _____ that this name came from the idea that twelve new members are elected every year.
4 As a _____ , members have meetings once a week.
5 It's usually the _____ that Apostles are undergraduates.
6 Apostles have a _____ to become Angels after they graduate.
7 It is often _____ that the Angels meet at a Cambridge college every few years.
8 It was _____ believed that some of the spies had been Apostles.

7 Write three opinions about each of the statements below, using language from Speak Out. Then compare and discuss your answers in groups.

- Nobody can ever keep a secret.
- Everybody needs their privacy.
- We all need somebody to confide in.

READING AND VOCABULARY

1 How do you usually choose a book? Discuss your answers in pairs, using the ideas below.

- recommended by a friend
- familiar with the author's work
- buy second-hand
- borrow from a library
- read a review
- like the cover
- other

2 Describe the picture using the words and phrases from the box. Use your dictionary if necessary.

a beehive   platforms and steps   immense
pierced by light   palatial   a high glass dome
a labyrinth of passageways

3 **CD ROM** In pairs, answer the questions about the picture. Then read Part 1 of the story and check your answers.

1 Where do you think this place is? What is it?
2 Who is the boy? What's he doing?
3 How does he feel? Why is he there?

4 **CD ROM** Before you read Part 2 of the story, discuss the questions. Then read and check your predictions.

1 What does Daniel's father do for a living?
2 Why is this place called the Cemetery of Forgotten Books?
3 What happens to a person who visits this place for the first time?
4 What's going to happen next? Will it be positive or negative?

5 Vocabulary Find words 1–7 in the story and guess their meaning from the context. The line numbers are given in brackets. Then match them to their definitions a–g.

1 stunned (line 27) ☐
2 make out (line 30) ☐
3 hushed (line 35) ☐
4 gaze (line 56) ☐
5 timidly (line 77) ☐
6 gleam (line 79) ☐
7 caress (line 79) ☐

a in a shy way
b just able to see something
c quiet
d touch gently
e shine softly
f a long steady look
g too shocked to speak

'Come, Daniel, get dressed. I want to show you something,' said my father.
'Now? At five o'clock in the morning?'
'Some things can only be seen in the shadows,' he said,
5   with a mysterious smile.
We stepped out of the front door into the misty streets. The lamps along the Ramblas marked out an avenue in the early morning haze as the city awoke, like a watercolour slowly coming to life. I followed my father
10 through the narrow streets until at last he stopped in front of a large door of carved wood. Before us rose what to my eyes seemed like an ancient palace, a place of echoes and shadows.
'Daniel, you mustn't tell anyone about this. Not even
15 your friend Tomás. No one.'
A smallish man with thick grey hair opened the door.
'Good morning, Isaac. This is my son, Daniel,' my father announced. 'He will be eleven soon, and one day the shop will be his. It's time he knew this place.'
20 The man called Isaac nodded and invited us in. We followed him through a palatial corridor and arrived at an enormous round hall, the shadows pierced by light from a high glass dome above us. A labyrinth of passageways and bookshelves rose like a beehive, with
25 platforms, steps and bridges that suggested an immense library of impossible geometry. I looked at my father, stunned. He smiled at me and winked.
'Welcome to the Cemetery of Forgotten Books, Daniel.'

PART 2

Among the library's corridors and platforms, I could
make out about a dozen human figures. Some of them
turned to greet me from a distance, and I recognised the
faces of various booksellers, colleagues of my father's. To
my ten-year-old eyes, they looked like a brotherhood of
alchemists in secret study. My father knelt next to me, with
his eyes fixed on mine, and spoke in the hushed voice he
reserved for promises and secrets.

'This is a place of mystery, Daniel, a sanctuary. Every book
you see here has a soul. The soul of the person who wrote
it and of those who read it and lived and dreamed with it.
Every time a book changes hands, every time someone runs
his eyes down its pages, its spirit grows and strengthens.
This place was already ancient when my father brought
me here for the first time many years ago. Perhaps as old
as the city itself. How long has it existed? Who created
it? Nobody knows that for certain. I will tell you what my
father told me, though. When a library disappears, or a
bookshop closes down, when a book has been completely
forgotten, those of us who know this place, its guardians,
make sure that it gets here. In this place, books no longer
remembered by anyone live forever, waiting for the day
when they will reach a new reader's hands. In the shop, we
buy and sell them, but in truth books have no owner. Every
book you see here has been somebody's best friend. Now
they only have us, Daniel. Do you think you'll be able to
keep this a secret?'

My gaze was lost in the immensity and magic of the light. I
nodded, and my father smiled.

'And you know the best thing about it?' he asked.

I shook my head.

'According to tradition, the first time someone visits this
place, he must choose a book, any book, and adopt it.
That's a big responsibility. He has to make sure that it will
never disappear, that it will always stay alive. It's a very
important promise. For life,' explained my father. 'Today it's
your turn.'

For almost half an hour, I wandered within the labyrinth,
breathing in the smell of old paper and dust. Among the
titles, I could make out words in familiar languages and
others I couldn't identify. I walked through galleries filled
with hundreds, thousands of volumes. After a while it
occurred to me that between the covers of each of those
books was a boundless universe waiting to be discovered,
while beyond those walls, in the outside world, people
allowed life to pass by in afternoons of football and radio
soaps. At that precise moment, I knew that I had already
chosen the book I was going to adopt, or that was going to
adopt me. It stood out timidly on one corner of the shelf,
bound in wine-coloured leather. The gold letters of its title
gleamed in the light from the dome above. I caressed them
with the tips of my fingers, reading to myself.

The Shadow of the Wind

JULIÁN CARAX

I had never heard of the title or the author, but I didn't
care. I took the book down with great care and leafed
through the pages. Once liberated from its prison on the
shelf, it released a cloud of gold and dust. Pleased with my
choice, I put it under my arm and walked back through the
labyrinth, a smile on my lips. I felt sure that *The Shadow of
the Wind* had been waiting there for me for years, probably
since before I was born.

6 Read the story again and choose the correct answer.

1 When Daniel and his father left the house
  a the streets were very dark.
  b it had been raining.
  c they arrived at their destination quickly.
  d it was beginning to get light.

2 When they arrived at the door of the building
  a Isaac was expecting them.
  b Daniel's father gave him a warning.
  c Daniel knew why he was there.
  d Isaac was reluctant to let them in.

3 When Daniel went into the library, he was
  a frightened and upset.
  b excited and surprised.
  c astonished and shocked.
  d bored and disappointed.

4 Some of the people in the library
  a were friends of Daniel's father.
  b came to say hello to Daniel.
  c were studying to be alchemists.
  d knew Daniel.

5 The library was created
  a by Daniel's grandfather.
  b to preserve old books.
  c for people to buy and sell books.
  d by the owners of the books.

6 Daniel
  a was confident he'd chosen the right book.
  b found it very difficult to choose a book.
  c preferred football to books.
  d found the right book immediately.

7 Work in pairs and follow the instructions.

Find sentences a–d in the story. What do the underlined words refer to?

a Daniel, you mustn't tell anyone about this.
b Nobody knows that for certain.
c … those of us who know this place, its guardians
d In the shop, we buy and sell them …

Sentences e–g are different from the ones in the story. Find them and underline the differences here.

e Perhaps this place was as old as the city itself.
f After it was liberated from its prison on the shelf, it …
g I was pleased with my choice and I put it under my arm …

8 Read Train Your Brain and match sentences a–g from Exercise 7 to the rules.

TRAIN YOUR BRAIN | Reading skills

Avoiding repetition in a text

To avoid repetition the writer can use two techniques.

Referencing

Every time a book changes hands, every time

someone runs his eyes down its pages …

The writer uses pronouns (eg *they, its, us, this/that*) to refer
1 forwards to information in a text. ☐☐
2 backwards to information in a text. ☐☐

Ellipsis

If the meaning is clear, the writer often:
1 leaves out the subject and verb in the following sentence if it is the same as the previous one. ☐
2 leaves out the subject and verb *to be* before adjectives and past participles. ☐☐

9 Follow the instructions. Use Train Your Brain to help you.

1 What do the underlined words in sentences a–c refer to in the story?

  a Some of them turned to greet me from a distance.
  b Do you think you'll be able to keep this a secret?
  c And you know the best thing about it?

2 Rewrite the sentences d–f from the story including the words that were left out.

  d I looked at my father, stunned.
  e It's a very important promise. For life.
  f It stood out timidly on one corner of the shelf, bound in wine-coloured leather.

10 How far do you agree with these statements? Discuss your opinions in groups. Then summarise your ideas about *one* topic and present them to the class.

• Books have 'souls' and should be preserved.
• It's not worth keeping books once you've read them.
• We'll be able to download books from the Internet soon so won't need to buy them.
• Reading books is a waste of time. All the knowledge you need is online.

VOCABULARY

1 Write the words and phrases from the box in the correct column to make common idioms. Use your dictionary to help you. Then match six of the expressions to the cartoons.

the funny side   eye to eye
somebody up and down   daggers at
down your nose at   the point of   at a glance
the light   somebody in the eye   red

look	see

2 Circle the correct phrases.

1 He was so embarrassed, he couldn't look me *in the eye / up and down*.
2 When I walked in, I saw *eye to eye / at a glance* that they'd been arguing.
3 She's always looked *down her nose at / daggers at* less well-off people.
4 We all thought it was hilarious, but he didn't see *the point of / the funny side*.
5 I was so furious when he criticised my work, I saw *red / the light*.

3 Complete the sentences with the correct forms of five expressions from Exercise 1.

1 I don't know what I did wrong but she _____ me when she arrived.
2 When I walked in, he _____ as if there was something wrong with my clothes.
3 When he didn't call, I finally _____ and ended the relationship.
4 They got home so late that they didn't _____ going to the party.
5 We don't _____ on anything. We can't even agree on what film to see.

4 Match sentences a–h to 1–8 and underline the phrasal verbs with *look* and *see*. What do they mean?

1 He's always so attentive and polite. ☐
2 Oh, do you have to go so soon? ☐
3 I haven't got time to wash up, Mike. ☐
4 It doesn't matter if you don't know his number. ☐
5 Role models are important to kids. ☐
6 Don't worry. We'll find out who stole it soon. ☐
7 She's such a terrible snob. ☐
8 Sorry, can't stop. Tom's leaving in half an hour. ☐

a You can look it up in the phone book.
b The police are looking into it.
c I have to see him off at the airport.
d She looks down on everybody.
e They need people to look up to.
f But I can see through his charm.
g Could you see to it, please?
h Hang on. I'll see you out.

5 Complete the questions with five phrasal verbs from Exercise 4. Then, in pairs, ask and answer the questions.

1 Who do you _____ to? How are they important to you?
2 When you have a party with friends, who _____ the arrangements?
3 Who or what do you _____ on? Why?
4 When did you last _____ somebody _____ ? When? Who?
5 Do you trust everybody or are you good at _____ people?

The Big Read

LOVE. AT ANY COST.

THE CONSTANT GARDENER

THE HIGHLY ANTICIPATED INTERNATIONAL THRILLER FROM JOHN LE CARRÉ & FERNANDO MEIRELLES THE ACADEMY AWARD® NOMINATED DIRECTOR OF *CITY OF GOD*

RALPH FIENNES   RACHEL WEISZ

A Frightening, heartbreaking, and skilfully written, ¹_____ John le Carré's eighteenth novel, *The Constant Gardener*, in spite of the tragic events at the heart of it. The story is set in Kenya and the plot ²_____ the dark side of globalisation, with its greed and cynicism.

B ³_____ the brutal murder of the young and beautiful Tessa Quayle, who's married to Justin, a shy British diplomat. Unlike her husband, Tessa is an idealistic heroine and passionate reformer. Before her death, she sends a report to Justin's bosses about a sinister British pharmaceutical company. The company is secretly testing a new drug on innocent African villagers, and some of them die. But the report disappears. Justin, the 'constant gardener' of the title, is deeply shocked by his wife's murder and eventually suspects his superiors.
⁴_____ , when they try to stop his investigations, he cleverly escapes, setting off on a personal crusade to find the killers.

C ⁵_____ about the book, apart from the thrilling action and convincing story, was the vivid descriptions of the places Justin visits in search of answers: from Africa to Italy to Canada and back. Le Carré also creates a range of entirely believable English characters, from absurd bureaucrats to heartless businessmen. ⁶_____ of the book is that the author has a tendency to introduce too many new characters and names, so it was occasionally rather confusing.

JOHN LE CARRÉ
THE RUSSIA HOUSE
A classic le Carré *Sunday Times*

JOHN LE CARRÉ
TINKER TAILOR SOLDIER SPY
A great thriller, the best le Carré has written
Spectator

JOHN LE CARRÉ
ERFECT SPY

D All in all, though, ⁷_____ spy thrillers, you'll love this book. And if you're not, ⁸_____ it because *The Constant Gardener* is also a profoundly moving love story, of a man who discovers not only his own strengths, but also the incredible courage of the woman he loves.

Author bio: John Le Carré

John le Carré's real name is John Moore Cornwell. He was born on October 19 1931 in Poole, England. He was fascinated by foreign languages and graduated from Lincoln College, Oxford, in 1956. He then taught at Eton, the elite British public school, for two years before joining the British Foreign Service. He subsequently worked abroad, mainly in West Germany, for MI6, the British secret service.
Le Carré is the author of twenty-one novels, mostly spy thrillers. Nine of his books have so far been made into films, including *The Tailor of Panama* and *The Constant Gardener*. He has been married twice, has four sons and lives in Cornwall.

WRITING AND VOCABULARY

1 What types of books do you like reading most? Why? Choose from the box or think of other types.

crime   spy thriller   science fiction
suspense   fantasy   classics   biography
historical fiction   humorous   romantic
mystery   adventure

2 Look at the photos, book covers and short bio. Then answer the questions in pairs.

1 What can you find out about this author and his books?
2 Predict what the books are about from their titles. Which do you think seems most interesting? Why?
3 If you've read *The Constant Gardener*, what did you think of it?

3 Read the review and complete it with the phrases in the box.

One of the things I liked best
I would still recommend   My only criticism
centres on   I thoroughly enjoyed
The book opens with   if you're a fan of
Consequently

4 Match paragraphs A–D to 1–4 below. If you know the book, do you agree with the review?

1 Conclusion and recommendation ☐
2 Main events in the story ☐
3 Introduction ☐
4 Positive and negative comments ☐

5 Answer the questions about the review.

1 Which tense is most often used? Why?
2 Is the style of writing neutral or informal?
3 Which definition describes the meaning of 'constant' in the title?
   a happening regularly   b loyal and faithful

6 Find the nouns that collocate with these adjectives in the review.

1 tragic _____	6 convincing _____
2 brutal _____	7 vivid _____
3 idealistic _____	8 believable _____
4 personal _____	9 heartless _____
5 thrilling _____	10 incredible _____

7 Underline the adverbs in phrases 1–3 and match them to their uses a–c. Find five more examples in the review.

1 entirely believable
2 is secretly testing
3 eventually suspects

a describes how something happens ☐
b describes an adjective ☐
c is a time adverb ☐

8 Circle the correct adverbs in the review below.

Susan thinks that she and her husband are [1] *wonderfully / skilfully* happy. One day, a stranger tries to murder her. She is [2] *slowly / profoundly* shocked. She [3] *consequently / happily* discovers that her husband planned it. He [4] *secretly / quickly* wants to kill her. She [5] *occasionally / cleverly* plans to find out the truth. She [6] *finally / unfortunately* proves that he is guilty.

9 Make notes about a book you have enjoyed reading, using the prompts below. Then talk about your book in groups.

1 I thoroughly enjoyed …
2 It's a … and was written by …
3 The story is set in …
4 The plot centres on …
5 The thing I liked best was …
6 My only criticism of the book is …
7 All in all, …
8 If you're a fan of … , you …
9 I would recommend it because …

10 Expand the information from Exercise 9 and write a review of your book (200–250 words). Use Train Your Brain to plan and check your review.

TRAIN YOUR BRAIN | Writing skills

A book review

Organisation
Introduction: include the title, type of book, author, your overall impression and a brief summary of the setting and plot.
Summary of the plot: outline the main characters and events in the story.
NB: Don't say too much and spoil the ending!
Opinions: say what you particularly liked/disliked about the book.
Conclusion: recommend/don't recommend the book.

Style and language
• Use present tenses to describe the main events of the story.
• Write in a neutral style, not too formal or casual.
• Vocabulary: use a variety of adjectives, adverbs and linking words to make your review more interesting and engaging.

VOCABULARY AND GRAMMAR

1 Match the phrasal verbs with the phrases to make common collocations. Then write your own sentences with each collocation. Add all the necessary details.

turn down   come up with   see through
look up   look down on   see off
cheer up   do away with

a good suggestion   a word in a dictionary
poorer relatives   old possessions
at the train station   a marriage proposal
his lies   an upset friend

2 Complete the letter with one word in each gap.

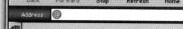

Q I'M WORRIED ABOUT MY ROOMMATE

Dear Agony Aunt,

I'm worried that my roommate may soon find himself in serious financial difficulty. He's always liked buying things off the Internet but now he spends the whole day surfing the net for, as he puts it, irresistible bargains. I know how easy it is to get addicted ¹_____ things like this and I'm afraid he's totally ²_____ on it already. I'm worried it might turn into a serious addiction one day and that he'll become a compulsive ³_____ or something. What can I do to help him? I know that I should confront him about it but I'm almost sure he would ⁴_____ daggers at me and deny everything. And then he would start talking about my shopping ⁵_____ and call me a shopaholic. We just don't seem to ⁶_____ eye to eye on anything. So what's your advice? Should I look him in the ⁷_____ and discuss my suspicions, or should I ask his parents or friends to raise this issue with him?

Confused Steven

3 Complete the sentences with the correct forms of the verbs in brackets.

1 Yoga makes me _____ (feel) great.
2 I find it challenging _____ (keep) track of my finances.
3 For one thing, _____ (overeat) causes obesity and heart disease.
4 Once again they attempted _____ (reach) the summit, this time successfully.
5 He'll never forget _____ (win) the invitation to the MTV Music Awards.
6 I would never risk _____ (book) a flight with a newly set up airline company.
7 The Prime Minister suggested _____ (adopt) a more pragmatic approach to international relations.
8 Jogging made Jack dizzy, so he stopped _____ (take) a few deep breaths.

University Life

While at university, students often choose to join a sorority or fraternity. They create a feeling of community because they let ¹___ others with similar interests. They also enable students to ²___ new activities and find out their strengths and abilities. There are however a few things you may want to know before you choose the one you want to join.

- I encourage ³___ all the houses. Talk with the members and remember ⁴___ what it's like to live there for real.
- Some sorority and fraternity chapters ⁵___ have their own houses. Think about whether you would prefer to live with the other members of your chapter or have the freedom to live elsewhere (especially if you ⁶___ to sharing your accommodation with others).
- Once an active member, don't despair if your initial enthusiasm for sorority or fraternity life ⁷___ . It's ⁸___ that sometimes you'll feel a bit discouraged.

4 Read the text above and choose the correct answers a–d.

1 a that students meet   **c** students meet
  b students meeting   **d** students to meet
2 a take up   **c** pick at
  b come across   **d** part with
3 a you visit   **c** you to visit
  b you visiting   **d** that you visit
4 a that you check out   **c** checking out
  b check out   **d** to check out
5 a mustn't   **c** are bound not to
  b shouldn't   **d** may not
6 a didn't use   **c** don't use
  b aren't used   **d** aren't getting used
7 a pigs out   **c** works out
  b sets off   **d** wears off
8 a inevitable   **c** believable
  b overwhelming   **d** immense

5 Use the words in capital letters and rewrite the sentences so that they mean the same as the original ones.

1 It is becoming normal for me not to see my parents every weekend.   USED
_____

2 Being extremely sensitive, she will probably be easily influenced by her peers.   LIKELY
_____

3 It was an invitation she couldn't refuse.   ABLE
_____

4 If you are an EU student, you won't have to pay entrance fees.   OBLIGED
_____

5 They didn't succeed in stopping the demonstrations.   MANAGE
_____

6 Visitors to the National Park mustn't walk dogs without a lead.   FORBIDDEN
_____

7 I'm sure it will be the best book ever written.   BOUND
_____

PRONUNCIATION

1 **CD2.14** Listen to a question asked in four different ways. Pay attention to where the main stress falls each time and match each question with one of the answers a–d.

So, you've been on the Cabbage Soup Diet for two weeks?

a No, but my best friend Ana has. ☐
b No, I've been on the Atkins diet. ☐
c No, I've been on it for two days. ☐
d No, but I'm thinking about going on it. ☐

2 **CD2.15** Listen and check. Then practise in pairs.

LISTENING SKILLS

1 **CD2.16** Listen to the radio programme about obesity. Are the statements true (T) or false (F)?

1 In Britain obesity has recently become a much bigger problem than smoking. ☐
2 Britain holds the title for being the fattest nation in the developed world. ☐
3 The number of obese people in the UK is now twice as high as twenty years ago. ☐
4 Experts are very clear as to why people's calorie requirement is much lower now than before. ☐
5 Scientists believe that the sensation of hunger is genetically determined. ☐
6 People's claims about how much they eat and exercise are often misjudged. ☐
7 The results of the studies show that overweight people should be much more careful with what they eat than slim people. ☐

SPEAKING SKILLS

1 Express two general opinions connected with topics 1–4. For each answer use the words/expressions in brackets.

1 Most young people nowadays are obsessed with diet and exercise.
(common belief) _____
(said) _____

2 A book is man's best friend.
(generally agreed) _____
(the case) _____

3 A feeling of belonging to a group is a very important aspect of a human's life.
(tendency) _____
(thought) _____

4 Vegetarians have found the secret of good living.
(view) _____
(whole) _____

2 Look at the visuals and get ready to present the material and discuss:
– people's reading habits and preferences;
– the future of traditional books and newspapers.
Then answer the teacher's questions.

Teacher's questions:
1 What information do you get from the graph, the photos, the short comments and the quote?
2 What kinds of books are the most popular among children, teenagers and young adults in Poland?
3 What role does reading play in people's lives?
4 Why are alternative forms of reading gaining more and more popularity?
5 In your opinion, how will reading habits change in the near future?

'Books, like friends, should be few and well chosen.' *Samuel Paterson*

Are traditional books and newspapers dying? Your reaction

HAVE YOUR SAY

+ Post a comment

Well, just answer these simple questions for yourself. How much time do you spend each day reading newspapers? And how much time do you read on-line?

Tim Brown, UK

Why should they be? Because of the influence of the Internet? It is just a big library. Of a different kind.

T K Serghides, USA

Read all comments

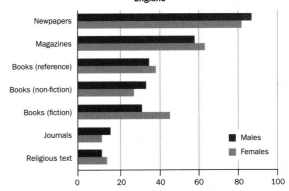

Reading preferences[1]: by sex, 2001
England

(Newspapers, Magazines, Books (reference), Books (non-fiction), Books (fiction), Journals, Religious text — Males / Females)

[1] Adults aged 16 and over. Respondents were asked what they had read in the last seven days. More than one response could be given.

Express yourself

Read, listen and talk about self-expression, culture and the arts.
Practise reported speech and reporting verbs; vocabulary related to arts and culture.
Focus on justifying opinions.
Write a haiku.

Back Forward Stop Refresh Home AutoFill Print Mail

Address www1.a novel in a year.com

A novel in a year

Search [   ]

Home

Comment
Your view
Blogs
News
Picture galleries
Magazine
Features

↘ SERVICES

RSS feeds
Email
Mobile
Podcasts
Contact us

Novelist Louise Doughty invited you to join her creative fiction class by writing the first sentence of a novel – the first step towards helping you create a novel in a year. She gave you these words to start with: 'The day after my eighth birthday, my father …' and asked you to finish the sentence. And you did – in your thousands. Here's a selection of your responses.

Your responses …

The day after my eighth birthday, my father …

Response **a** … asked whether I'd seen him hide the money the day before.

Response **b** … told me to meet him there that night.

Response **c** … asked when I would be back there, and I answered 'Next week.'

Response **d** … informed me that he had found me a husband.

Response **e** … asked me if I could write.

Response **f** … asked me to take the fish finger out of the soup, wrap it in a cloth and take it to Grandma.

Response **g** … announced that from then on, everything would be different.

Response **h** … said he would like to tell me something very important.

Response **i** … told me that we must leave the house immediately because they were coming.

Response **j** … said I should pack my things because we had to go to Hong Kong the following day.

Response **k** … said that secrets always come out in the end.

Quote Unquote

The truth is that many of us write novels for the same reason that George Mallory gave for climbing Everest – 'Because it's there.'
Louise Doughty

A writer is a person for whom writing is more difficult than it is for other people.
Thomas Mann, German writer (1874–1965)

You learn as much by writing as by reading.
Lord Acton, 19th-century historian

GRAMMAR AND LISTENING

1 Read the introduction to the website and answer the questions.

- Who is Louise Doughty?
- What did she invite people to do?
- Would you be interested in a course like this? Why?/Why not?

2 Read some of the responses that were sent in. Which make you want to read on, and why? Use the adjectives from the box.

scary silly dull engaging disturbing
amusing intriguing upsetting
far-fetched

3 Think Back! Look at the responses again and answer the questions.

1 In responses a–g, which report(s)
- an affirmative sentence? ☐☐
- a *wh-* question? ☐
- a *yes/no* question? ☐☐
- an imperative sentence? ☐
- a request? ☐

What verbs are used to report each of them? What other verbs can be used?

2 What happens to tenses and pronouns in reported speech? Give examples.

3 What two words are used to start *yes/no* questions?

Work it out

4 Find the reported versions of sentences 1–3 on the website. Which <u>underlined</u> modal verb can change in reported speech, and what does it change to?

1 You <u>should</u> pack your things. We <u>must</u> go to Hong Kong tomorrow.
2 I <u>would</u> like to tell you something very important.
3 We <u>must</u> leave the house immediately because they're coming.

5 Complete the table with the highlighted words from the website.

direct	reported	direct	reported
1 here 2 yesterday 3 this 4 that	that/the	5 tomorrow 6 now 7 today 8 tonight	that day

6 Look at the reported sentences a–d. Why don't the <u>underlined</u> words change? Match explanations 1–3 to each sentence a–d.

Secrets always <u>come out</u> in the end.
a Dad **says** that secrets always <u>come out</u> in the end. ☐
b Dad **said** that secrets always <u>come out</u> in the end. ☐

I'll be back <u>next week</u>.
c He **said** he'<u>ll be</u> back <u>next week</u>. ☐
d He **has said** he'<u>ll be</u> back <u>next week</u>. ☐

1 the reporting verb is in the present (present simple or perfect)
2 the statement is reported soon after it was said so the situation is still relevant
3 the reporter believes that the original fact/opinion is still true

➤ **Check it out page 155**

7 Report the sentences using the prompts.

1 Sea levels will rise in the next fifty years. Experts have said that _____ .
2 Did you hear about the accident last week, Jon? He wanted to know _____ .
3 Dinosaurs lived for 250 million years. My teacher explained that _____ .
4 What time are you having your Spanish class this evening? She asked them _____ .
5 Sally, I'll meet you here tomorrow night. (Sally that night) Bob said _____ . (Sally the next day) Bob said _____ .
6 I would go there now if I could. She said _____ .

8 Correct the two mistakes in each sentence. Which responses on the website do they follow?

1 So I told him I would get the suitcases and said what time were we leaving.
2 I asked him what did he mean and how would it be different.
3 I asked that I should go alone or if I can bring my sister.
4 I told that I was too young and that I had already had a boyfriend.
5 I replied that I haven't but he told me I had been lying.

9 CD2.17 Listen to stories A–C and match them to the correct sentences in Exercise 8. How do you think each story will continue?

A ☐   B ☐   C ☐

10 CD2.17 Listen to story A again and write as much of the dialogue as you can remember. Then change it to reported speech.

11 Read the quotes on the website. In groups, discuss what they mean. Which do you like best and why?

VOCABULARY

1 Read the entertainment guide. In pairs, discuss which event you would prefer to go to, and why.

2 Complete the table with the <u>underlined</u> words in the guide. Some belong to more than one category.

Art	Music	Dance/Musical	Theatre
paintings			

[ARTS]
London entertainment guide

Canaletto in Venice

Canaletto (1697–1768) established the definitive image of Venice with his breathtakingly convincing <u>paintings</u>. Fourteen of them form the core of this <u>exhibition</u>, with seventy works on paper, the largest number of his <u>drawings</u> ever shown.
Queen's Gallery, until Sunday

The Grand Canal

+ BBC Symphony <u>Orchestra</u> and <u>Chorus</u>

Mozart's 250th anniversary celebrations continue with this <u>performance</u> of his glorious, eternally popular Mass in C Minor, with <u>soloists</u> Laura Aikin and Jeremy Ovenden, and <u>conductor</u> David Robertson.
Barbican, Fri

+ Billy Elliott: The Musical

Smash hit *Billy Elliot* is a funny, heart-warming celebration of one young boy's dream. Based on the film, with a spectacular <u>cast</u>, brilliantly inventive <u>choreography</u> and clever <u>sets</u>, this exhilarating <u>production</u> continues its record-breaking run at the Victoria Palace. To top it all, the music is by <u>composer</u> Elton John.   *Victoria Palace, daily except Sun*

+ Jeremy Irons onstage

Jeremy Irons returns to the West End <u>stage</u> for the first time in nearly twenty years. He plays the <u>leading role</u> in <u>playwright</u> Christopher Hampton's critically-acclaimed <u>drama</u>, *Embers*, adapted from the international best-selling novel by Sandor Marai.   *Duke of York's Theatre, <u>previews</u> now*

3 Add the words in the box to the table in Exercise 2. Use a dictionary to help you.

still life   string quartet   dress rehearsal
watercolour   duet   score   abstract
box office   the stalls   sonata   concert
percussion   portrait   audition   landscape
backstage   dressing room   sculpture
understudy   supporting role

4 In pairs, decide which word or phrase is the odd one out in each group. Give reasons.

1 portrait   drawing   abstract   landscape
2 solo   duet   score   chorus
3 conductor   composer   playwright   choreographer
4 cast   dressing room   supporting role   understudy
5 dress rehearsal   backstage   stalls   box office

5 Complete the sentences with the correct forms of the verbs in capital letters.

1 What I like best is the _____ of the painting.   COMPOSE
2 Henry Moore was Britain's greatest twentieth-century _____ .   SCULPT
3 He was much better as a songwriter than as a _____ .   PERFORM
4 We encourage our dancers to develop their _____ talent.   CHOREOGRAPH
5 He not only wrote the script, but was also the _____ .   PRODUCE

6 Circle the correct verbs.

1 Lloyd Webber's latest musical has *broken / made* box office records again.
2 Don West *stars / plays* the leading role as the heroic husband.
3 I thought he *did / gave* a poor performance in his last part.
4 Paula North is *showing / putting on* her new work at the local gallery.
5 Our school Drama Club is *playing / putting on* a musical next month.
6 I think I'll *make / go for* an audition for this new production.

7 CD2.18 Listen to five conversations. What are the people talking about? What words helped you to decide?

8 Check the meaning of the words in the box in a dictionary. Then answer the questions in groups.

culture vulture   opera buff   philistine
arty type   theatre-goer   balletomane

- Do you know anybody who fits these descriptions? If so, how do they fit, and why?
- What artistic or cultural events have you been to recently? What did you enjoy/not enjoy about them?

READING AND VOCABULARY

1 In groups, write down as many different kinds of dances as you can in one minute.

2 Discuss the questions in pairs. Then read the introduction to the text on page 76 and check your answers.

1 When and why did people begin to dance?
2 What roles has dance played in our society and culture?
3 What sorts of dances are popular nowadays?
4 Do you know any TV programmes which popularise dancing? What are they?
5 Why is dancing good for us?

3 **CD ROM** Work in groups of three. Read your text on pages 76–77 and answer questions 1–5. Then exchange information with the other two members of your group.

Student A, read the text about flamenco.
Student B, read the text about capoeira.
Student C, read the text about salsa.

1 How did the writer first find out about the dance?
2 Where did the dance come from and what is it about?
3 What does the writer like about it? How does it make them feel?
4 What has he/she learnt from it?
5 What benefits does it bring to the people who do it?

4 In groups, match the dances from all three texts to sentences 1–9.

1 This dance is usually performed in public by full-time, professional dancers. ☐
2 You don't need to have much professional training to do this dance. ☐
3 This has helped the writer take a more relaxed attitude to life. ☐
4 This goes beyond being just a dance or means of entertainment. ☐
5 You usually do this in a club as a way of relaxing and enjoying yourself. ☐
6 The writer is attracted to this dance because of its pride and passion. ☐
7 It still retains its original purpose but has developed its own philosophy. ☐
8 It is now being adapted to incorporate other dance forms and rhythms. ☐
9 This dance has a ritual formality associated with it. ☐

5 Vocabulary Look at the underlined words and expressions in the texts and match them to their definitions.

1 so worried and tired that you can't relax
2 really surprised and impressed me
3 feelings of shyness or embarrassment
4 talk about something you like in an excited way
5 have a very different opinion or attitude to something
6 express feelings you wouldn't normally talk about
7 relax completely and enjoy yourself
8 behave in an angry way because you are nervous or worried
9 put your feet down on the floor loudly and with force

6 **CD2.19** Find two adjectives in each text that best describe each dance. Then listen to the dance music and add other adjectives to describe it.

1 Flamenco _____ , _____
2 Capoeira _____ , _____
3 Salsa _____ , _____

7 **CD2.20** Listen to more dance music. How would you describe it? Choose adjectives from the box or your own. Justify your opinions.

peaceful   dramatic   energetic   rhythmic
graceful   soporific   depressing   uplifting
relaxing   monotonous

1 tango   3 hip hop   5 Irish jig
2 ballet   4 waltz

8 Discuss the questions in groups.

• Which of the dances you have read about or heard would you like to try? Why?
• What role does dance play in your life and your culture?
• Why do you think dance is often a performance?
• Read the quotes and choose the one you like best, saying why.

'Socrates learned to dance when he was seventy because he felt that an essential part of himself had been neglected.'

Source unknown

'Dance is the hidden language of the soul.'

Martha Graham, pioneer of modern dance

'I do not try to dance better than anyone else. I only try to dance better than myself.'

Mikhail Baryshnikov, Russian ballet dancer

'A sense of humour is just common sense, dancing.'

Clive James, Australian writer

MOVE TO THE MUSIC

People of all ages and walks of life are dragging themselves away from their sofas and TVs and discovering the pleasures of moving their bodies to the rhythms of music. Is this a temporary craze or a sign of the times?

Moving to music appeals to our most primal instincts. Throughout history, people have expressed themselves through dance in rituals and ceremonies, on social occasions with friends and family, and as professional artists. Nowadays clubbing is one of the most popular forms of socialising for young people. And added to this, the huge popularity of TV programmes like *Strictly Come Dancing*, where even the clumsiest celebrities are turned into graceful ballroom dancers, has encouraged people of all ages to try it for themselves. Meanwhile, a leading medical journal applauds the benefits: 'Dancing is a great way to build physical activity into our lives. It stimulates the senses, it's great fun and it's good for our bodies and minds.'

'It's really a performance art and takes years to perfect.'

I go to a flamenco club every Friday just to watch the dancing. The British love flamenco and I'm one of them. I happened to be in Andalucia on holiday when the Jeréz flamenco festival was on, and it just <u>blew me away</u>. Now there's an annual festival in London and it's getting more popular every year, partly because flamenco's changing so much. There are still those who perform it the traditional gypsy way, but others have experimented with a fusion of styles, mixing flamenco with jazz, modern dance, even ballet. But what I love most is the pride and fiery passion of the gypsy temperament. I'm sure this is its basic appeal – we have nothing like it in British culture.

I go to classes every week and more people are joining all the time, both men and women. Some come to get rid of stress after a day's work, some are very committed and want to be professionals. It's really a performance art and takes years to perfect. Still, I find it exhilarating to <u>stamp</u> out passionate rhythms with twenty other people. It's the only place I can use that kind of aggressive energy, but at the same time I'm allowed to be so feminine, and feel proud and free. To me, flamenco is the ultimate in self-expression. It's all about the way people feel. When I watch flamenco, I see the dancers <u>make confessions</u> on stage. When I dance flamenco, I feel as if I'm dancing my life.

Monika, 21

A: FLAMENCO

'A big city person might see it as a form of self-defence, while for others it's a way of life.'

It was a sunny winter's day in London when I first heard the music. Exotic instruments, hypnotic rhythms. I turned round. Was it a dance? Some sort of fight? Acrobatics? 'What is it?' 'Capoeira.' 'Capo-what?' 'Ca-po-ei-ra. A Brazilian martial art.' As I later discovered, it's all of these things and more. It originated nearly 400 years ago as a form of self-defence amongst African slaves. They disguised it as a folk dance to make it acceptable, and it developed from there. Brazilians say they 'play' capoeira, like a game, not a fight. It's quite difficult to learn, but I don't do it just to get physically fit; it's the mind-body-spirit connection that begins to change you. You meet so many different people, especially Brazilians, and they have a completely different take on life. I used to be very shy but I've lost some of my inhibitions – and I don't get uptight when things go wrong. I enjoy life and appreciate the good things. Anyone can find some form of identity in capoeira. For instance, a big city person might see it as a form of self-defence, while for others it's a way of life. Its philosophy is to release good energy. When everybody's facing each other in the circle, and the instruments are playing, and everybody's focusing on the two players in the middle, singing and clapping to the music, you're definitely going to feel something. And if you don't, then you're not doing it right.

Keith, 24

B: CAPOEIRA

'There's no 'right' way of doing it, you just dance for the joy of it.'

I first heard about salsa a couple of years ago when a friend came back from Cuba raving about it. Finally, he persuaded me to go to a salsa club in the West End. It was hot and crowded, and the music was deafening, but I just couldn't believe the energy and vitality of the place – it was magic. One thing that surprised me was how courteous it all was. Complete strangers will politely ask you to dance, then after five breathless minutes on the dance floor, just as politely thank you and move on. But it was the dance itself that was so intoxicating. There's no 'right' way of doing it, you just dance for the joy of it.

It's very sensual and the only philosophy is to delight in the music and let yourself go. I found out that 'salsa' means 'hot sauce' in Spanish, and Latin American people in New York began to use it to describe their music in the '70s. It's a mix of Afro-Cuban and Latin rhythms like mambo and rumba – with lots of spice! If you're not a confident dancer, have a few lessons to learn the basic steps. As well as learning something new, it's a great way to meet people. You'll feel so free and happy, and it's a fantastic release when you're feeling a bit stressed out. I was amazed to find that I was quite good at it. Now I'm training to be a salsa teacher.

Joanne, 19

C: SALSA

GRAMMAR

1 Read the article and match the visuals 1–4 to texts A–D. Which was NOT a success story, and why?

2 Match the sentences to texts A–D in the article. Who do you think regretted their actions, and why?

1 She <u>suggested</u> getting a job as a secretary. ☐
2 Publishers <u>criticised</u> her book for being too long. ☐
3 She <u>advised</u> her not to become a model. ☐
4 He <u>offered</u> to pay them $130 for the rights. ☐
5 He <u>explained</u> that four-member bands were out. ☐
6 They <u>apologised</u> for rejecting her book. ☐
7 He <u>warned</u> him that he was wasting his time. ☐

Work it out

3 Add the <u>underlined</u> verbs in Exercise 2 to the table according to their patterns.

Reporting verb patterns	
+ (that) + reported sentence	promise, admit, agree, regret, 1_____
+ object + (that) + reported sentence	remind, 2_____
+ infinitive	agree, promise, 3_____
+ object + infinitive	recommend, 4_____
+ gerund	admit, advise, regret, recommend, 5_____
+ preposition + gerund	insist on, object to, 6_____
+ object + preposition + gerund	congratulate sb on, accuse sb of, 7_____

4 Circle six verbs in the table in Exercise 3 that have more than one pattern. Then rewrite sentences 1–6 using a different pattern from the table.

1 She admitted giving Norma Jean the wrong advice.
   She admitted (that) she had given Norma Jean the wrong advice.
2 The executive recommended him to give up.
3 The boys regretted not making a better deal.
4 The publishers promised that they would look at her book again.
5 He advised taking the money as they wouldn't get a better offer.
6 Epstein agreed that he would become their manager.

Who's sorry now?

It's often difficult to imagine that immensely successful people ever had a moment's doubt or rejection in their lives. Read on …

A ☐

March 1996
Dear Ms Rowling,
Thank you for sending your manuscript. We are sorry we are not able to publish your book but it's far too long for children. If you cut it, we'll look at it again.
Yours sincerely,
A Publisher

B ☐

Eighteen-year-old Norma Jean Baker applied to the Blue Book Modelling Agency in 1944. However, Emmeline Snively, the agency's director, gave her some friendly advice: 'Why don't you learn secretarial work?' She also suggested that she should get married. Norma Jean ignored this and eventually became the sensational Marilyn Monroe.

C ☐

After discovering The Beatles playing in a Liverpool club in 1961, Brian Epstein became their manager. Among the rejections he received from record companies was one from a Decca executive, who said: 'You're wasting your time, Mr Epstein. Four-member groups are out. Give up and go back to Liverpool.'

D ☐

The first issue of *Action Comic* in the US in 1938 featured a new character called Superman. He was the creation of two seventeen-year-olds, Joe Shuster and Jerry Siegel. Their publisher saw some potential in the character and said: 'I'll give you $130 for the rights. Take it now – you won't get a better offer.' Seeing the chance to earn $65 each, the boys accepted the deal.

Books – News

Worldwide Bestsellers 2005 ❹

1 Harry Potter and the Half-Blood Prince
J K Rowling (300+ million copies)

5 Read the pairs of sentences below. What extra information do the <u>underlined</u> words provide?

1 a The woman suggested <u>that Norma Jean should</u> get married.
  b The woman suggested getting married.
2 a They recommended <u>that she should</u> make the book shorter.
  b They recommended making the book shorter.

➤ **Check it out** page 155

6 Rewrite the sentences. Sometimes more than one pattern is possible. Check the verb patterns on page 155 to help you.

1 I didn't cause the accident. It was the other driver.
  He denied _____ .
2 Come on, I know you can do it, Mike.
  Mike's teacher encouraged _____ .
3 It was Dan who broke the window.
  Mary accused _____ .
4 No, I'm not going out for a walk today. It's too cold.
  He objected _____ .
5 That's a terrible cough, Alan. You should see a doctor.
  Alan's mother suggested _____ .
6 I won't help you if you don't try harder.
  His dad threatened _____ .
7 You really must read this book, Lisa. It's his best yet.
  Her friend insisted that _____ .

7 Write seven sentences about Judy's conversation with her art teacher, using the verbs in the box.

> advise congratulate recommend remind insist
> warn admit

T Well done, Judy! You've painted another brilliant picture.
J I think it's awful.
T No, believe me, I know you'll be a great artist!
J But my parents don't think so …
T Well, you'll have to work hard. It's difficult to get into art college these days. But remember, you love painting.
J Yes, you're right. What can I do?
T First, you should have a serious talk with your parents. Then look for a good art college …

8 Complete the text with the correct forms of the words in brackets.

In mid 1997, film critics insisted that the new *Titanic* film ¹_____ (be) a flop. The director, James Cameron, however, thought differently. Originally, the studios wanted Matthew McConaughey to play Jack, but Cameron ²_____ (insist on/have) Leonardo DiCaprio, who was perfect for the role. Then Cameron complained that Céline Dion's song ³_____ (be) too sentimental and ⁴_____ (refuse/include) it. But James Horner, who wrote the film score, ⁵_____ (persuade/him/use) it. When several stunt people were injured during filming, critics ⁶_____ (accuse/Cameron of/be) ruthless and ⁷_____ (criticise/him for/put) people's lives in danger. When the film finally opened in December, critics still ⁸_____ (warn/filmgoers/it/be) a disaster. Four months later, *Titanic* won eleven Oscars. Everybody ⁹_____ (congratulate/Cameron on/make) such a marvellous film, which earned nearly two billion dollars. But some critics never ¹⁰_____ (admit/make) a mistake.

9 Work in pairs. Student A, look at page 147. Student B, look at page 149.

SPEAKING AND LISTENING

SHOWTIMES

MISSION IMPOSSIBLE III 12A
New Release

SHREK 3 U
New Release

CHARLIE AND THE CHOCOLATE FACTORY PG

TAXI DRIVER 18

BOOK NOW!
THE CONSTANT GARDENER 15

1 Look at the film listing. What do the symbols represent? Match them to the definitions.

1 Universal – anybody can see it
2 Parental guidance needed for children under 8
3 For under 12s accompanied by an adult
4 For teenagers over 15
5 For adults over 18

2 In pairs, discuss the questions about your country.

1 Are the film ratings the same as in Britain? If not, what are they?
2 Which newspaper has the highest circulation? What makes it so popular?
3 What are the most widely viewed TV programmes? Why?

3 CD2.21 Listen to Part 1 of a radio programme. Are the statements true (T), false (F) or is there no information (NI)?

1 The programme is a debate about freedom of speech. ☐
2 James Harmer thinks the 12A film rating is not always strict enough. ☐
3 The BBFC expects everybody to decide for themselves what films they see. ☐
4 Eighteen percent of young people in the survey are fifteen-year-olds. ☐
5 Kelly thinks that there should be more control over what kids watch on TV. ☐
6 She accepts the fact that the newspapers take a lot of interest in her life. ☐

4 CD2.21 Listen again and tick the phrases you hear in Speak Out. Then summarise the main points each speaker makes.

SPEAK OUT | Justifying opinions

1 You have to admit that … ☐
2 You can't deny that … ☐
3 You have to bear in mind that … ☐
4 It goes without saying that … ☐
5 As far as I can see … ☐
6 I really don't see the point of … ☐
7 That might not necessarily be *good/the case* … ☐
8 The way I see it … ☐
9 The truth (of the matter) is … ☐
10 To be *frank/honest* … ☐
11 On the other hand … ☐

5 CD2.22 Before you listen to Part 2, complete the sentences using Speak Out. Then listen and check.

1 _____ it, it's all about money – it's pure greed.
2 _____ admit that most people are not interested in being informed.
3 _____ without _____ that the stories are usually exaggerated.
4 And _____ can't _____ she's absolutely right – we need more control.
5 But _____ might_____ in many homes.
6 _____ be _____ , parents can't constantly screen what their children watch.
7 _____ can _____ from what Tommy and James said, there's a lot wrong …
8 _____ of having ratings for so many different age groups.
9 You have to _____ in _____ that to learn responsibility, we need more freedom, not less.
10 Though on _____ , you could argue that they only buy pirate movies because they were banned.

6 CD2.22 Listen again and summarise the main point that each person makes. Who do you agree with and why?

7 Work in pairs. Student A, look at page 148. Student B, look at page 150.

8 Discuss the questions in pairs.

• In your country, how much control is there of TV programming, newspaper content, film ratings, the Internet?
• Do you think there should be more or less control? Why?
• What sort of rights do young people have when they are eighteen?

WRITING

1 In pairs, answer the questions.

- Do you like poetry? If so, which poets do you read, and why?
- Have you ever written poetry? If so, do you show it to other people? Why?/Why not?

2 Read the haiku and match them to topics 1–4. Which one do you like best? Why?

1 Walking in a snowstorm ☐
2 A computer crash ☐
3 Getting older ☐
4 A solitary walk ☐

A *No one else travels*
Along this way, only me
This autumn evening.

B *No sky and no earth*
But still snowflakes fall softly
As I walk along

C *First snow, then silence*
This thousand-dollar screen dies
So beautifully

D *First winter morning*
the mirror I stare into
shows my father's face

3 CD2.23 Read the tips for writing haiku and guess what could be put in the gaps, using the haiku in Exercise 2. Then listen and check.

Top tips for writing haiku

- Write in three lines of five, ¹_____ and five syllables each.
- Use the ²_____ tense.
- Refer to the time of day or ³_____ .
- Use ⁴_____ images that show harmony or contrast, like earth and ⁵_____ .
- Write about ordinary events in ⁶_____ .
- Write from personal experience or ⁷_____ .
- Write about experiencing life through your five ⁸_____ !

4 CD2.24 Complete the haiku with the words from the box. Listen and check. What are these haiku about?

wind   yesterday   working   Windows
summer   walk

1 *Cool* ¹_____ *and cold sand*
I ²_____ *along at sunset*
Remembering ³_____

2 ⁴_____ *it worked.*
Today it is not ⁵_____ .
⁶_____ *is like that.*

5 Look at the painting and write a haiku about it. Read the haiku to each other in groups. Discuss which you like best, and why.

Love

Good progress?

Read, listen and talk about inventions, science and technology.
Practise passives; compound nouns and adjectives.
Focus on interpreting graphs and charts.
Write a 'for and against' essay.

GRAMMAR AND LISTENING

1 In pairs, match the inventions in the photos to the headlines 1–4. Then discuss what you think these inventions can do.

Your body – the conductor 1 ☐

Text me a coffee 2 ☐

This bag will more than surprise you! 3 ☐

Mirror, mirror on the wall, who'll be the ugliest of them all? 4 ☐

2 Read sentences 1–10 and match inventions A–D to them.

1 It is going to be shown at the 'New Inventors' show next month. ☐
2 It can be switched on by text message. ☐
3 A transmitter is worn on the body and digital messages are sent via the body's electrical field. ☐
4 Once a profile of your lifestyle has been built up, a computer shows you how your appearance will be affected in the future. ☐
5 'Fresh Brew' was created by British coffee company 'Beans R Us'. ☐
6 When Lois realised she had been followed to her front door, she quickly activated her bag. ☐
7 Music and games could be downloaded in seconds via your right arm. ☐
8 When we last heard, the 'mirror' was still being developed in a lab in France. ☐
9 According to a spokeswoman, the invention is being welcomed by coffee-lovers and couch potatoes everywhere. ☐
10 It should not be used as protection from wild animals. ☐

3 **CD2.25** Listen and check your answers to Exercise 2. Which inventions could be really useful, and which are a waste of time, do you think? Why?

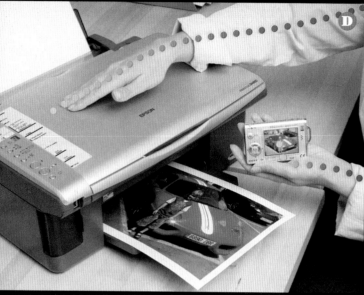

Work it out

4 Underline all the passive forms in the sentences in Exercise 2 and complete the table.

Present Simple	
Present Continuous	
Present Perfect	
Past Simple	
Past Continuous	
Past Perfect	
Modal verbs	
going to	

5 Complete the rules about the passive with one word in each gap. Use the sentences in Exercise 2 to help you.

1 A passive verb has a form of the verb _____ and a _____ participle.
2 We use the passive to move the focus of attention from the subject of an active sentence to the _____ .
3 If we want to mention the agent, or the 'doer' of the action, we use the preposition _____ .
4 We don't mention the _____ if it is obvious, unknown or unimportant.
5 The passive is common in newspaper reports and academic writing because it makes the style more _____ .

6 Sentences a–d come from the texts you listened to in Exercise 3. Answer questions 1–3 about them.

a The company **expects** Body Download <u>to be launched</u> next year.
b It's a 'must have' if you are worried **about** <u>being attacked</u>.
c There's one drawback: it **needs** <u>to be filled</u> with coffee and water first.
d Nobody **likes** <u>being told</u> about their bad habits, especially by a computer.

1 Which inventions do they refer to?
2 Which contain a *passive infinitive* and which a *passive gerund*?
3 Why are passive infinitives and gerunds used? Look at the words in **bold**.

7 Look at sentences a–b and follow the instructions.

a It will show people the consequences of an unhealthy lifestyle.
b It gives anyone who touches it an electric shock.

1 <u>Underline</u> the two objects of the verbs *show* and *give*.
2 Rewrite the sentences in the passive in two ways, starting with the words given.
  a People _____ .
   The consequences of an unhealthy lifestyle _____ to _____ .
  b Anyone who touches it _____ .
   An electric shock _____ to _____ .

➤ **Check it out** page 156

8 Rewrite the sentences, starting with the words given. What is a possible context for each sentence? Discuss in pairs.

1 They offered us seats in Business Class.
 We _____ .
2 They will send her a cheque for £10,000.
 She _____ .
3 Is somebody paying them for their work?
 Are _____ ?
4 They give the contestants four ingredients to use.
 The contestants _____ .
5 They might ask you how you heard about the job.
 You _____ .
6 They have promised compensation to the residents.
 The residents _____ .
7 When are they going to tell us the results?
 When are we _____ ?
8 He was handing her the money from the till when we walked in.
 She _____ .

Accidental Inventions

Did you know that many familiar household items were invented by accident? Here are the stories of three of them.

Coca-Cola

In 1886 a pharmacist called John Pemberton made a medicinal syrup. He intended it [1] *to use / to be used* as a cure for headaches. At first, Pemberton [2] *used / was used* cold water to dilute the syrup, but one day he found that it [3] *had accidentally mixed / had accidentally been mixed* with carbonated water by his assistant. This made it fizzy and [4] *gave / was given* it a more interesting flavour. In the first year Pemberton [5] *sold / was sold* twenty-five bottles of the drink, for a total of $50. Nowadays, 834 million Coca-Cola products [6] *consume / are consumed* every day.

Scotchguard

Scotchguard is a substance that [7] *prevents / is prevented* fabric from [8] *marking / being marked* by dirt. It [9] *discovered / was discovered* when a scientist was experimenting with a synthetic rubber that [10] *would use / would be used* in airplane fuel lines. He accidentally [11] *spilt / was spilt* some of the substance on his canvas shoe, and it [12] *couldn't remove / couldn't be removed*. As the shoe got older, it got dirtier, except for the area where the substance [13] *had spilt / had been spilt*.

Crisps

One day in 1853 a New York chef called George Crum made some chips for a customer. The chips [14] *sent / were sent* back because the customer wanted them [15] *to slice / to be sliced* a little thinner. This [16] *happened / was happened* twice, and Crum [17] *became / was become* rather annoyed. He sliced the potatoes so thin that, once they [18] *had fried / had been fried*, they [19] *couldn't eat / couldn't be eaten* with a fork. Well, the customer loved the crisp potatoes, and soon they [20] *were requesting / were being requested* by other diners.

9 Read the article above and circle the correct forms. Which story did you find most interesting? Why?

10 Complete the advertisement with the correct forms of the verbs in brackets.

Does your dog or cat hate [1]_____ (wash)?
Did you know that you are more likely [2]_____ (injure) while trying to wash a pet than during any other household activity?
If you answered 'yes' and 'no' to these questions, you need our remarkable Pet Cleaner. We know that it's horrible [3]_____ (soak) in water or [4]_____ (cover) in scratches. When using our bath the pet [5]_____ (not/need/hold) at all because its body is completely enclosed in the box. However, the animal's head [6]_____ (must/not/put) inside the bath, or it may panic. We also recommend that the pet [7]_____ (should/keep) in the box for at least fifteen minutes after [8]_____ (rinse), so that it calms down and you avoid [9]_____ (attack) when it comes out. A further advantage of the Pet Cleaner is that it [10]_____ (can/use) as a carrier for your pet when you are travelling.

NEW!

11 In pairs, write some sentences about the Weight Loss Spoon, using the passive. Compare your sentences with other students. How similar/different are they?

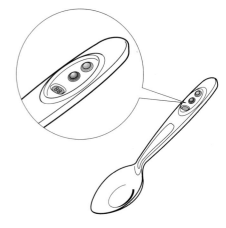

- Who was it invented for?
- How is it activated?
- What can you do when you are given the green light? What about the red light?
- What can it also be used for?
- What shouldn't be done with it?

12 Work in pairs. Student A, look at page 148. Student B, look at page 150.

SPEAKING AND LISTENING

1 Look at the bar chart and the graph and answer the questions.

1 What information is given in each of them?
2 Which durable does not show a rising trend? Why, do you think?
3 Which of the durables do you think will be used less in the future? Why?
4 How many people have access to the Internet in your country? Is the trend similar?
5 Did any of the trends in the chart and graph surprise you? Why?

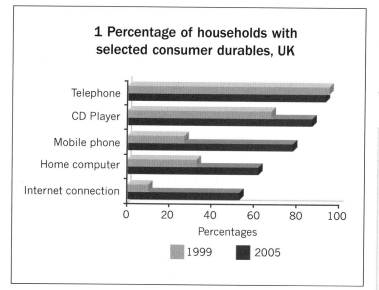

1 Percentage of households with selected consumer durables, UK

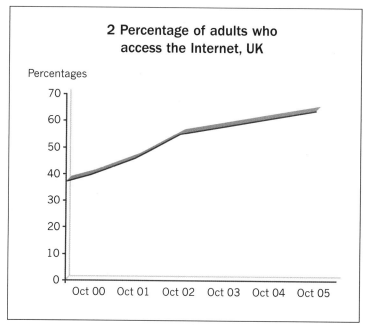

2 Percentage of adults who access the Internet, UK

2 **CD2.26** Listen to Maria talking about the bar chart and the graph. She makes four mistakes. Mark them 1–4 on the chart or graph.

3 **CD2.27** Correct Maria's mistakes with the phrases in the box. Then listen and check.

> less than half   increased gradually   tripled
> about twice as many had

1 the number of households with a telephone fell slightly between 1999 and 2005, whereas the number of mobile phones nearly doubled
2 five times more households had an Internet connection in 2005 than in 1999 and there was a similar increase in the number of home computers
3 between 2000 and 2002 there was a significant rise in the percentage of people who used the Internet, while between 2002 and 2005 the number stayed the same
4 more than half the adult population used the Internet in 2005, compared with a small minority in 2000

4 Use Speak Out to complete the gaps in sentences 1–4 about the chart and graph.

SPEAK OUT | Visual material: graphs/charts

Describing trends

- to rise/increase   slightly/gradually/
  to fall/decrease   significantly/sharply

- a slight/gradual/   rise/increase   in ...
  significant/sharp   fall/decrease

- (nearly/more than) halve/double/triple
  stay the same
  change very little

- twice as many ... as ...
  (X) times more/fewer ... than ...

Describing proportions

- (X) percent of (households) ...
- one in (five/ten ...) ...
- more/less than (a quarter/a third/half) of ...
- the (vast) majority/a (small) minority of ...

1 _____ _____ of households had an Internet connection in 1999.
2 _____ _____ _____ households had a telephone than a mobile phone in 1999.
3 Between 2001 and 2002 the number of people who used the Internet _____ _____ .
4 Between 2003 and 2004 there was a _____ _____ in the number of people who used the Internet.

5 Work in pairs. Use the language from Speak Out to talk about the two pie charts on page 146.

READING AND LISTENING

1 Read the profile of the kingdom of Bhutan and answer the questions.

- How is Bhutan different from other countries?
- Would you like to visit the country? Why?/ Why not?

2 In 1999 the first TV and Internet services were introduced into Bhutan. What effect do you think this had on the country? Discuss in pairs.

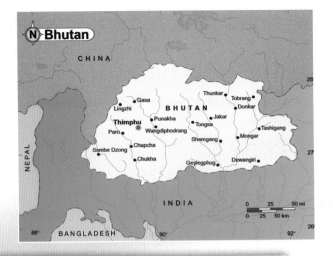

COUNTRY PROFILE: BHUTAN

THE KINGDOM OF BHUTAN is a tiny, remote and impoverished country nestling in the Himalayas between its powerful neighbours, India and China. Almost completely cut off for centuries, it only began to open up to outsiders in the 1970s. Its breathtaking scenery and ancient Buddhist culture make it a natural tourist attraction, but tourism is restricted: visitors must travel as part of a pre-arranged package or guided tour.

The king, partly educated in Britain and having travelled abroad, has continued the policy of limited modernisation adopted by his father. He has gone to great lengths to preserve the country's deep-rooted Buddhist culture and ancient traditions from the rapidly-developing world outside its borders. National dress is compulsory – a robe with a belt, or 'gho', for men and a long dress or 'kira', with a short jacket, for women.

National Dress

Bhutan Countryside

Open TFN News in audio and video

✉ Email this to a friend

Part 1
Culture Clash?

It was the World Cup Final of France '98 that sparked the introduction of television into Bhutan. The 3–0 victory of the home side over Brazil was watched by thousands on a big screen in Bhutan's National Square. ¹_____ Six months after that, global TV broadcasting was allowed in. It was this second

5 development that really made people wake up to life in the twentieth century and caused profound change, according to TV analyst Shockshan Peck. 'Young people are now much more in tune with globalisation and what is happening around the world,' she says. 'The risk is that the more we learn about the world, the more we lose of our own culture.'

10 Bhutan has no film industry to speak of, and after a diet of cultural and educational programmes from BBS, some Bhutanese began to look for something a little more spicy. ²_____ The TV avalanche began, and along with it came a change in people's lifestyles. Residents of the capital, Thimphu, say they are now glued to the TV for several hours a day, and often stay up late

15 to watch the non-stop stream of programmes. Long-running Indian soap operas beamed from across the border are hot favourites. One viewer, Choki Wangmo, says that her children go out and play less, and that television dominates family discussions these days. Her son, Ugyen, admits that his studies are affected because he cannot concentrate in the classroom. 'I keep thinking about what will happen next in the story,' he says.

20 Also popular are cartoons, football matches, and the wrestling series from the US. ³_____ Kinley Dorji, editor of Bhutan's only newspaper, says that when TV first came in, he received several pained letters from students, saying they were shocked. 'Bhutanese kids who have grown up in this quiet country, this very rustic society, suddenly saw these big men beating each other up on television. They couldn't understand it.' ⁴_____ 'We received a report from a school where a student broke his arm after being thrown to the ground by his friend, who was emulating the wrestlers.'

25 Kinley Dorji says that television is 'splitting' Bhutanese society. He explains that the thinking in the country is that it will never be a military or economic power, so its strength must be its unique society. He believes that TV represents a direct threat to this. ⁵_____ 'If you look at the items being stolen, like TV sets, tape recorders and clothes, it's directly related to what they're seeing,' he adds.

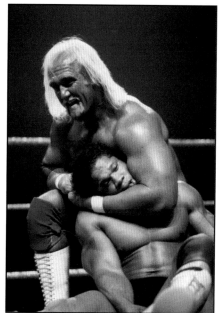

3 **CD ROM** Read Part 1 of *Culture Clash?* Were your predictions about the effect of television correct?

4 Complete the article with five of sentences a–h. There are three extra sentences.

a The latter is at the centre of a debate about the influence of television on Bhutan's young people.
b He also links television to a rise in crime over the period that it has been broadcasting.
c Some people see what happened next as an aerial invasion of Bhutanese society.
d It was such a success that a year later, on the twenty-fifth anniversary of his coronation, the king decided to begin the Bhutan Broadcasting Service (BBS).
e The family cannot take their eyes off a soap on the television set in their tiny living room.
f However, it was not long before the children started doing it themselves.
g So they turned to multi-channel TV, through satellite in the countryside and cable in the towns.
h But some of the cartoons were considered too violent.

5 Vocabulary Words and phrases 1–8 are used in a figurative way in the article. In pairs, discuss what they mean in the text. Then match them to definitions a–h.

1 sparked (line 1) ☐
2 wake up to (line 5) ☐
3 be in tune with (line 7) ☐
4 a diet (line 10) ☐
5 spicy (line 12) ☐
6 an avalanche (line 12) ☐
7 be glued to (line 14) ☐
8 a stream (line 15) ☐

a a long and continuous series
b something you are given regularly
c caused
d a large number
e exciting
f become aware of
g be able to understand
h look at something with all your attention

87

Part 2

So is it too late to stop the damage that television is doing to
30 Bhutanese society? And what about the spectre of destructive
external forces raised by the Internet? How much of a threat do
they pose?

Well, first of all, it is worth remembering that for hundreds
of years, Bhutan enjoyed its self-imposed isolation, at pains
35 to protect its culture from the world outside its borders. So
the country is hardly likely to sit back and let outside forces
endanger it, and the government is already working on an
Information, Communication and Technology Act to regulate what
the people can watch. One of the first programmes to be taken
40 off the air will probably be the US wrestling series.

As far as the Internet is concerned – well, though it is hard to
believe, the headquarters of Druknet, Bhutan's only Internet
service provider, is a space the size of a living room. It hosts the
country's entire Internet traffic. Perhaps this is not surprising,
45 since there are only about 5,000 computers in the whole country.
Few people can afford the luxury of a home PC, and so Bhutan's
connected generation is catered for by what must be some of the
highest Internet cafés in the world. Inside, young netizens send
emails, play online games and generally explore the world beyond
50 the Himalayan peaks.

When it comes to regulating TV and the Internet, we should
also consider the Buddhist culture of Bhutan. Shockshan Peck
argues that it is a key part of this culture that people decide
for themselves what is right and wrong. She quotes the King
55 of Bhutan, who said on the launch of television that he was
confident people would pick the best from the media. 'Both good
and bad are there – it's up to you to decide what is good and
what is bad,' she stresses. 'There's inherently a great confidence
in people understanding what is good.'

60 Other people see the debate as largely irrelevant. They point
out that, outside the towns of Thimphu and Paro, the country
is sparsely populated across a mountainous terrain, and most
Bhutanese lead a simple rural existence. Also, nearly 60% of
Bhutan's population does not even have electricity, let alone a
65 television or computer.

88

6 **CD ROM** **Read Part 2 of *Culture Clash?* and answer the questions.**

1 According to the article, do TV and the Internet pose a threat to Bhutan's culture?
2 What four reasons support the argument?

7 **Complete the sentences with the correct forms of the words in capital letters. All the new words are in the article.**

1 Many people are worried about the
effect of _____ on local culture.   GLOBAL
2 We felt like complete _____
when we first moved here.   OUTSIDE
3 I sometimes feel as if Toby isn't even
aware of my _____ .   EXIST
4 I wonder what qualifications you
need to be a business _____ .   ANALYSE
5 Despite the money they spent on
_____ , the building is still ugly.   MODERN
6 Last night's storm was the most
_____ we've had all year.   DESTROY
7 We all listened carefully as the
writer explained the _____
behind her book.   THINK
8 It's amazing how many people
_____ their health by smoking.   DANGER

8 **CD2.28** **Listen to the radio programme and circle the correct answer.**

1 Lucy
  a had no idea where Bhutan was.
  b did a lot of research into Bhutan.
  c was disappointed by Bhutan when she got there.
  d was influenced by the Bhuddist religion.

2 Bhutanese people
  a wear jeans and T-shirts in the evening.
  b wear western clothes because they see them on TV.
  c aren't allowed to wear western clothes at work or school.
  d see a lot of western tourists.

3 During her stay in Bhutan, Lucy was most impressed by
  a the local architecture.
  b the government's concern with people's health.
  c the way that the country has allowed some progress while protecting its traditions.
  d the fact that the country has banned the sale of tobacco.

In groups, discuss these questions.

• In what ways can TV and the Internet influence people's behaviour?
• Should the government regulate what TV programmes people watch, or should they be left to decide for themselves? Why?
• What important aspects of your country's culture should be protected from change?

VOCABULARY

1 In groups, answer the quiz questions. Guess if you are not sure. Then check your answers on page 147.

2 <u>Underline</u> the compound nouns and compound adjectives in the quiz (fifteen in total).

Science and Inventions Quiz

1 Which of these inventions came first?
a the swimming pool
b toothpaste
c the lawnmower
d the pencil

2 Which artist is also well-known for his groundbreaking work in science?
a Pablo Picasso
b Michelangelo
c Leonardo da Vinci

3 When was the first radio-controlled device invented?
a 1898
b 1904
c 1915

4 Who choked on his own invention?
a Booth (vacuum cleaner)
b Smythe (false teeth)
c Branston (pickled onions)

5 Which of these labour-saving devices was not invented by a woman?
a the ironing board
b the automatic dishwasher
c the sewing machine
d correction fluid

6 How many of these scientists were left-handed?
a Marie Curie
b Albert Einstein
c Ivan Pavlov
d Albert Schweitzer

3 How many compounds from the quiz match each 'pattern' in Train Your Brain?

TRAIN YOUR BRAIN | Compounds

Compound nouns

1 noun + noun: *Internet café, soap opera*
2 gerund + noun: *writing paper, running shoes*
3 adjective + noun: *loudspeaker, frozen food*

Compound adjectives

4 adjective/adverb/noun + past participle: *high-powered, badly-paid, air-conditioned*
5 adjective/adverb/noun + present participle: *good-looking, never-ending, mouth-watering*
6 adjective/number + noun + -ed/-d: *absent-minded, two-faced*

Mind the trap!

Compounds can be written as one word, two words joined by a hyphen, or two separate words. As there are no rules for this, you need to check in a dictionary.

4 Think Back! Find six compounds in the profile of Bhutan on page 86. Which pattern in Train Your Brain does each one match?

5 Cross out one word in each group which cannot be used to make a compound with the word at the end. Use a dictionary to help you.

1 absent   narrow   closed   open   -minded
2 big   small   empty   level   -headed
3 full   empty   even   right   -handed
4 energy   labour   health   time   -saving
5 high   solar   battery   electric   -powered

6 Match each word in group B to three words in group A to make compound nouns.

A		B
life (x2)	phone	agent
secret	smoke	card
security	body	insurance
travel (x3)	estate	alarm
burglar	car (x2)	guard
boarding		

7 Complete the gaps in these questions with your ideas. Then work in pairs, and ask and answer the questions.

1 Would you prefer to work as a _____ agent or a _____ guard?
2 Is it worse to be _____-headed or _____-minded?
3 What _____-powered objects have you got at home?
4 Is it more important for a parent to be _____-minded or _____-handed?
5 Which of these inventions do you think is more important, _____ , _____ or _____ ?

Which person is a street robber more likely to steal from?

D&G

It doesn't take a genius to stop street crime

WRITING

1 In pairs, look at the visual material and the essay question, and think of some ideas for the essay. Decide what to put in the following paragraphs.

- The introduction
- Arguments for the statement in the question
- Arguments against the statement in the question
- The conclusion, including your personal opinion

2 Read the essay. How many of your ideas did the student include? Do you agree with the conclusion?

Essay question

'Mobile phones should be banned from schools.' Write an essay giving arguments for and against this statement, and also state your own opinion.

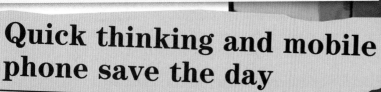

Quick thinking and mobile phone save the day

Mobile phones are here to stay. According to a recent survey in the UK an overwhelming number of teenagers (eighty-seven percent in fact) own one. Even so, there is considerable disagreement over whether they should be allowed on school premises.

The advantages of banning mobile phones are undeniable. To begin with, they disrupt 5 lessons and, to quote a British secondary school teacher, 'destroy learning'. Students text each other during lessons and have even been known to use SMS messages to cheat in exams. What is more, supporters of a ban point out that mobile phone theft is a serious issue in many schools. A final key argument is the disturbing rise in the number of cases 10 of bullying by text message. Research has shown that fourteen percent of teenagers have been bullied or threatened in this way at some time.

On the other hand, the arguments against a ban are extremely convincing. Teenagers and their parents alike are concerned about the question of safety, both in schools and on public transport nowadays, and see mobile phones as a vital way of keeping in touch. It 15 could also be argued that mobile phones may soon actually be used in class, for instance as a means of finding out information if the Internet is not available.

All in all, although people have some strong arguments against allowing mobiles in schools, I feel that the issue of safety is of overriding importance. To my mind, it should be possible to introduce clear rules to make sure that phones are not misused.

254 words

3 Look at the essay again and follow the instructions.

1 For each of the <u>underlined</u> linkers, think of an alternative with the same meaning.
2 Look at the adjectives in red. What effect do they have on the student's arguments?
3 Decide why the student uses:
   a a short statement in the first line,
   b a direct quote in line 5,
   c percentages in lines 2 and 9,
   d *in fact* (line 2), *even* (line 6) and *actually* (line 14).
4 What phrases are used instead of the following?
   A survey said …   A teacher said …
   Supporters of a ban say …
5 How many examples of the passive can you find? What effect does it have on the style of the essay?

4 In Train Your Brain match the sentence beginnings (1–7) with their endings (a–g) and check your answers to Exercise 3.

TRAIN YOUR BRAIN | Writing skills

For and against essays: arguing persuasively

1 Start the essay with a short, 'punchy' statement or question ☐
2 Use a variety of linking words and phrases ☐
3 Use the passive ☐
4 Include words like *even*, *actually* and *in fact* ☐
5 Include a variety of 'strong' adjectives ☐
6 Use phrases like *according to, to quote (x)* and *point out* ☐
7 If possible, include direct quotes and percentages or statistics ☐

a to make the style of the essay more impersonal.
b to catch the reader's attention.
c to support your points.
d to add emphasis to what you are saying.
e to avoid repeating the word 'say'.
f to organise your arguments.
g to make your arguments more persuasive.

---

5 Find a sentence in the essay that means the same as the three sentences below. What follows *in spite of/despite* in each of these examples?

- In spite of/Despite some strong arguments against allowing mobiles in schools, …
- In spite of/Despite people having some strong arguments against allowing mobiles in schools, …
- In spite of/Despite the fact that people have some strong arguments against allowing mobiles in schools, …

6 Rewrite sentences a and b using *in spite of/despite* in the three different ways.

a Although they are friends, Gill and Hannah often disagree.
b Although the ring cost a lot of money, Paul decided to buy it.

7 Study the use of *even though, even if* and *even so* in a–c. Then complete sentences 1–3 with the correct phrase.

a <u>Even though</u> he didn't like Science, Matt got a grade A in his Science exam.
b I don't think Lola will pass her History exam, <u>even if</u> she studies hard.
c Tim had an important exam in the morning. <u>Even so</u>, he went out with his friends the night before.

1 I know you can find useful information on the Internet. _____ , you're spending too much time on the computer.
2 Sue started checking her emails, _____ it was very late when she got home.
3 _____ you're right about who stole my mobile phone, we can't prove it, can we?

8 Discuss these questions in small groups. Make a note of any interesting points other students make, which could be useful for an essay on this subject.

- Have you visited an Internet chatroom, or do you know anyone who has?
- How common is it for young people in your country to spend time in chatrooms?
- Why do people visit them?
- What do people talk about?
- Why are they sometimes considered anti-social, or even dangerous?

9 Look at the essay question. Make a list of arguments for and against the statement, and decide whether you agree with it or not. Then write your essay in 200–250 words. Use Train Your Brain to help you.

Essay question

'Internet chatrooms do not serve a useful purpose.' Write an essay giving arguments for and against this statement and also state your own opinion.

VOCABULARY AND GRAMMAR

1 **Circle the correct words or phrases.**

1 Don't be so naive! How could you believe such a *dull / far-fetched / disturbing* story?

2 It's a shame he was taken ill and couldn't play today. But that *understudy / producer / conductor* was exceptionally good.

3 Their refusal to use technological inventions is very *open / absent / narrow* -minded.

4 There were no tickets available on the balcony, so we chose seats *in the stalls / at the backstage / in the dressing room.*

5 It's the *costume / clothes / dress* rehearsal for the school play today. I'm really excited.

2 **Complete the text with one word in each gap.**

Technology
A technology blog from
ScienceTimes Blogs

Technological progress = cultural regression?

Do new technologies and the world of art go together? Can we still expect audiences to sit still during a whole film or theatre ¹_____ ? Will they want to go to an art ²_____ to silently admire (with their mobiles off!) the ³_____ of Picasso, Monet and many others? Or will they prefer to play interactive games with their eyes ⁴_____ to all sorts of screens? It's a matter of choice, of course. But even if we opt for the 'old-fashioned' art, do we still remember how to behave in a proper, 'old-fashioned' way?

I have never been much of a theatre ⁵_____ . Recently though, I decided to see *Three Days of Rain* (written by an American ⁶_____ Richard Greenberg) at the Jacobs Theatre with Julia Roberts starring in the ⁷_____ role. It might not be a box ⁸_____ success and you can argue about the quality of Roberts' acting (this being her first time on ⁹_____). But it's no excuse for the appalling behaviour of several of the people in the audience. From the moment the lights went out, I could hear text messages and people answering their mobiles. Appalling! Don't you think we should all ¹⁰_____ up to the dangers that modern technologies bring to contemporary culture?

3 **Complete the text using the correct form of the words in brackets.**

The new play *The* ¹_____ (destroy) *Beast* is a drama based on the problems of ²_____ (globe) and how man (the 'beast' in the title) is threatening the ³_____ (exist) of our planet by his constant need to ⁴_____ (modern) and grow richer. A few weeks ago, I went to see a ⁵_____ (rehearse) for the play and met some of the actors backstage. They seemed to be very sincere, pleasant people, but sitting through the play was too ⁶_____ (depress). After about half an hour, I settled down for a nice, ⁷_____ (peace) sleep and that was the last I saw of the play. I was ⁸_____ (wake) up by a cleaner about half an hour after the play had finished.

4 **Complete the sentences so that they mean the same as the original sentences.**

1 We do not really know how much global warming will increase in the next fifty years. Researchers have admitted that _____ _____ .

2 'You've passed with an A. Well done!' My professor congratulated _____ _____ .

3 'Did you stay at home or go out yesterday?' Tom asked me _____ .

4 At that time they were still renovating the exterior of the hotel. At that time the exterior of the hotel _____ _____ .

5 'We'll do our best to resolve the situation.' They offered _____ .

6 'Don't leave your luggage in a rental car.' At the car rental desk, they told _____ _____ .

7 'I'm sorry I haven't been able to give you much support lately.' Their brother apologised _____ _____ .

8 You are required to fill in visa application forms online. Visa application forms _____ .

5 **Complete the text with the correct forms of the verbs in brackets.**

Stained-glass windows ¹_____ (admire) for their utility and beauty since ancient Rome, when pieces of coloured glass ²_____ (assemble) into patterned window frames. In Europe, the art of stained glass reached its height between 1150 and 1500, when magnificent windows ³_____ (create) for great cathedrals.

Throughout the centuries the way stained glass ⁴_____ (make) has changed because of improved tools and growing knowledge, but the technique is essentially the same as in medieval times. A full-size drawing of the design ⁵_____ (use) as a pattern for cutting the glass. After ⁶_____ (cut), the pieces can temporarily ⁷_____ (hold) together by beeswax, and then they are painted. Next the paint needs ⁸_____ (stick) to the surface of the glass by firing in a special oven called a kiln. The final firing ⁹_____ (follow) by the glazing process. The pieces of glass ¹⁰_____ (join) by strips of lead.

PRONUNCIATION

1 **CD2.29** Listen to these compounds and in each <u>underline</u> the word with the main stress. Then circle the correct words in rules 1–2.

travel agent   phone card
Internet café   pickled onions
parental guidance frozen food
film ratings   automatic dishwasher

  1 With adjective + noun compounds the main stress is on the *adjective / noun*.
  2 With noun + noun compounds the main stress is on the *first / second* noun.

2 **CD2.29** Listen again and repeat the compounds.

READING SKILLS

1 Read the text and choose the correct answers a–d.

by Jane Reichhold

Today a neighbor brought us some fresh fish he had caught on his last boat trip. As we thanked him, he said, 'They are not from me; they only come through me.' At that moment I noticed the similarity between fish and haiku.

Nowadays, if Mom doesn't ever serve fish for dinner at least the kids get a taste of haiku at school. For most of us, our first introduction comes from reading translations from Japanese, which is a bit like comparing sushi to frozen fish sticks. Even with the knowledge of the exotic, most poets stick to the meat and potatoes of English literature. It often isn't until we get older that we accept the simple goodness of fish, adding them to the menu more often.

Having acquired a taste for fish and learned how to cook them, one is better able to appreciate the short form of haiku. Like fishing, haiku writing can be done with minimal equipment. A pin or a pen, and a scrap of paper, is enough, but it is tempting to go all out and buy a rod and reel (even study Zen, visit a monastery or take a trip to Japan). If one goes in for deep sea fishing, a computer and laser printer are soon on the list of 'must haves'.

Like fishing, to catch haiku you have to go where they are. Unlike fish, haiku are everywhere. Still, you have to know the secret places where they hide and how to get there. Wearing old comfortable clothes (usually thought of as a meditative state) we look around just where we are. It does little good to only read of fishing off the coast of Japan when sitting beside the lake by our own front door. It does help to know which fish are edible and which are not. There are two ways of finding this out. We can either eat everything we catch and publish what feels right, or we can read books containing others' experiences while making up our minds about what kind of fish to go for.

If we compare spending days on rough seas to fish or strolling on the beach writing haiku; it is very easy for me to decide where my interest lies. Still I do love a fish dinner and I hope my neighbor enjoys my latest poems.

---

1 The similarity between fishing and writing haiku the text does NOT mention is
  a the freedom to choose what we do with the product of each activity.
  b the delayed appreciation of both activities.
  c the thrill experienced when engaging in them.
  d the limited resources required for practising them.

2 In paragraph 2, the author refers to *sushi*
  a to point out that the American eat frozen fish sticks more often.
  b to contrast it with meat and potatoes.
  c to give an example of an exotic dish.
  d as a metaphor for original Japanese texts.

3 According to the author, haiku writers have to
  a read about the process of haiku writing.
  b be observant of what is around them.
  c try to have their poems published.
  d get acquainted with Zen philosophy.

4 The best title of this text would be
  a Something fishy about haiku.
  b The forgotten skill of fishing.
  c Writing haiku is easy.
  d The art of writing haiku.

SPEAKING SKILLS

1 Look at the line graph and describe the trends.

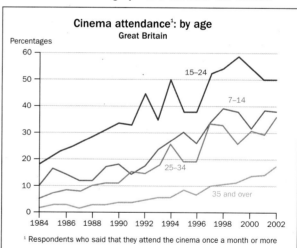

Cinema attendance[1]: by age
Great Britain

[1] Respondents who said that they attend the cinema once a month or more

2 Choose <u>one</u> of the topics and prepare a three-minute presentation.

1 Some people see art as an important feature in the primary education of all children. Others claim that art should be something you learn outside school, along with other hobbies. What, in your view, should the place of art be in the school curriculum? Give reasons.

2 What do you understand by David Rockefeller's words: 'If necessity is the mother of invention, discontent is the father of progress'? Explain.

Why risk it?

Read, listen and talk about risk, money and business.
Practise expressing dissatisfaction and regret, conditionals; money vocabulary.
Focus on criticising and showing annoyance.
Write a summary.

GRAMMAR

1 Which situation in the cartoons involves the most risk? What are the people thinking in each case? Discuss in pairs.

2 Match two of thoughts 1–8 to each cartoon.

1 I wish I'd gone first. ☐

2 If only I'd done some market research. ☐

3 If only I had a knife. ☐

4 I could have been a taxi driver. ☐

5 I should be selling umbrellas. ☐

6 I'd better turn off the TV. ☐

7 I wish he'd sing something different. ☐

8 I should have bought her some jewellery. ☐

"HOLD ON, DAPHNE!"

"...AND THE LATEST NEWS COMING IN. A PUPIL FROM ST. MARK'S SCHOOL HAS BEEN ARRESTED FOR SELLING STOLEN iPODS..."

3 Think Back! **Look at sentences 1–3 in Exercise 2 and complete the rules below.**

1 We use *I wish/If only* + _____ to talk about present regrets.
2 We use *I wish/If only* + _____ to talk about past regrets.

Work it out

4 **Match sentences 4–8 in Exercise 2 to definitions a–e.**

a I want this to happen now or in the future. ☐
b This was possible, but didn't happen. ☐
c I am unhappy about a past action. ☐
d I think this is the best thing to do in the situation. ☐
e I am unhappy about a present situation. ☐

5 **What does *'d* replace in sentences 1, 2, 6 and 7 in Exercise 2?**

➤ **Check it out** page 156

6 **Complete the sentences with the correct forms of the verbs in brackets. Then match them to the cartoons.**

1 We should _____ (join) a walking club instead. ☐
2 If only the rain _____ (stop). ☐
3 I'd better _____ (not look) down. ☐
4 I wish I _____ (can) swim. ☐
5 I could _____ (arrest), too. ☐
6 I wish the news _____ (finish). ☐
7 I should _____ (not spend) all my savings on this shop. ☐
8 They should _____ (pay) us extra money for doing a job like this. ☐

7 **Rewrite the sentences so that they mean the same, using the words in capital letters.**

1 I think it's best if I don't phone Dave again. BETTER
2 It was stupid of me to buy that old motorbike. SHOULD
3 Why didn't I work harder for the exams? ONLY
4 Steve regrets having split up with Rosie. WISHES
5 It was lucky that I didn't hurt myself on that glass. HAVE
6 Why am I walking through the park in the dark? SHOULD
7 I really don't want our neighbours to make so much noise. WISH
8 I'm sorry that I don't live near the sea. IF

8 CD2.30 **Read about Ally and write seven things that she might say using *I wish, If only, I should, I could, I'd better*. Then listen and compare.**

Ally and her friend Ed bought three tickets in a raffle for a Caribbean holiday. A few days later the winning number was announced in the paper and Ally was sure that she had it – except she couldn't find the tickets. She looked in all the sensible places, like her purse, and the drawer of her desk, then she remembered that they were in the pocket of her jeans … but her jeans were in the washing machine! She rushed to get them out, but it was too late – the tickets were there, but they had almost disintegrated and the numbers were impossible to read. She tried talking to the competition organisers, but they said that since she'd forgotten to write her name and phone number on the receipt for the ticket, there was no proof that she'd won. She hasn't told Ed about what happened yet.

I should've …
If only …
I should be …

9 **Work in pairs. Student A, look below. Student B, look at page 150.**

Student A, read the notes (think of answers to the questions in brackets) and tell Student B about your situation. Then listen 'actively' to Student B's situation (ask questions, show sympathy, etc).

You missed an interview for a job (what was the job?) because you woke up late (why?).
You really want this job (why?) so you've tried to arrange another interview, but the personnel manager at the company refused.

What are your regrets? What do you wish would happen? What had you better do in future?

10 **Complete the sentences so that six are true for *you*, and two are false. Read your sentences to a partner: can he/she guess which two are false?**

1 I wish I hadn't …
2 When I get home, I'd better …
3 I should be … this week.
4 I could've …, but I didn't.
5 I wish I didn't have to …
6 I should've … over the weekend.
7 I wish my friends would …
8 I shouldn't have …

SPEAKING AND LISTENING

1 Who could the people in the photo be and what might happen next? Discuss in pairs.

2 **CD2.31** Listen to three phone calls and answer questions 1 and 2 about each one.

    1 Who is speaking?
    2 What is the purpose of the phone call?

3 **CD2.31** Listen again and match a–h to 1–8 in Speak Out. Which phrases refer to the present, and which to the past?

    a let Alec drive.
    b phoned me.
    c leave it lying around.
    d speak up.
    e let her hear you talking.
    f told her what you do for a living.
    g turned your phone off.
    h get another car from somewhere.

SPEAK OUT | Criticising/showing annoyance

1 I wish you'd … ☐
2 You could've … ☐
3 You should've … ☐
4 You shouldn't have … ☐
5 You'd better … ☐
6 I wish you wouldn't … ☐
7 It's about time you … ☐
8 You'd better not … ☐

---

4 **CD2.32** Listen to the sounds and complete the sentences with the correct forms of verbs in column A and nouns in column B.

A	B
turn down	the neighbours
go to	the door
slam	a sweater
feed	the cat
apologise to	that music
wear	the doctor

    1 You could …
    2 I wish you …
    3 It's about time you …
    4 You'd better …
    5 I wish you …
    6 You should have …

5 **CD2.33** Listen to the complete sentences from Exercise 4 and repeat them, paying attention to your intonation.

6 Work in pairs. Decide what to say in the following situations. Use the correct phrases from Speak Out.

    1 Your friend says he/she is broke. You know that he/she spends a lot of money on takeaway meals, because he/she can't cook.

    2 Your friend went to a job interview, but he/she didn't get the job. He/She always looks untidy, and you know that he/she didn't prepare for the interview at all.

    3 Your friend has argued with his/her girlfriend/boyfriend, and they've split up. This is the fifth time it has happened.

    4 Your friend has lost a watch that was a present from his/her parents. He/She was at the swimming pool this morning and can't remember where he/she put it.

    5 You arrive at a friend's house for a party, but he/she tells you it's been cancelled because not many people could come. You know that he/she only sent out the invitations a few days ago.

Ⓐ   Ⓑ   Ⓒ

Cautious Carl   Lucky Lorna   Reckless Ralph

VOCABULARY

1   **Cautious Carl, Lucky Lorna and Reckless Ralph got involved in business. What happened to each of them? Match each person to three sentences from 1–9.**

1 ___ came into a lot of money when his/her uncle died.
2 ___ sold the family home to raise money for the business.
3 ___ got a loan from the bank and put it into a savings account with a high interest rate.
4 ___ blew half of the money on expensive office furniture and bet the rest on a horse that came last.
5 ___ was careful with his/her money and paid off the loan quickly.
6 ___ found a painting in the attic that turned out to be worth £500,000.
7 ___ saved up enough to put a deposit on some business premises.
8 ___ invested in a new company just before it took off.
9 ___ borrowed money from a loan company and is still heavily in debt.

2   **Answer the questions about Carl, Lorna and Ralph.**

1 Who ... is broke? ... gets by? ... is well-off?
2 Whose business ... is doing well? ... went bankrupt? ... is breaking even?

3   **Which pairs of phrases do NOT have a similar meaning? Explain the difference. Use a dictionary to help you.**

1 get a loan/borrow money
2 inherit money/come into money
3 go bankrupt/break even
4 be in debt/owe money
5 make a profit/take off
6 pay off a loan/repay a loan
7 blow money on sth/spend money on sth
8 bet money on sth/donate money to sth

4   **Complete the sentences with words or phrases from Exercises 1–3.**

1 My brother _____ all his money on an engagement ring for his girlfriend, and now he's _____ .
2 I decided to open a _____ account instead of a cheque account, because it has a better _____ rate.
3 Ken asked me if he could borrow some money but he still _____ me £50!
4 My mum's shop isn't making a profit, but at least it's _____ _____ .
5 I have to be very _____ with money, otherwise I can't _____ _____ on my salary.
6 When his grandmother died, Phil _____ some of the money he _____ to charity.

5   **CD2.34 Listen to a news story and complete the sentences. Which findings do you think are true of teenagers in your country?**

The report reveals that two thirds of British teenagers know the exact [___1___] an iPod.
Seventy-five percent of teens work [___2___] to repay loans from their parents.
Two thirds of those who took part in the survey realise that it's not sensible to get into [___3___] .
More than half admitted that they [___4___] to their parents in order to get money.
The report also found that fifty-eight percent of teenagers are [___5___] about money than their appearance.
The book *Money Money Money* deals with a variety of topics relating to [___6___] .
The editor wants to help teenagers to understand that [___7___] can be dangerous.
All secondary schools and colleges in Britain will receive a [___8___] .

6   **Work in pairs. Student A, look at page 148. Student B, look at page 150.**

GRAMMAR AND SPEAKING

1 In pairs, think of a risky situation related to each of the topics.

business   relationships   sport   travel   money

2 Do the quiz. Choose the best answers for *you*. Then compare your answers with your partner. How similar/different are you?

3 **Think Back! Match conditionals a–d from the quiz with their types and meanings. Then find one more example of each in the quiz.**

a I <u>wouldn't do</u> it if you <u>paid</u> me!
b If I <u>meet</u> someone in a situation like that, I <u>get</u> very nervous.
c If I'<u>d been able</u> to afford it, I'<u>d have gone</u> with them.
d I'<u>ll lend</u> you the money, provided that you <u>pay</u> it <u>back</u> by the end of the month.

1 Zero Conditional: a situation that is always true ☐
2 First Conditional: a possible situation in the future ☐
3 Second Conditional: an unlikely or imaginary situation in the present or future ☐
4 Third Conditional: an imaginary situation in the past ☐

1 Would you go on a blind date?
a No – if I meet someone in a situation like that, I tend to get very nervous.
b I'd go as long as I could take a friend with me.
c Yes – who knows, I might meet the love of my life!

2 A friend invites you to go parachuting. How do you reply?
a If I'd had more time to prepare myself for it, I'd go.
b Why not? I'll never know what it's like unless I try it.
c I wouldn't do it if you paid me!

3 Some friends have gone on a boat trip in Antarctica. How do you feel about it?
a If I'd been able to afford it, I'd have gone with them.
b I can't imagine why they went there. It's not my idea of a holiday.
c If I didn't get seasick, I'd have gone too.

4 What is your opinion about people who start up 'dotcom' companies?
a Too many 'dotcom' companies have gone bankrupt: it's very risky.
b Companies like Google and eBay might never have existed if those people hadn't taken the risk.
c If you get proper financial advice, it can be a good investment.

5 What do you think about singers who insure their voices for millions of dollars?
a Why do they need to insure their voices: haven't they got enough money already?
b Well, if I had a really great voice, I'd have done the same.
c I don't think anyone's voice is worth that much!

6 A friend of yours needs to borrow some money, but you know that he's unreliable and has a lot of unpaid debts. What do you say?
a I'll lend you the money, provided that you pay it back by the end of the month.
b I'd lend you the money if you'd paid off some of your other debts.
c I'm sorry, I haven't got any spare cash at the moment.

Work it out

4 Find conditionals in the quiz that mean the same as sentences a and b and complete the table. Why are they known as 'mixed' conditionals? Then find one more example of each in the quiz.

a I didn't have time to prepare myself for it, so I'm not going.
b I get seasick, so I didn't go.

	if clause	Main clause
a	If I'd had time to prepare …	
b	If I didn't get …	

5 Match patterns a and b from the table in Exercise 4 to their uses.

1 to talk about the consequences in the present of an imaginary past situation ☐
2 to talk about the effects of an imaginary present situation/state on the past ☐

➤ **Check it out** page 157

6 Join the sentences in 1–6 to make two types of conditional in each case: one 2nd or 3rd, and one mixed.

1 My best friend went on a blind date.
   a She met her future husband.
   b She's engaged.

2 My sister can't keep a secret.
   a I get annoyed with her.
   b She told Jackie about the surprise party.

3 Craig isn't afraid of heights.
   a He goes bungee jumping every weekend.
   b He went parachuting with us yesterday.

4 Luke didn't invest in that 'dotcom' company.
   a He didn't lose all his money.
   b He doesn't have a lot of debts.

5 I'm so shy.
   a I don't know what to say when I meet people.
   b I didn't talk to Kim's brother at the picnic.

6 I told Ruth the truth about her boyfriend.
   a We had a big argument.
   b She isn't speaking to me.

7 Complete the conditionals with the correct forms of the verbs in brackets.

1 If Tony _____ (offer) me a lift on his bike, I always say 'no'.
2 If he _____ (keep) driving like that, he'll have a crash.
3 I _____ (risk) riding a motorbike in this weather if I were you.
4 I'd lend you my car if I _____ (take) it to be serviced.
5 I'd have called an ambulance if I _____ (have) my phone with me.
6 If he _____ (wear) a crash helmet, his injuries would be much worse.
7 If he _____ (be) a more careful driver, he wouldn't have skidded off the road.
8 These days if it rains, Tony _____ (catch) the bus.
9 He won't ride a motorbike again unless the bank _____ (agree) to lend him the money for a new one.

8 Work in pairs. Read about Eric, then take turns to say conditional sentences about his story.

Eric went on holiday to South America. He went parasailing and broke his leg, so now he's in hospital. Eric didn't take out travel insurance, so he has to pay for a flight home. But he hasn't got any money. He left his wallet and passport in his hire car and they were stolen while he was parasailing. Luckily, one of the nurses speaks English, and she phoned Eric's family. His father is flying to South America to fetch him. Eric's father is angry because his son is so irresponsible. Eric isn't looking forward to seeing his father.

If Eric hadn't gone parasailing, he might not have broken his leg. And if he hadn't broken his leg, … .

99

READING AND WRITING

1 Look at the photos on pages 102–103. Which four phrases from the box describe the crime that the young man is committing?

> steal someone's identity   blackmail someone
> impersonate someone   take someone hostage
> masquerade as someone
> assume a false identity

2 Vocabulary Match visuals a–f to sentences 1–6. Use a dictionary to help you. Which of the crimes does NOT involve getting money or property from someone by dishonest means?

1 The young man who said he was from the gas company <u>swindled</u> the old lady <u>out of</u> her life savings. ☐

2 A local gang has <u>defrauded</u> more than one hundred people of thousands of pounds. ☐

3 My sister paid a £50 fee to an Internet company so that she could work at home for them, but it was all <u>a scam</u>: the company didn't even exist! ☐

4 I think the signature on this certificate has been <u>forged</u>. ☐

5 We discovered that the accountant had <u>embezzled</u> £200,000 of the company's money. ☐

6 I realised that the man wasn't a real insurance expert and that he had played a clever <u>confidence trick</u> on me. ☐

3 In pairs, discuss these questions.

1 Which of the crimes in Exercises 1 and 2 are the most/least serious? Why?

2 What kind of personality do the people who commit these crimes have?

4 CD ROM Read the text on pages 102–103 and choose the correct answers.

1 What kind of text is it?
 a a news story   **c** a biography
 b a report   **d** a review

2 Why did the author write the text?
 a to entertain us
 b to inform and interest us
 c to warn us about identity theft
 d to surprise us

3 Which of the following crimes did Frank Abagnale NOT commit?
 a forgery   **c** identity theft
 b fraud   **d** hijacking

4 Which of the following statements is NOT true of Frank Abagnale?
 a He did not pass any exams.
 b People found him attractive.
 c He committed his crimes between the ages of sixteen and twenty-one.
 d He did not intend to harm people through his crimes.

5 What is the main point that the author is making?
 a Abagnale has always used his talents to make himself rich.
 b Identity theft poses a serious threat to society nowadays.
 c Abagnale is a very talented man who was misdirected when he was young.
 d The life of a criminal is not glamorous.

6 Look at the <u>underlined</u> words and phrases in the text and choose the best description of the author's attitude to Frank Abagnale.
 a He is amused by him.
 b He is critical of him.
 c He is sceptical about him.
 d He is impressed by him.

Show me mail from: Everyone

	From	Subject
✉	☐ **Unknown sender**	**Earn hundreds of pounds working at home for a few hours a day.**

Insurance Policy

5 Put these events in Frank Abagnale's life in chronological order. Use the text to help you.

a He changed his date of birth on his driving licence. ☐
b He masqueraded as an airline pilot. ☐
c He started his own consultancy company. ☐
d He used his father's credit card to make money for himself. ☐
e He was arrested and spent five years in prison in Europe. ☐
f He ran away from home. ☐
g He worked in a hospital and a university. ☐
h He made $40,000 by depositing other people's money into his bank account. ☐

6 Vocabulary **Use the context to help you guess the meaning of words 1–8 in the text. Then match them to synonyms a–h.**

1 rooting for (line 3) ☐
2 ingenious (line 25) ☐
3 stunt (line 35) ☐
4 credentials (line 42) ☐
5 malicious (line 66) ☐
6 perpetrating (line 67) ☐
7 warrants (line 69) ☐
8 legitimate (line 86) ☐

a qualifications
b genuine
c clever
d committing
e risky act
f supporting
g documents giving police particular powers
h mean and cruel

7 Read the text again carefully and <u>underline</u> the information which supports the author's main point.

8 Which two summarising sentences 1–6 should NOT be included in a summary of *Frank Abagnale: from Fraud to FBI*? Why?

1 Abagnale's father shouldn't have let him use his credit card.
2 He took advantage of the fact that he looked older than his years.
3 His first successful scam was working out how to get other people's money into his bank account.
4 He is best-known for masquerading as a Pan Am pilot, despite the fact that he couldn't fly a plane.
5 He also assumed several other false identities, including that of a doctor, a teacher, a stockbroker, and even an FBI agent.
6 He has always claimed that he was an opportunist, and didn't have any malicious intentions while perpetrating his crimes.

9 Read Train Your Brain **and check your answer to Exercise 8.**

> **TRAIN YOUR BRAIN** | Writing skills
>
> **Summaries**
>
> • **Start by naming the author and identifying the text type and the topic.**
> • **State the author's main point and summarise the information which supports it, in your own words.**
> • **Be objective: do not include your own opinions or thoughts on the subject.**
> • **Once the summary is written, read and check it for accuracy.**

10 Find three more pieces of information which should be in the summary but are not in Exercise 8.

11 Write a summary of the text in about 250 words, using Train Your Brain to help you. Then swap summaries with a partner and check each other's work for accuracy.

12 In groups, discuss these questions.

• What do you think of Frank Abagnale? Is the author of the biography too positive?
• Is Abagnale a suitable person to give advice on fraud? Would you trust him? Why?/ Why not?
• Why do criminals like Abagnale often seem attractive, despite their crimes?
• What other 'reformed' criminals can you think of, who have tried to do something positive for society?

Do not trust these men

FRANK ABAGNALE

FROM FRAUD TO FBI

BY BERNIE ALEXANDER

Ask any audience member of the hugely popular Spielberg film *Catch Me If You Can*, and they will probably admit that they were rooting for the young con artist. Although he was a criminal, Frank Abagnale was also a teenager who was simply too smart for his own good. 5

Born in 1948, Frank W. Abagnale was always a creative child. For example, he would buy items on his father's credit card only to sell them back to the shop for the cash. But his real life of crime began when his parents divorced. 10 A judge wanted him to choose between living with his mother or father and that was a decision he wasn't able to make. So he ran away and never looked back. Because he was only sixteen years old, work was hard to come by in New York, the city he had escaped to. Luckily for him, he 15 was six feet tall and his hair had begun to turn grey; he looked older than he really was. He changed a number on his driver's licence from a '4' to a '3' and all of a sudden he was ten years older.

With a total of $100 to his name, he went into a bank 20 to open an account. That's when he was first introduced to banking operation procedures. Being a new client, he did not have a cheque book with printed deposit slips in his name, so he had to use a blank deposit slip from a pile on the counter. And it was then that he had an ingenious 25 idea: what if he took a handful of the slips home and printed his account number on them in magnetic ink, then returned them to the counter? Tempted to see what would happen with a scheme like that, he did it on impulse. The result was that every time someone made 30 a deposit using these slips, the money went straight into Abagnale's own account. By the time the bank discovered the system, Abagnale had made over $40,000 and already changed his identity.

Abagnale's most famous stunt was impersonating a Pan Am pilot for two years. At first, he did it so he could travel around the world for free – although he had no idea how to fly. He would <u>simply</u> introduce himself at the airline counter, saying he needed a ride, and fly back using the spare seat behind the pilot. Everything, including his food and lodging, was billed to Pan Am. As far as credentials went, all he needed was a uniform and an identification card. For the former, he simply contacted the airline headquarters and made up a story about how his uniform had been lost, and they outlined the course of action for him. For the latter, he requested a sample with his name and picture from a company specialising in ID cards, and used a transfer of the Pan Am logo from a model plane to give authenticity to the card. He became known as 'The Skywayman'.

Over five years, he assumed the identities of Frank Williams, Robert Conrad, Frank Adams and Robert Monjo – Abagnale managed to forge and cash cheques for a total of $2.5 million

Using <u>the same remarkable skills,</u> he forged a Harvard Law diploma and managed to pass the bar exam of Louisiana, enabling him to get a job in a state attorney general's office. Impersonating a paediatrician, he became the temporary resident supervisor at a Georgia hospital. He also taught Sociology at Brigham Young University for a term (thanks to a false Columbia University degree), and masqueraded as a stockbroker and an FBI agent. <u>The best part of all</u> was that he didn't even have a high-school diploma! Over five years, he assumed the identities of Frank Williams, Robert Conrad, Frank Adams and Robert Monjo – Abagnale managed to forge and cash cheques for a total of $2.5 million. This money was used to support his lifestyle, which in turn was designed to make him seem more attractive. He has always claimed that he was an opportunist, and <u>didn't have any malicious intentions</u> while perpetrating his crimes.

Before long, he had defrauded people in all fifty states of the USA and twenty-six foreign countries. Warrants were issued for his arrest all over the world. After five years of these escapades, the law finally caught up with Frank Abagnale. When he was twenty-one, an Air France flight attendant recognised him from a wanted poster and the French authorities arrested him. He served a total of five years in prison in France, Sweden and finally the United States, where he was sentenced to twelve years. In 1974, the federal government approached him and offered him a deal; they released him on the condition that he would help the authorities, without payment, to understand the inner workings of fraud and confidence tricks.

After his release, Abagnale tried several jobs, but found them unsatisfying, so he approached a bank with an offer. He explained who he was and what he had done, and offered to speak to the staff and show them the various tricks he had used to defraud banks. <u>Naturally, they were impressed</u>, and he began a legitimate career as a consultant. He later founded Abagnale & Associates, which advises financial institutions and law enforcement agencies on how to prevent the same crimes <u>he so brilliantly committed</u>. More than 14,000 financial institutions and law enforcement agencies use his fraud prevention programmes, and he has become <u>one of the world's most respected authorities</u> on forgery, embezzlement and other forms of white-collar crime. He is now a multi-millionaire, and has <u>willingly paid back</u> all the money he stole. He is also a regular speaker on the conference circle, and was voted the No 1 Campus Speaker in America by the National Entertainment College Conference Association.

Abagnale admits that life on the run was lonely, and not as glamorous as it is sometimes portrayed in Hollywood. Now a family man, he regrets his past and confesses that although he still gets ideas about interesting scams, he would never act on them. He is certain the crime of the future will be identity theft and that today's technology makes it a lot easier. He claims that today he could flip open a slim laptop, power up a small printer and have access to your personal and financial information within five or ten minutes – all thanks to the Internet. His new mission in life is to convince the world of it. ▣

Where the heart is

Read, listen and talk about home, houses and places.
Practise relative clauses; vocabulary for describing houses.
Focus on identifying attitude; being tentative.
Write a description of a memorable place.

GRAMMAR AND READING

1   In pairs, look at photos A–C and answer the questions.

    1 Where do you think the places are? Why do you think so?
    2 What kind of people might live in or visit these places? Give reasons.
    3 Which place would you choose to live in if you could? Why?

2   Read the article and check your answers in Exercise 1. Which person did not live in the place he is associated with?

Antoni Gaudí

Ian Fleming

John Lennon

3   Think Back! **What are the <u>underlined</u> relative pronouns in the article used for? Complete the table.**

relative pronouns	used for
	people
	things
	possessive
	time
	place

4   Complete the article with sentences a–d.

    a He had just arrived home with his wife, Yoko Ono, **who** <u>had been recording a new single that afternoon</u>.
    b It's an area **which** <u>all Fleming's friends loved visiting because of its secluded beaches</u>.
    c The building, **which** <u>many considered ugly at first</u>, is today a UNESCO World Heritage site.
    d It was the man **who** <u>later killed him</u>, Mark Chapman.

A life of their own*

*There are countless places all over the world that have taken on a life of their own, far beyond the people who built or lived in them. This week in our series *Where the heart is* **we take a look at some of them.**

A Casa Milà, commonly known as La Pedrera (the Quarry), was commissioned as an apartment block in 1905 by Roger Milà, <u>who</u> was a rich Catalan businessman. It is one of several distinctive buildings in Barcelona <u>that</u> can be immediately identified as the work of Antoni Gaudí. The highly unconventional absence of any straight lines in his buildings is precisely what made Gaudí's work so original. He was fascinated by the natural world and incorporated nature's curves into his surrealistic architecture, <u>which</u> created much controversy at the time. Many people describe La Pedrera's undulating balconies as a series of waves or sand dunes, like sculptures. ¹___

B Goldeneye was the Caribbean home of the author Ian Fleming, <u>whose</u> 007 thrillers made him world famous. Fleming, who had worked in Jamaica during World War II and fallen under its spell, later built a house there. He moved there permanently in the early 1950s, and it is <u>where</u> he wrote all the James Bond novels. Surrounded by lush tropical vegetation, it is set on the magnificent Jamaican coastline. ²___ Since his death in 1964, however, the place has been sold. It has now been refurbished but the master bedroom still contains the desk he wrote at. He once said: 'Would these books have been born if I hadn't been living in the gorgeous vacuum of a Jamaican holiday? I doubt it.'

C The imposing nine-storey Dakota building is in West 72nd Street. It had little claim to fame until the early 1970s, <u>when</u> it was just another fashionable address for the wealthy New Yorkers <u>that</u> lived there. Then in 1973, the Dakota became well-known as John Lennon's residence. More notoriously, it was the site of his murder on December 8 1980. ³___ John had recently released his first album in five years, *Double Fantasy*, and had earlier signed a copy of it for a fan he'd shaken hands with. ⁴___ People from all over the world now visit the Dakota, which shows how deeply admired John still is. They also lay flowers at the Strawberry Fields Memorial, which is nearby in Central Park.

Work it out

5 Look at sentences a–d in Exercise 4 and follow the instructions.

1 Match the <u>underlined</u> relative clauses to the description of their use. Which do not need a comma?
- essential information which tells us exactly who or what the speaker is talking about (defining) ☐☐
- extra information which is not necessary to understand who or what the speaker is talking about, and can be omitted (non-defining) ☐☐

2 In which relative clauses could we replace *who/which* with *that*?

3 In which relative clause can *who/which/that* be left out? Why?

6 Read sentences a and b from the article. Match the <u>underlined</u> relative clauses to definitions 1 and 2. How do you translate *which* in both sentences in your language?

a People from all over the world now visit the Dakota, <u>which shows how deeply admired John still is</u>.

b They also lay flowers at the Strawberry Fields Memorial, <u>which is nearby in Central Park</u>.

1 It adds extra information about something in the main clause. ☐

2 It comments on the whole of the main clause. ☐

7 Compare the pairs of sentences. Why can you leave out the relative pronouns in b and what happens to the prepositions?

1 a The master bedroom still contains the desk **at which** he wrote.
 b The master bedroom still contains the desk he wrote **at**.

2 a John had earlier signed a copy of it for a fan **with whom** he'd shaken hands.
 b John had earlier signed a copy of it for a fan he'd shaken hands **with**.

➤ **Check it out page 157**

8 Complete the sentences with the correct relative pronouns. Where possible use *that*. Then decide where the sentences could fit into the article.

1 It's a garden _____ was built in his memory and _____ he and Yoko loved to walk.

2 He is also the architect _____ designed the Sagrada Familia Cathedral, _____ is still unfinished.

3 It has since become a luxury holiday haven for celebrities like Sting, _____ apparently wrote *Every Breath You Take* there.

4 The roof, _____ has a dream-like landscape, features surrealistic chimneys _____ look like figures from a science-fiction movie.

9 Join the sentences to make one, using relative clauses. Decide if they are defining or non-defining, adding commas where necessary.

1 Several new buildings have been constructed in the last decade. They may be the future wonders of the world.

2 The Burj Dubai will be the next tallest building in the world. It will be 705 metres high.

3 The new tower will be ready by 2010. It was commissioned to replace the Twin Towers in New York. It is called the Freedom Tower.

4 The architect Norman Foster designed the controversial 'Gherkin'. His Millennium Bridge had to be closed for repairs two days after opening.

5 The Gherkin won a prestigious architecture award in 2004. Its real name is the Swiss Re tower. It became an instant popular icon in 2004.

A Casa Milá

C Dakota

B Goldeneye

105

A LIFE OF THEIR OWN

Gherkin

10 Rewrite the sentences adding more information about the underlined words. Use *who, that, which, whose, where, when.* Then compare your sentences.

1 The house was by the beach.
*The house **where we lived as children** was by the beach, **which we played on every day**.*
2 Mark has moved to a new flat.
3 The bedroom overlooked a beautiful garden.
4 London is famous for its many monuments.
5 Pop star Kelly Malone had bought three homes by the age of seventeen.

11 Complete the sentences with a comment on the whole of the main clause.

1 Many people spend their weekends decorating their houses, which *is a waste of time, in my opinion.*
2 Nearly all my friends want to travel before they settle down, which …
3 People nowadays constantly send emails when they're on holiday, which …
4 Critics of the Gherkin building think it's really ugly, which …

12 Delete the extra word from each sentence. Then rewrite them to make them more natural.

1 The man to whom we spoke to knew some fascinating stories about the place.
The man we spoke to knew some fascinating stories about the place.
2 The hotel in which we stayed was the best what I've ever been to.
3 Who was the woman that about whom you were talking?
4 The airport from which we left it was very crowded.
5 The people with whom we shared the taxi they were very helpful.
6 What was the name of the lovely castle that to which we went last summer?

Mind the trap!

what = the thing *that/which*

This is **what** made his work so famous.

NOT This is ~~that~~ what made his work so famous.

13 Complete the sentences to make them true for *you.* Then compare your answers in groups.

1 I love places which …
2 My dream house would be one that …
3 What I like about my favourite building is that …
4 A place I like to relax in is where …
5 Exploring new cities is what …
6 The most famous architect in my country is a person who …

Ⓐ

LISTENING AND VOCABULARY

1 Work in pairs and answer the questions. Use a dictionary to help you.

- Where are the creatures in the pictures living? Choose from box A below.
- What creatures live in the other places?
- Which adjectives from box B could the creatures in the pictures use to describe the places they live in?

A Places

nest   cave   hive   reef   pond   cage
kennel   burrow   iceberg

B Adjectives

dangerous   isolated   damp   cramped
peaceful   huge   secluded   draughty   airy
lonely   crowded   spacious   cosy   stuffy

2 **CD3.1** First, decide which creature from the pictures might say each of the following. Match two sentences to each creature. Then listen and check.

1 I've been sitting here for a week, and it feels like forever. ___
2 I need to feel part of the world, not just like an object in a box! ___
3 Nobody ever tells me anything, you know – I don't get out much, well not in the daytime, anyway. ___
4 I don't mind if she comes in here to keep dry. ___
5 After all, that's what man's best friend deserves, isn't it? ___
6 The views are absolutely spectacular. ___
7 I've got so much to do to get the place ready, but I haven't really managed to do any of it. ___
8 You never know what might be hiding round the corner. ___
9 Is there something I should know? ___
10 They don't really understand who I am, although I've tried to explain it to them. ___

3 Try to guess each creature's attitude, by looking at the language they use in Exercise 2. Choose from the box.

indignant   apprehensive   suspicious
bored   tolerant   self-pitying   sarcastic
thrilled   frustrated   condescending

4 Look at the attitude adjectives in Exercise 3 again. In each case, how do you think the person would speak?

• with high or low pitch?
• quickly or slowly?
• quietly or loudly?

5 **CD3.1** Listen to the creatures again and match two attitude adjectives from Exercise 3 to each.

the bird _____ , _____
the dog _____ , _____
the lion _____ , _____
the mole _____ , _____
the clownfish _____ , _____

6 Complete the gaps in Train Your Brain. Look back at Exercises 3 and 4 to help you.

TRAIN YOUR BRAIN I Listening skills

Judging attitude

To judge a person's attitude, we need to listen carefully to:
• the ¹_____ they use, eg do any of the words or phrases sound positive or negative?
• the ²_____ , speed and volume of their voice, eg if a person is feeling very emotional, he/she is likely to speak more ³_____ and more loudly, with a higher pitch.

7 **CD3.2** Listen to the conversation and choose the correct answer.

1 The two rabbits have escaped from a
  a zoo.   c pet shop.
  b garden.   d house.

2 At first they feel
  a frightened.   c surprised.
  b tired.   d elated.

3 At the top of the hill, Mops starts to feel
  a self-pitying. c optimistic.
  b terrified.   d pessimistic.

4 Peter's cousin is
  a sarcastic.   c patronising.
  b considerate. d tolerant.

5 In the end, Mops
  a realises she overreacted.
  b is confused.
  c apologises to Peter.
  d is annoyed.

8 **CD3.2** Listen again and answer the questions.

1 How does Peter make it possible for him and Mops to escape?
2 Why does he suggest that they hide in the garden for a while?
3 What terrifies Mops as they are going up the hill?
4 Why does Mops get annoyed with Peter at the top of the hill?
5 Why doesn't Peter join in and share the carrots with Mops?

No Place Like Home?

Lizzie and David Dickson give us first-hand accounts of the pros and cons of living away from home

Lizzie is studying History and American Studies at Nottingham University.

David recently completed Part One of a degree in Architecture at the University of Newcastle.

Lizzie

There is no doubt that starting university is a daunting experience. Aside from the fact that in two days you meet at least 300 people but can remember only two of their names, it is the first time in your life that you become anonymous. Until this point, someone has always been haranguing you. So it seems inconceivable that it should just all stop when you get to university.

There is something vaguely anarchical about living in a hall of residence in your first year. Freed from the constraints of family life, you suddenly find yourself in a place where the cheese toastie is seen as a valid source of nutrition, your music is not referred to as 'that awful racket', and you won't be judged for wearing your pyjamas to lunch. Or dinner.

1

Halls never sleep. Neither, it would seem, do the pizza delivery men who service them. No matter what time of the day or night, you will always find doors open, a bass thudding, or a kettle boiling. At first, you wonder how you will ever sleep with this constant noise. When you go home, you wonder how to sleep without it.

2

But then Monday comes. And there is life, you have a purpose, you've got hockey training, you've handed in an essay and you can get excited about the prospect of a full five nights of flinging your limbs around in an over-capacitated nightclub. You might actually never go home again.

David

One of the main things you learn from going away to university is that the grass is always greener. You can't wait to leave home to go there, but it only takes about a term for the novelty of life in halls to wear off.

While it was once exciting to be living with a thousand strangers, it doesn't take long to realise that you have nothing in common with the majority of them. Awkward conversations with people you still vaguely recognise from Freshers' Week become tiresome and you've had enough of people stealing food from the communal fridge. In short, you long to get into a place of your own.

3

Inevitably, these dreams of domestic bliss are short-lived when, a few weeks into independent living, you realise the house won't clean itself, bills don't go away if you just ignore them, and you're not quite the gourmet chef you thought you were. Early morning fire alarms are now replaced by housemates chucking stuff at your window when they've locked themselves out. And now, when the washing machine floods, it's you that has to deal with it.

4

So, what have I learnt from leaving home? That I can bear a considerable amount of grime before feeling compelled to clean, and that it costs a lot to run a tumble dryer. And, strangely, that the home you so longed to get away from three years before, the one where someone else cooks and cleans and pays for the electricity, no longer seems quite so bad after all.

READING AND VOCABULARY

1 In pairs, discuss these questions.

  1 What are the advantages of living away from home, eg in a hall of residence?
  2 What things about living at home would you miss? Why?

2 Read the article: Who feels more positive about living away from home?

3 Complete the gaps in the article (1–4) with four of the paragraphs (A–E). There is one extra paragraph.

A And at university, the seven-day week becomes strangely inverted. The weekend starts on Monday, and at the real weekend, half the hall mysteriously disappears and nobody goes out because it's too expensive. At 5.30 on a cold, dark Sunday afternoon in November, a thought occurs to you. Wouldn't it be nice to be at home? To eat a proper meal and have a parent tell you to go to bed, because, really, you are quite run-down?

B Of course in the second year these minor inconveniences are easily ignored. Who cares about squalor and a diet of cereal when there is so much else going on? But, by the third year, going out every night of the week is no longer so alluring, and the pressure of work means that more time is spent at home. You realise it's quite nice to eat a good meal on a regular basis and that it isn't that difficult to keep a place clean.

C It can also prove difficult to understand the concept of taking responsibility for your own education. After a couple of weeks of dutiful lecture attendance, it dawns on you that you don't have to go, and what's more, that nobody will notice if you don't go. It's only much later on that you realise you really should have gone … but then it's too late.

D Even if you've had a gap year, this is a new kind of autonomy. It's somehow more reckless and infinitely more communal. For some, moving into halls will mean an amazing regression in maturity – for example, setting off a fire alarm at four in the morning never seemed so funny.

E Ah … a place of my own – every student's dream. Somewhere I can be with people I like, where I can eat food that I want, when I want. A place I can decorate to my taste, where I can watch what I want on TV, and have impromptu parties when the mood takes me. A place where fire alarms won't wake me at 5a.m. and the washing machine will clean my clothes.

4 Vocabulary Match the highlighted words in the article to the synonyms below.

  1 unthinkable   6 attractive
  2 much   7 lawless
  3 annoying   8 reversed
  4 spontaneous   9 obliged
  5 criticising   10 uncomfortable

5 Vocabulary Are these statements true (T) or false (F)? Find the underlined words and phrases in the article to help you.

  1 If something is short-lived, it doesn't last long. □
  2 If there is the prospect of something, it is likely to happen. □
  3 If the novelty of something wears off, it becomes more attractive. □
  4 The grass is always greener if other people's situation seems worse than yours. □
  5 I go out when the mood takes me means 'when I feel like it'. □
  6 If you have an idea early in the morning, you can say 'it dawned on me'. □
  7 A place that is over-capacitated has very few people in it. □
  8 A person who is run-down is tired and unhealthy. □

6 Complete the gaps with a word or phrase from Exercises 4 and 5. Sometimes you need to make changes to the phrase.

  1 Sheila felt quite _____ when she bumped into her ex-boyfriend with his new girlfriend.
  2 It suddenly _____ _____ me that Kim had been right all along.
  3 You look a bit _____ . Maybe you should take some extra vitamins.
  4 When the police started asking questions, Joe felt _____ to tell the truth.
  5 Do we really have to fill in all these forms? It's so _____ .
  6 At first I thought this new computer game was fun, but now the _____ has _____ _____ .
  7 Cherie seems quiet, but she can be very entertaining when the _____ _____ _____ .
  8 Paul and his friends gave an _____ performance of the song they had been practising.

7 In groups, discuss these questions.

  • Which things mentioned in the article would you find most worrying, tiresome or alluring about living away from home?
  • What 'house rules' would you have if you were sharing a house with other students?
  • What life skills do you think people learn when they first leave home?

8 CD3.3 Song Look at the song on page 147 and follow the instructions.

A

It's a lovely little house, and really near the river, in fact the garden [1]_____ it – you'll have to come rowing in the summer! We're beginning to [2]_____ now, although it's been chaos since we moved in because Mum and Dad have already started doing it up. The best part of it is that they're going to [3]_____ the loft into a bedroom – *my* bedroom I hope, especially since Charlie is off to university in September …

B

For rent: spacious studio flat on top floor of 1950s [4]_____ block in the city centre. Small balcony off bedroom, facing Monroe Park. [5]_____ floors throughout.

C

All our cabins are comfortably furnished and fully equipped with bed linen, crockery, cooking [6]_____ , etc. Relax in front of a cosy log fire in winter, or on warmer days, take in the view from your private [7]_____ overlooking the lake.

D

Melinda took her cup of tea and walked into the [8]_____ , which had always been her favourite room in the house. She opened the [9]_____ to let the sun flood in, and immediately felt her mood lift. She thought about Randolph's note, which was still propped on the [10]_____ in the sitting room. No – she wouldn't read it yet.

VOCABULARY

1 Read extracts A–D and match them to text types 1–4. Justify your answers.

1 A newspaper advert ☐
2 A novel ☐
3 An email to a friend ☐
4 A holiday brochure ☐

2 Complete the extracts with the words from the box. Which place appeals to you most? Why?

tiled   settle in   mantelpiece   convert
utensils   backs onto   conservatory
apartment   verandah   blinds

3 **CD3.4** Choose the odd one out in each group, giving reasons. Then listen and check.

1 cutlery   ornaments   crockery   utensils
2 shelves   windowsill   bookcase   mantelpiece
3 do up   convert   renovate   settle in
4 mansion   cabin   studio flat   apartment block
5 shed   basement   loft   conservatory
6 curtains   shutters   net   blinds
7 balcony   lawn   terrace   verandah
8 tiles   marble   lino   carpet
9 wardrobe   sideboard   dressing table   cabinet
10 run-down   overlook   back onto   face

4 **CD3.5** Listen and decide where the people are. Choose from the places in the box, and write down three words that helped you decide in each case.

hall   bedroom   loft   study   basement
kitchen   dining room   shed   terrace
utility room

5 Work in pairs and follow the instructions.

1 **Student A**, you rented the studio flat advertised in Exercise 1. Tell Student B about the advantages and disadvantages of living there.
Student B, you spent a weekend in one of the cabins advertised in Exercise 1. However, the cabin was not exactly as it was described in the brochure. Tell Student A about it.

2 **Student A**, there is a room to rent in the shared student house that you live in. Be prepared to answer Student B's questions about the room and the house.
Student B, you are interested in renting a room in the house where Student A lives. Think of some questions to ask Student A about the room and the house.

Act out the conversation. Student B, decide whether you want to rent the room or not. Then swap roles.

6 In groups, discuss these questions.

• What order would you put the following in when choosing a place to live? location, decoration, views, neighbours, outdoor space, price
• If you were going to rent a place to live, what three things would you not be able to live without? Why?
• Would you prefer to live on your own or share with other people? Why?
• What is the difference between a house and a home?

A | Before

B | After

SPEAKING AND LISTENING

1 In pairs, look at the photos and answer the questions.

- How has the room been changed? (colours, furniture, objects)
- Which one do you prefer? Why?
- Would you have redecorated it differently? How?

2 **CD3.6** Listen to the conversation between Gemma's parents. Write what they say about the following things in her flat.

- colour of the walls
- curtains and blinds
- furniture in the bedroom
- ornaments
- bathroom tiles

3 **CD3.7** Using your notes from Exercise 2, decide what suggestions Gemma's parents might have made to her on their first visit. Then listen and check.

Why don't you paint the walls in plain colours?

4 **CD3.7** Listen again. Are the statements true (T) or false (F)?

1 Gemma's new flat is cramped and lacks some basic equipment. ☐

2 Both the basement and the lawn are well looked after. ☐

3 Gemma's mum thinks the living room looks bare and exposed. ☐

4 Gemma is enthusiastic about having some of her mother's ornaments. ☐

5 The colour scheme in the bathroom hasn't been changed for twenty years. ☐

6 Gemma is considering changing the colour of the furniture to white. ☐

5 **CD3.7** Complete sentences 1–8 with phrases from Speak Out. Then listen again and check. Who do you agree with: Gemma or her parents? Why?

SPEAK OUT | Being tentative

If/I hope you don't mind me saying so …
I don't want to interfere but …
It's nothing to do with me but …
It's none of my business, I know, but …
I wasn't going to mention it but …
While we're on the subject, …
Perhaps what you *should/could* do is …
I think it might be even better if …
I wonder if you'd thought of (painting) …
Would you mind if I made a suggestion?
I was wondering if …

1 I _____ it but if you're going to redecorate anyway, I've got an idea.

2 _____ is put some nice curtains up.

3 And if _____ , it would make it much more private.

4 I don't _____ but it might be a good idea to paint them a nice bright white.

5 _____ if the doors and windows were a slightly darker shade.

6 And _____ on _____ , what about the bathroom tiles?

7 _____ painting them white.

8 It's _____ of _____ , but I wonder what the landlord would say.

6 Work in pairs and roleplay the conversations. Use language from Speak Out. Student A, look at page 148. Student B, look at page 150.

111

Living in the past

If you want to go somewhere memorable, you can't beat the Living History Centre in Wales. A friend of mine, who's an archaeology enthusiast, invited me to go there with him last summer. I'd always fantasised about being a time traveller and jumped at the chance. The Centre, which is set in magnificent countryside with gently rolling hills and green valleys, is about 100 kilometres northwest of Cardiff. Arriving there was literally like stepping into another world. The Iron Age village they've reconstructed is totally authentic, with its roughly-built wooden huts and thatched roofs. We saw a bustling scene of women cooking over open fires, men chopping wood and children struggling with heavy buckets of water. Then after storing our twenty-first-century gear and dressing in scratchy tunics and trousers, we were ready to face the first century. What was so stimulating was how much we learnt.

It didn't take us long to get to know our fellow time travellers, who willingly showed us the ropes. Every experience was a steep learning curve, from shooting a bow and arrow to weaving a simple piece of cloth. We even learnt how to make bread, which meant painstakingly grinding the flour first! We couldn't just open the fridge when we felt peckish. The weirdest thing of all was going home – total culture shock! The Centre was a truly remarkable place that taught me not to take things like electricity for granted. I highly recommend it to anyone who's ever wondered what it would be like to travel back in time.

Busy Iron Age villagers!

Map of the Living History Centre

Our hut!

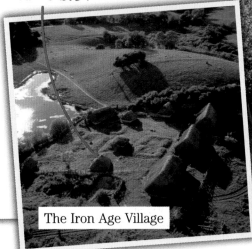
The Iron Age Village

Fishing in a dugout canoe

WRITING AND READING

1 In pairs, look at the photos and the lists below. Answer the questions.

1 What period of history do the photos represent and what was life like then?
2 Which activities in the list would you find most interesting, mundane, laborious, difficult? Which would you like to try and why?
3 If you could live in another time, when would it be and why?
4 What would it be like to live then? What would you miss?

Time	Activities
the Stone Age	hunting animals
the Iron Age	weaving baskets/cloth
Ancient Rome	building huts
the Middle Ages	grinding flour
the Renaissance	forging tools
Napoleonic times	carving bows and arrows
the year 2200	ploughing

2 Read the text and check your predictions to question 1 in Exercise 1. Then work in pairs and follow the instructions.

1 Divide the text into four paragraphs and match them to their purpose a–d.
  a to describe the place and your first impressions ☐
  b to reflect on the experience and make recommendations ☐
  c to specify the place and reason why you went there ☐
  d to describe what made it memorable ☐

2 The text was written as an answer to an exam question. What was it?
  a Describe a famous place and what you saw there.
  b Give an account of your last holiday and what you did.
  c Describe a place and say why it was memorable.

3 Decide the best place in the text to put each of the sentences 1–5. In pairs, explain your reasons. Would you enjoy staying in this place? Why?/Why not?

1 It covers over one hundred acres and includes pre-historic burial mounds and an archaeological dig of Celtic remains.
2 What I missed most was the community life, and the pleasure you get from achieving simple tasks.
3 As the name suggests, it's a place where you can experience living in another time, which in this case was the Iron Age.
4 I suddenly realised what I'd let myself in for!
5 Of course, there were difficult moments.

4 Find these words in the text. What do they mean and what effect do they have on style of the text?

literally   bustling   struggling
painstakingly   peckish

5 Complete the sentences with the words from Exercise 4.

1 Although it was early, the town was already _____ with people.
2 It took us all morning to _____ weave a basket.
3 I took some chocolate in my rucksack in case I felt _____ .
4 As soon as we arrived, the rain _____ poured down.
5 We saw an old woman _____ with a heavy suitcase.

6 Look at the highlighted expressions in the text and match them to definitions 1–4.

1 eagerly accept the chance to do something
2 things you need to know how to do
3 something you had to learn very quickly
4 won't find anything better

7 Find all the relative clauses in the text. What is their function? Then rewrite sentences 1–5 using *which*, *whose* and *where*. Which countries/cities could the sentences be describing?

1 The medieval castle was set on a cliff top. It had panoramic views of the bay.
2 The seventeenth-century mansion was surrounded by magnificent parkland. We saw ancient oak trees and tame deer there.
3 We found the museum in the centre of the bustling city. It was crowded with people and cars.
4 My first impression was of an industrial wasteland of smoking chimneys. It was very depressing.
5 The ancient temple was situated in a hot, deserted part of the country. Its columns were crumbling to dust.

8 Read Train Your Brain. Which exercise helped you with organisation and which exercises helped you with style and language?

TRAIN YOUR BRAIN | Writing skills

Description of a place

Organisation: In four paragraphs
1 Information about the place and why you went there
2 Description of the place and your first impressions
3 Reasons why it was memorable/exciting, etc and personal anecdotes
4 Reflections on your experience and why you would recommend it

Style and language
• Write in a neutral style, adding personal anecdotes.
• Choose a variety of adjectives and adverbs to make your description more vivid.
• Use some colloquial words and expressions to add colour and interest.
• Use relative clauses to link your ideas in more complex sentences.

9 Read the phrases in the diagrams below and choose a heading for each one from the box.

people   buildings and gardens   cities
atmosphere   countryside   weather

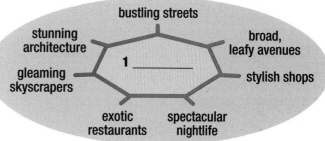

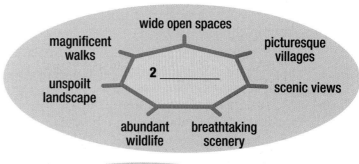

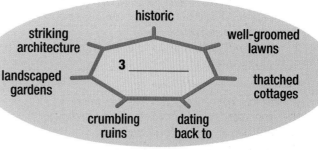

10 Write a description of a memorable place you once visited. Use Train Your Brain to plan and check your review, and include descriptive language from the lesson. Write 200–250 words.

VOCABULARY AND GRAMMAR

1 Read the leaflet and choose the correct answers a–d.

> ### How to survive away from home? Advice for first-year college students.
>
> + Choose your accommodation carefully. If you like peace and quiet, look for a place away from the ¹___ streets of the city centre.
> + Think twice before deciding who to share your place with. You probably don't want to end up ²___ with your roommate because he or she doesn't help with the household chores.
> + Learn how to manage your finances early on. It's simple – be ³___ with your money and don't ⁴___ it on unnecessary things. Always try to ⁵___ by on what you have and never be tempted to borrow money from a loan company. The interest ⁶___ is usually very high.
> + If you decide to combine work and studies – don't expect too much. Yes, some students have even started their own companies but it can take them months just to ⁷___ even. Be realistic and remember that these are your college years and you are here not to ⁸___ a financial profit but to study and have some fun!
>
> If you need any help, contact Office of

1 a crumbling	**c** bustling		
b stunning	**d** abundant		
2 a thrilled	**c** self-pitying		
b apprehensive	**d** frustrated		
3 a confident	**b** broke	**c** careful	**d** saving
4 a bet	**b** blow	**c** pay	**d** donate
5 a get	**b** pass	**c** go	**d** take
6 a rate	**b** level	**c** ratio	**d** worth
7 a be	**b** survive	**c** go	**d** break
8 a gain	**b** make	**c** achieve	**d** do

2 Put the words into the correct categories. Then add two more words to each category. The first and last letters of each word have been given.

hive   draughty   detached house   kennel
frying pan   dressing table   run-down   hall
basement   studio flat   cabinet   cutlery

1 Animal homes: _____ , _____ ,
n _ _ t, b _ _ _ _ w
2 Places in the house: _____ , _____ ,
u _ _ _ _ _ y room, l _ _ t
3 Kitchen items: _____ , _____ ,
u _ _ _ _ _ _ s, c _ _ _ _ _ _ y
4 Adjectives to describe places: _____ ,
_____ , c _ _ _ _ _ d, c _ _ y
5 Furniture: _____ , _____ ,
w _ _ _ _ _ _ e, b _ _ _ _ _ _ e
6 Places to live: _____ , _____ ,
m _ _ _ _ _ n, c _ _ _ n

3 Complete the text with one word in each gap.

> Are you one of those people ¹_____ house just isn't right? Do you ²_____ you had a bigger house? Is it about ³_____ you decorated your bedroom or have you seen some furniture ⁴_____ would look great in the living room? Are your friends telling you that you'd ⁵_____ get the roof fixed soon?
>
> Well, ⁶_____ the answer to any of these questions is 'yes', you will need money. You could go to the bank and ⁷_____ a loan and be in ⁸_____ for the next five years. Or, I ⁹_____ if you'd thought of …
>
> ## MIRACLE FINANCING
>
> The painless way to borrow money.

4 Combine the sentences with the correct relative pronoun, leaving it out where possible. Are the relative clauses defining or non-defining?

1 San Gimignano is within half-an-hour's reach from here. Its towers can be seen clearly from Belsole.
_____

2 The house was spacious but stuffy. We used to live in the house as children.
_____

3 Tom's signature was forged on one of the documents. This was a great shock to him.
_____

4 The roommate should be able to cook well. I'm looking for a roommate.
_____

5 Barcelona has a truly spectacular nightlife. We used to go there every year.
_____

5 Complete the sentences so that they mean the same as the original sentences.

1 I really don't think you should go on a date with her.
You'd _____ .
2 Tamara only lives and works in London because she married an Englishman.
If _____ .
3 Josh regrets choosing black tiles for his bathroom.
Josh wishes _____ .
4 I want you to stop biting your nails – it drives me mad!
If only _____ .
5 They swindled Mrs Parsons out of her life savings because she is very naive.
If _____ .
6 She had a chance of winning but she withdrew from the race due to a serious injury.
She could _____ .

PRONUNCIATION

1 **CD3.8** Listen to each sentence said in two different ways. In each case, is the speaker neutral or emotional? Write N for neutral and E for emotional.

1 a ___   b ___   3 a ___   b ___
2 a ___   b ___

2 **CD3.8** Listen again and repeat the sentences.

LISTENING SKILLS

1 **CD3.9** Listen to the BBC Radio 4 programme and circle the correct answers a–d.

1 Derek Bond was in the headlines because
  a thousands of people have had a similar experience to his.
  b he was the latest victim of identity theft.
  c his case of identity theft was unusual.
  d a lot of money has been stolen from him.

2 Which of the following statements is NOT true of Tom Craig?
  a He used to work as a detective.
  b He has access to people's credit records.
  c He worked for Scotland Yard.
  d He consults people on security issues.

3 Quite a number of people have experience of
  a having their identity documents stolen at the airport.
  b being accused of identity theft.
  c having to wait for new documents for three weeks.
  d being suspected of something they haven't done.

4 What, according to the experts in the studio, is true about fraudsters?
  a They might add data to those of their victims.
  b Most often they get hold of their victims' identity by stealing their mail.
  c They often commit serious crimes such as murder in the name of their victims.
  d They need to steal just one document.

SPEAKING SKILLS

1 What can you say in these situations? Try to sound tentative. Use words from the box.

wondering   mind   business   interfere

1 Your sister wants to spend her holiday in a tent. You know that wet weather is forecast for most of the summer.
2 Your best friend plans to lend a lot of money to Tom (another friend of yours). You've heard that Tom is heavily in debt.
3 Your cousin wants to settle in Florida. She hasn't got any friends there.
4 Martha is moving in with Joanna. You know Joanna is untidy and irresponsible.

2 Look at the visuals and get ready to present the material and discuss:
– possible reasons why people choose to live in mobile homes;
– advantages and disadvantages of mobile home accommodation.
Then answer the teacher's questions.

Teacher's questions:
1 What information do you get from the advert, the table and the headline?
2 Would you like to live in the advertised house? Why?/Why not?
3 What are some pros and cons of mobile home accommodation?
4 Statistics show that there is an increase in the number of people choosing to live in mobile homes. Why do you think that is?
5 Could this kind of accommodation be a good solution to a housing problem in Poland? Why?/Why not?

Southminster, Essex £20,000

Luxury static mobile home for sale

Luxury mobile home for sale at St Lawrence Bay, Essex, 1 bed, sleeps 4, on large plot, parking 3/4 cars, paved area, large fenced garden with 2 sheds to remain, alarmed, site fees paid 2006, many extras, sea views, ideal for boating with a small beach on site. Price negotiable.

Mobile Homes: 1990–2000

	1990		2000		Percentage Change 1990–2000
	#	% of All Housing Units	#	% of All Housing Units	
South Carolina	235,863	16.6	355,499	20.3	50.7
United States	7,324,154	7.2	8,779,228	7.6	19.9

NEWS |
Daily News July 14

CARS MAY BE LESS DANGEROUS THAN MOBILE HOMES AND THE OUTDOORS DURING TORNADOES

according to study by Kent State University Researchers

Give me a clue

Read, listen and talk about riddles, mysteries and crime.
Practise past modal verbs; impersonal report structures; expressions with *live/die*.
Focus on problem solving, reaching a decision.
Write headlines and short articles.

1 Romeo and Juliet were found dead on the floor of the living room. There is some broken glass and spilt water around them. How did they die?

2 A man walked into a bar and asked for a glass of water. The barman took out a gun and pointed it at him. The man said 'Thank you' and walked out. Why?

3 A woman went to a party and drank some of the punch. She left the party early. Everyone else at the party later died of poisoning. Why didn't the woman die?

GRAMMAR AND LISTENING

1 In pairs, discuss which of these games and puzzles you have tried.

Sudoku, word squares, hangman, crosswords, battleships, noughts and crosses, spot the difference, riddles

2 Read riddles 1–3. Which riddle does the picture illustrate? In pairs, discuss possible solutions to it.

3 CD3.10 Listen to two students trying to solve the riddle in the picture. What possible solutions do they give? Do you think they're plausible? Why?

4 Think Back! Look at the <u>underlined</u> past modals in sentences a–g and match them to definitions 1–3.

a The barman <u>can't have liked</u> the look of the man.
b No, it <u>couldn't have been</u> that. It's too obvious.
c The man <u>must've been</u> thirsty or he wouldn't have asked for some water.
d He <u>might've</u> just <u>walked</u> across the desert and was dying for a drink.
e The barman <u>could've been</u> scared, so he took out his gun.
f The barman <u>may have recognised</u> him from the newspapers.
g He <u>might not have known</u> his photo was in the papers.

1 you are almost certain that something happened ☐
2 you think it's possible that something happened/didn't happen ☐☐☐☐
3 you are almost certain that something did *not* happen ☐☐

116

5 CD3.11 Listen and repeat the sentences, paying attention to the contracted forms.

6 CD3.12 Discuss how the modals change the meaning in each sentence. Then listen to the solution to the riddle and circle the correct modals. Were your ideas in Exercise 2 similar?

1 The barman *could / can't* have been playing a joke on him.
2 The barman *must / might* have been insulted by the man in some way.
3 They *may / can't* have been working in the same place.
4 The man *could / might* have helped him – but he refused.
5 The man *must / couldn't* have been threatened because he said 'thank you'.
6 The barman *could / mightn't* have wanted just to scare him.

Work it out

7 Look at the sentences in Exercise 6 and follow the instructions.

1 Underline two passive and two continuous forms of past modals.
2 Look at two different uses of *could* in sentences 4 and 6. Which *could* means that it was possible for something to happen but it didn't?
3 In which sentence, 4 or 6, can we replace *could* with *might* and *may*?

Mind the trap!

We use *needn't have* + past participle to say that something was done but it wasn't necessary.
We use *didn't need* + infinitive to say that something wasn't necessary, and it wasn't done.

He **needn't have pointed** a gun at him. (but he did it)
That's why he **didn't need to** drink the water. (and he didn't)

➤ **Check it out** pages 157–158

8 Rewrite the sentences using past modals. Sometimes more than one modal is possible.

1 It wasn't necessary for me to go to the meeting because it was cancelled.
   I didn't need to go to the meeting because …
2 I'm sure the accident was caused by speeding.
3 Perhaps she was having a shower when you called.
4 It was possible for him to post the letter yesterday but he forgot.
5 I cooked a lot of food for the party but it wasn't necessary because nobody was very hungry.
6 It's almost certain that he wasn't murdered – it was probably suicide.
7 Maybe the TV wasn't working yesterday.

9 Read the riddle and discuss what the solution might be. Use past modals.

> A man was found dead in the middle of a field. He was holding a broken match. What happened?

10 CD3.13 Complete the sentences with the correct forms of the verbs in the box. Then listen and check. Was your solution to the riddle correct?

murder   break   approach   test   train
stab   kidnap   push   damage   take

1 He might _____ the bomb there.
2 He could _____ , and they were going to shoot him.
3 Yes, but they needn't _____ him to a field to shoot him.
4 It might have been an accident or he may _____ .
5 He could _____ or strangled!
6 He might _____ to be a parachutist, and his parachute didn't open!
7 So he may _____ from the plane!
8 The match could _____ in two pieces, and he only had half of it!
9 The balloon could _____ by a bird, or it was too heavy.
10 They might _____ some mountains and were going to crash.

11 Read the situations and write down at least two things you might say in each one, using past modals. Compare your answers in groups.

1 You get home and find the house is in a terrible mess.
2 You spent all day preparing a presentation for school the next day. The teacher was ill and the class was cancelled.
3 You phone a friend but nobody answers, which is strange because there's always someone at home at that time.

12 Work in groups of three to solve riddles 1 and 3 in Exercise 2.

Riddle 1: Students A and C, look at page 147.
Student B, look at page 150.
Riddle 3: Student A, look at page 148.
Students B and C, look at page 147.

READING AND VOCABULARY

1 In pairs, read the list of situations and answer questions 1–3.

- You strike up a conversation with someone and discover you have a friend in common.
- You think about someone, and shortly afterwards they phone or email you.
- You go shopping alone and buy the same clothes as a close friend.
- Twin brothers have girlfriends with the same name.

1 Have you experienced any of these coincidences, or others like it? If so, how and when?
2 Which was, or would be, the strangest or most unusual for you? Why?
3 Do you think coincidences happen for a reason, or are purely chance events? Why?

2 Read the blurb on the back of the novel and look at the sketch. What's the central plot of the book?

Isabel Dalhousie, the charming, well-intentioned editor of a philosophy journal in The Sunday Philosophy Club, is back in Alexander McCall Smith's new book, *Friends, Lovers, Chocolate.*

Isabel's inability to ignore people in need inevitably involves her in unusual situations. By chance she meets Ian, a psychologist, who recently had a heart transplant. Ian tells her about a serious problem, which might prevent his recovery. He's been having disturbing visions of an unfamiliar face – a face he thinks his new heart might remember …
Isabel is intrigued, and finds herself involved in a dangerous investigation. But she still has time to think about the things that possess her – like love and friendship, and, of course, chocolate …

ISBN 978-1-405-85191-6

9 781405 851916

PART I

'What are you getting involved in now?'

Over the next few minutes, Isabel told him about her chance meeting with Ian and about their conversation at the Scottish Arts Club. Jamie was interested – she could tell that – although he, like Isabel herself, seemed 5 incredulous when she mentioned cellular memory.

'There's a rational explanation for these things,' he said when she had finished talking. 'There always is. And I just don't see how anything other than brain cells could store memory. I just don't. And that's on the 10 strength of my school Biology course. It's that basic.'

'But that's exactly the problem,' retorted Isabel. 'We're all stuck with the same tried and trusted ideas. If we refused to entertain the possibility of something radically different, then we'd never make any progress 15 – ever. We'd still be thinking that the sun revolved round the earth.'

Jamie affected surprise. 'Isabel, don't start challenging that now!'

Isabel accepted his scepticism good-naturedly. 20 'I should point out that I'm completely agnostic on all this,' she said. 'All I'm doing is trying to keep an open mind.'

'And where does this take you?' asked Jamie. 'So what if the cells in the transplanted heart or whatever 25 think they remember a face. So what?'

FRIENDS, LOVERS, CHOCOLATE

Isabel looked about her, for no reason other than that she felt a slight twinge of fear. That was in itself irrational, but she felt it.

'The face that he remembers could be the face of 30 the driver who killed the donor,' she said. 'It could have been imprinted in memory – whatever sort of memory – after he'd been knocked down and the driver came and looked down at him.'

Jamie's lip curled. 'Really, Isabel!' 35

'Yes,' she said quickly. 'Really. And if it is the face of the driver, then we may have a description of the person responsible for the death.'

Jamie thought for a moment. It was now obvious to him what Isabel had been doing in the library. 'You've 40 found a report of the accident?' he asked. 'You know who the donor was?'

'I think so,' said Isabel. 'We know that the donor was a young man. That's as much as Ian knows. So I put two and two together and concluded that a sudden, 45 violent death on the day on which they called Ian in for his transplant would probably supply the identity of the donor. And it has. There's nothing brilliant in that. It's all pretty obvious.'

But was it? It crossed her mind that she was 50 assuming too much, and too readily. There might have been other incidents, other young men who could have been donors, but no, Edinburgh was not a very large place. It would be unlikely that two young men had died a sudden death that night. Her assumption, 55 she decided, was reasonable.

3 **CD ROM** **Read Part 1 of the extract. Complete sentences 1–9 with *Isabel, Jamie, Ian* or *the donor*.**

1 _____ was willing to consider theories that have not been scientifically proved.
2 _____ might've died in a car accident.
3 _____ was troubled by strange visions.
4 _____ was sceptical about the idea that heart cells can remember events and images.
5 _____ had a heart transplant.
6 _____ had been doing some research before this conversation took place.
7 _____ might've seen the face of the driver before he died.
8 _____ knew the heart donor was young.
9 _____ believed the person who'd died in the accident was the heart donor.

4 **Vocabulary Match 1–5 with a–e to make phrases from the extract.**

1 tried and ☐   **a** possibility
2 entertain the ☐   **b** and two together
3 keep ☐   **c** of fear
4 a twinge ☐   **d** trusted ideas
5 put two ☐   **e** an open mind

5 **Complete the sentences with the correct forms of the phrases from Exercise 4.**

1 When she heard footsteps behind her, she couldn't help feeling _____ .
2 I'm not sure whether I like him or not. I _____ at the moment.
3 Ann's not a very adventurous cook. She always sticks to the same _____ recipes.
4 He loved his home town and had never even _____ of living abroad.
5 After she'd seen him with the same girl for the third time, she _____ .

6 **Before you read Part 2, discuss these questions.**

• Are Isabel's assumptions about the identity of the donor reasonable? Why?/Why not?
• Will Jamie support Isabel in her investigations? Why?/Why not?
• What will Isabel do next? Why?

7 **CD ROM** **Read Part 2 of the extract on page 120. Are the statements true (T) or false (F)? Were your predictions correct?**

1 Jamie had become involved in Isabel's investigations before. ☐
2 Isabel had already assumed that Jamie would want to help her. ☐
3 Neither of them knew if the police had identified the driver. ☐
4 Ian had described the face of the man he kept imagining to Isabel. ☐
5 Isabel believed that the police would act on the information she had. ☐
6 She felt obliged to take responsibility for the problems of people she met. ☐
7 Isabel believed that justice must be done. ☐

119

PART 2

Rather against his better judgment, Jamie felt himself being drawn in. He could not resist Isabel, he had decided. There was something about her that fascinated him: the intellectual curiosity, the style, the verve. 60

'So?' he said. 'So who is he? And what do we do?'

We do, he thought. I should've said *you* do, but once again, I've played straight into Isabel's hands. I'm trapped. In nets of golden wires.

Isabel was oblivious of Jamie's struggle with himself. 65 She had invited him to meet her to discuss what she had found out; she had not asked him to join her in her inquiry. Of course, if he wished to do so, then that would be very helpful, but she had not asked him.

'Well,' she began, 'we now know who that unfortunate 70 young man was and where he lived. We know that the police appealed for information.'

'And that's it,' said Jamie. 'We … you don't know whether they ever found the driver.' Isabel conceded that this remained unknown. But now, at least, they 75 had a description of the person who might have been responsible.

'But what do you do with that?' asked Jamie. 'Go to the police? What would you tell them? That somebody else is having visions of a face and here's a drawing?' He 80 laughed. 'You can imagine the reception you'd get.'

Isabel thought about this. She had not imagined going to the police – just yet. Jamie was right in thinking that it would be difficult to convince them to take her seriously and that they would be unlikely to pursue the 85 matter further; unless, of course, the push came from the family of the victim. If they could be persuaded to do something about it, then the police could hardly refuse a request from them, at least to consider Ian's story.

Her thoughts were interrupted by Jamie. 'Why are you 90 doing this, Isabel?' he asked mildly. 'What's the point?'

She looked at him. It was her duty, was it not? If this was really information about who was responsible for the hit-and-run incident, then surely she had a duty to do something about it – any citizen would have that duty, 95 simply because he or she was a citizen. And there was more to it than that. By listening to Ian's story, she felt she had been drawn into a moral relationship with him and his situation. Isabel had firm views on moral proximity and the obligations it created. We cannot choose the 100 situations in which we become involved in this life; we are caught up in them, whether we like it or not. If one encounters the need of another, because of who one happens to be, or where one happens to find oneself, and one is in a position to help, then one should do so. It was 105 as simple as that.

She shrugged. 'The point is that I have to do this,' she said. 'I can't walk away from it. That driver needs to be called to account. And Ian needs to know why he's seeing that face. In each case, the solution lies in the 110 uncovering of the truth.'

---

8 Vocabulary **Complete the table. Some of the words are in the text. Then complete sentences 1–6 with the correct words.**

adjective	noun	verb
judgemental		
conclusive		
	rationale	
assumed		
conceding	concession	
	oblivion	

1 She instinctively made the _____ that he was telling the truth.
2 The results of the tests were _____ . There was no doubt about it.
3 I try not to make _____ about people until I get to know them better.
4 In the end, I was forced to _____ that he was right.
5 We were _____ of the fact that she was deeply hurt by our remarks.
6 I just don't understand the _____ behind his behaviour.

9 Vocabulary **In the extracts, find the words that match definitions a–h.**

a unable to believe something (line 6)
b reply quickly and angrily (line 12)
c move one's lip upwardly showing scepticism (line 35)
d energy and excitement (line 60)
e completely unaware of (line 65)
f admit reluctantly that something is true (line 74)
g nearness in distance or time (line 99)
h move one's shoulders upwardly showing you don't know or care (line 107)

10 **Discuss your opinions in groups.**

- Whose point of view do you sympathise with most – Jamie's or Isabel's?
- What would you do in her place?
- Do you ever find yourself in a dilemma? In what way?
- Do you find it easy to make up your mind about things or people? Why?/Why not?

120

VOCABULARY

1 In pairs, look at the cartoons and answer the questions.

- What do the <u>underlined</u> expressions mean? Do you have similar ones in your language?
- Which cartoon do you like best? Why?

2 **CD3.14** Lines a–e each finish five different dialogues. Listen and match the dialogues to the correct lines. Justify your choice.

a I wouldn't be seen dead with him! ☐
b Over my dead body! ☐
c I'm dead tired tonight. ☐
d You mean larger than life? He's sure to be the life and soul of the party. ☐
e But I couldn't for the life of me remember his name! ☐

3 Which sentences a–g follow on from sentences 1–7?

1 Have you bought the newspaper? ☐
2 I knew I shouldn't have gone there. ☐
3 I've just heard that Bob wore two different-coloured shoes to school. ☐
4 I've never worked so hard in my life. ☐
5 I've just had a pay rise! ☐
6 She really should look for a job nearer home. ☐
7 That hat is <u>to die for</u>! ☐

a I'm <u>dying for</u> a holiday.
b She's been <u>living out of a suitcase</u> for the last six months.
c I nearly <u>died of</u> boredom.
d But look at the price. I'd probably <u>live to regret it</u>!
e I'm <u>dying to</u> check the answers to yesterday's crossword.
f Let's go out and <u>live it up</u>!
g I nearly <u>died laughing</u>.

4 In pairs, write a sentence to follow on from sentences 1–6. Use the correct expressions from Exercise 3. Then compare your answers.

1 I wouldn't buy that jacket if I were you.
2 That new comedian at the club is brilliant.
3 He's just spent six months backpacking around Asia.
4 I heard they've got a new CD out.
5 Take my advice and don't go to see it.
6 The exams are over! Now we can relax.

5 Complete the phrasal verbs with the correct particles from the box. Use a dictionary to help you.

down (x2)   up to   with   off   out   away

1 Hundreds of species are thought to be dying _____ every day.
2 Once the press find out his secret, he'll never live it _____ .
3 We had a terrible storm last night but it soon died _____ .
4 I know you hate your job, but you'll have to live _____ it for the time being.
5 When our excitement finally died _____ , we realised what the million-pound win meant.
6 My boss is so demanding, I can never live _____ his expectations.
7 Students who go to university usually have to live _____ their parents.

6 In groups, discuss your answers to each prompt. Then compare your answers with other groups.

Something or someone …
- you can never remember for the life of you
- you might live to regret
- that makes you die of boredom
- you're dying to do or to have
- you might find hard to live down
- you find difficult to live with
- you find difficult to live up to

121

GRAMMAR AND READING

1 In pairs, look at the photos and the title, and answer the questions. Then read the article and check.

> 1 In which aspects of life can DNA be useful?
> 2 What kind of information can be obtained from it?

Work it out

2 <u>Underline</u> the equivalents of sentences 1–4 in the article. Then compare them to sentences a–d and circle the correct form in *italics*.

> 1 It was said that he had died in prison …
> 2 They thought that the hairs were from a cat.
> 3 It is believed that they identified fake Olympic souvenirs …
> 4 They expect that the new technology will ensure the authenticity of sports items …

> a He *is / was* said *to die / to have died* in prison during the French Revolution.
> b The hairs *are / were* thought *to be / to have been* from a cat.
> c They *are / were* believed *to identify / to have identified* fake Olympic souvenirs …
> d The new technology *is / was* expected *to ensure / to have ensured* the authenticity of sports items for years to come.

3 Look at sentences a–d in Exercise 2 and follow the instructions.

> 1 Match the sentences to patterns a and b.
> a subject + passive + infinitive ☐☐
> b subject + passive + perfect infinitive ☐☐

> 2 Which sentence reports a fact/situation that
> a happened at the *same time* as it was reported?
> b happened *before* the time it was reported?
> c is expected to happen in the *future*?

> 3 What verbs can be used to introduce patterns 1 a and b?

4 Which sentence, 1 or 2, contains a passive and which a continuous form? Find their equivalents in the article.

> 1 Louis XVII was claimed <u>to have been rescued</u> and replaced by an impostor.
> 2 Famous brand names are increasingly thought <u>to be using</u> DNA technology to protect their products.

➤ **Check it out** page 158

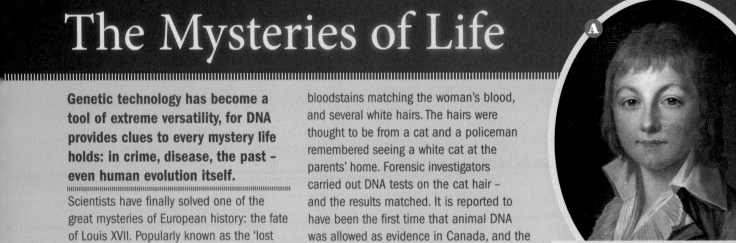

The Mysteries of Life

Genetic technology has become a tool of extreme versatility, for DNA provides clues to every mystery life holds: in crime, disease, the past – even human evolution itself.

Scientists have finally solved one of the great mysteries of European history: the fate of Louis XVII. Popularly known as the 'lost dauphin', Louis was the son of King Louis XVI and Queen Marie Antoinette. He was said to have died in prison during the French Revolution but many people claimed that he had been rescued and replaced by an impostor. Recently, however, DNA was extracted from the preserved heart that was thought to be Louis's. It matched conclusively to his living relatives, thus disproving claims from those who say they are descendants of the 'true' king.

A young mother was found murdered in Canada. Among the suspects was her ex-husband, who was living with his parents nearby. Police found a jacket with bloodstains matching the woman's blood, and several white hairs. The hairs were thought to be from a cat and a policeman remembered seeing a white cat at the parents' home. Forensic investigators carried out DNA tests on the cat hair – and the results matched. It is reported to have been the first time that animal DNA was allowed as evidence in Canada, and the man was convicted.

It is thought that famous brand names are increasingly using DNA technology to protect their products from unauthorised copying. In order to reduce the threat of fraud, all official goods for the 2000 Australian Summer Olympic Games were labelled with ink containing DNA taken from an unnamed athlete. A team of 'logocops' armed with special DNA scanners was sent out to investigate. They are believed to have identified fake Olympic souvenirs worth millions of pounds. The new technology is expected to ensure the authenticity of sports items for years to come.

5 Rewrite the sentences so that they mean the same.

1 Scientists now believe that Beethoven died of lead poisoning.
Beethoven _____ .

2 It was reported that fruit found at the crime scene had led police to the murderer.
Fruit found at the crime scene _____
_____ .

3 It is said that US Super Bowl organisers are using DNA marking in their footballs.
US Super Bowl organisers _____
_____ .

4 Archaeologists expect that the frozen mummy will provide vital information about Inca civilisation.
The frozen mummy _____ .

5 Geneticists claim that a local Bristol man is a descendant of a 9,000-year-old skeleton.
A local Bristol man _____ .

6 Many people at the time alleged Mozart had been poisoned.
Mozart _____ .

6 Complete the text with the correct forms of the words in brackets.

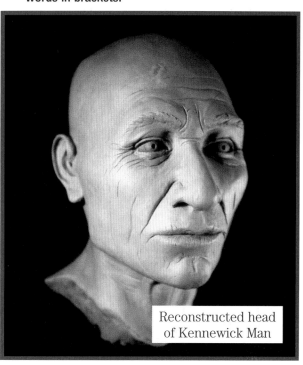

Reconstructed head of Kennewick Man

Kennewick Man
When two boys found the skeleton of Kennewick Man in 1995, it ¹_____ (think/be) the remains of a murdered man, but ²_____ (later/discover/be) over 9,000 years old. Then a legal battle over the remains delayed further analysis for years. Scientists ³_____ (report/be) extremely anxious about this. It was the oldest complete skeleton ⁴_____ (find) in North America and ⁵_____ (expect/provide) crucial information about the mysterious origins of the first Americans. Scientists finally gained access to Kennewick Man in 2005, and have made important discoveries. He ⁶_____ (understand/be) about 1m 70 tall and ⁷_____ (die) around the age of forty. Most interestingly, he ⁸_____ (say/bury) deliberately. Further analysis and DNA tests ⁹_____ (expect/determine) not only his diet but whether he was from Polynesia, not NE Asia.

7 **CD3.15** Listen to two news items and write down five more statements using the patterns from Exercise 3. Then rewrite them using *It is* + a reporting verb.

Paintings worth over forty million pounds are reported to have been stolen.
It is reported that paintings worth over forty million pounds have been stolen.

8 **In groups, discuss at least two possible uses of DNA in the areas below.**

• health and medicine
• crime detection
• famous historical figures
• our ancestors

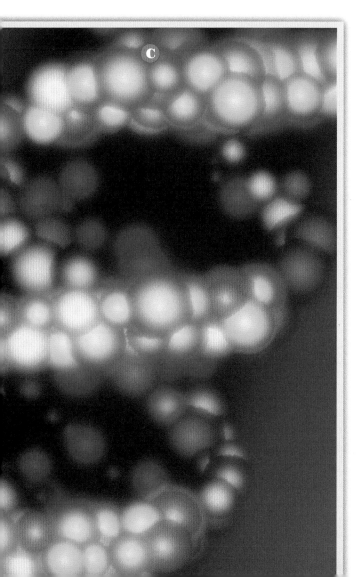

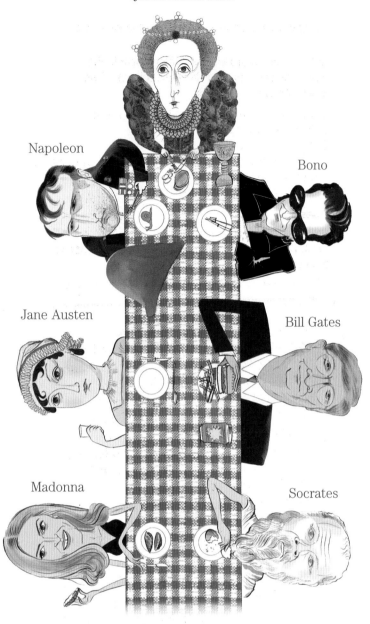

Queen Elizabeth I

Napoleon

Bono

Jane Austen

Bill Gates

Madonna

Socrates

3 **CD3.16** Listen to three people discussing the seating plan. Complete sentences 1–6 with the correct famous person's name.

1 _____ was said not to care about his appearance.
2 _____ can talk about intelligent, amusing and interesting things.
3 _____ lived a sheltered life in a rural area.
4 _____ could discuss his/her ambitions with Elizabeth I.
5 _____ believes in equality of the sexes.
6 _____ wouldn't agree with Napoleon's military ambitions.

4 **CD3.16** Complete Speak Out with words from the box. Then listen again and check. Draw their seating plan so far.

moving   hitch   getting   round   far
pitfalls   point

SPEAK OUT | Problem solving

To refer to a problem
The trouble is …
I can already see quite a few ¹_____ .
I've just realised there's a ²_____ here.
Yes, that could work!/I don't think it would work.

To refer to decisions made so far
Just to go back to the ³_____ you made about …
We don't seem to be ⁴_____ very ⁵_____ , do we?
So where are we now, then?
We'll get ⁶_____ it somehow.

To move the discussion on
Let's move on, shall we?/⁷_____ on …
Let's leave that for now and come back to it later.

5 How would *you* organise the seating plan? Discuss in pairs, using language from Speak Out. Then draw your plan. For information about the people, Student A, look at page 148. Student B, look at page 150.

6 **CD3.17** Listen to the end of the conversation and draw the seating plan *they* decide on. How similar/different is it to yours?

7 Work in groups of five. Imagine you have been invited to the dinner party. Decide which famous people you should sit next to and why. Use language from Speak Out.

SPEAKING AND LISTENING

1 In pairs, look at the picture and answer the questions.

• What do you know about these people?
• What sort of personality do you think they have/had? Use the words in the box. Justify your opinions.

strong-willed   charismatic   outspoken
argumentative   short-tempered   innovative
manipulative   quick-witted   inscrutable
a good conversationalist   astute   witty

2 Look at how the people are seated. Is the seating plan a good one? Why?/Why not?

WRITING

1 Read the headlines and, in pairs, discuss what the articles might be about.

1 Fish found in miracle escape

2 Thief caught by cartoon

3 Parrot held in jail

4 Woman fakes death over fines

2 Match the headlines to articles A–D. Then answer questions 1–3.

1 What were the key words that helped you match the headlines?
2 Which stories do you think are true? Why?
3 Which story do you think was the funniest, saddest, most ridiculous? Why?

A
A judge in Argentina ordered a parrot to ¹_____ held in custody until he said the name of his owner. Two neighbours, Jorge Machado and R Vega, ²_____ both claimed Pepo was theirs. After five days, Pepo ³_____ Jorge's name and sang the anthem of his favourite football team. Mr Machado said: 'I knew he wouldn't let me down. He's a real friend and we ⁴_____ support San Lorenzo.'

B
A burglar who stole from a cartoonist in Australia was arrested after his victim drew his picture. Bill Green, 82, saw the man take a bicycle ⁵_____ his shed. He gave his sketch to police, who matched ⁶_____ to a man arrested ⁷_____ a different theft. Policeman Michael Henry said: 'We were amazed. The cartoon was the spitting image of ⁸_____ man we'd just caught.'

C
A woman from Iowa is alleged to have faked her ⁹_____ death to avoid paying $500 in parking tickets. Police say Kimberly Du, 36, was caught after she got ¹⁰_____ ticket a month after her 'death'. She had faked her own obituary and forged a letter saying she had died ¹¹_____ a car crash. She now faces up to five years in prison ¹²_____ fraud.

D
A goldfish carried from its garden pond by floods has ¹³_____ found alive in a water-filled hole by the roadside more ¹⁴_____ a mile away. Farmer Ab Oskam, 66, was ¹⁵_____ his dog when he recognised the fish ¹⁶_____ one of three belonging to his neighbours. 'It was a miracle such a delicate little thing survived,' he said. The fish has now been named Nemo.

3 Complete the articles with one word in each gap.

4 Look at the list of features. Which apply to the headlines and which to the short articles? Find examples of each feature.

1 articles (*a, the*) are usually missed out
2 there is usually a quote
3 the age of the person is mentioned
4 the Present Simple is used to refer to present and past events
5 the past participle is used for the passive
6 the passive is often used

5 Read the article and write three different headlines for it. Compare your headlines in groups and choose the best ones.

In July 2005, the chocolate-loving community in Sydney was threatened by a blackmailer who claimed to have poisoned seven Mars Bars. As a result, all Mars Bars were taken off the shelves, causing panic among many consumers who feared they wouldn't be able to buy their favourite chocolate. Company manager Paul Rivers, 35, said, 'The situation is under control now. Mars Bars will be back in the shops tomorrow.'

A&E

CHOCOLATE REPLACEMENT PILLS

WE'VE ONLY GOT ENOUGH TO LAST UNTIL TOMORROW!

6 Choose a headline and write a short article about it, using 60–70 words.

1 Thieves caught in stolen clothes
2 School burglar takes Maths test
3 Burglar sleeps on the job
4 Stolen painting recovered

7 Read your article to the class who decide which headline it refers to, and why.

125

Newsworthy?

Read, listen and talk about news and media, photography, films.
Practise quantifiers; singular and plural nouns.
Focus on taking notes while listening, presentation skills: emphasis.
Write a report.

a 'Journalism is literature in a hurry.'
Matthew Arnold, British writer

b 'The man who reads nothing at all is better educated than the man who reads nothing but newspapers.'
Thomas Jefferson, American president

c 'No news is good news. No journalists is even better.'
Nicolas Bentley, British author and illustrator

d 'I believe in equality for everyone, except reporters and photographers.'
Mahatma Gandhi, political and spiritual leader

e 'It's amazing that the amount of news that happens in the world every day always just exactly fits the newspaper.'
Jerry Seinfeld, American comedian

GRAMMAR AND LISTENING

1 Read quotes a–e about journalism and discuss the questions in pairs.

Which …
1 is the funniest?
2 is the most negative?
3 do you agree with?
4 do you like best?

2 You are going to listen to an interview with Alastair, a news reporter. First, read the questions. Try to predict as many of his answers as you can.

1 Why did you become a reporter?
2 What qualities does a reporter need?
3 What are the easiest and most difficult types of story to write?
4 What's the most interesting story you've covered?
5 How easy is it to get a story on the front page?
6 What are the best and the worst things about the job?
7 Is it a glamorous job?

3 **CD3.18** Listen to Alastair's answers to the questions in Exercise 2 and make notes. Where is Alastair in the photo?

4 **CD3.18** Listen again and circle the quantifiers that Alastair uses in sentences 1–8.

1 There are *a number of / several / a few* reasons, if I think about it.
2 *The whole / Most of the / All the* family used to read newspapers.
3 She or he needs to have *a lot of / lots of / quite a lot of / a great deal of* curiosity.
4 As I've often found in *quite a few / a few / few / very few* cases, this may annoy or upset them.
5 *Any / Every / No* story is easy but I suppose there are some which reporters find particularly difficult.
6 *Each / Every* front page article is a special moment.
7 There is *a little / little / very little / no* time to feel frustrated.
8 *Most reporters / All reporters / Any reporter* will tell you that they are too busy to think about glamour.

Work it out

5 Write the quantifiers you circled in Exercise 4 in the gaps in the diagram below.

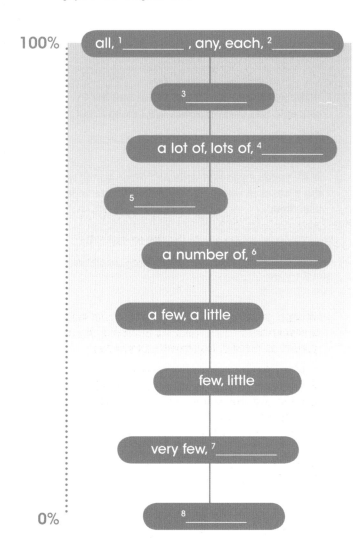

6 Look back at Exercises 4–5 and circle the correct options in the sentences below.

1 'the whole family used to read newspapers': 'the whole family' means *all the family / every family*
2 'any reporter will tell you': 'any reporter' means *no reporters / all reporters*
3 'a few' and 'a little' mean *more / less* than 'few' and 'little'
4 'quite a few' means *more / less* than 'a few'
5 'very few' and 'very little' mean *more / less* than 'a few' and 'a little'

7 Look at sentences a and b and complete rules 1 and 2 with *each* and *every*.

a Ned was waiting for me after school <u>every</u> day last week.
b My sister's friend has got five earrings in <u>each</u> ear.

1 We use _____ to refer to two things or more.
2 We use _____ to refer to three things or more.

Mind the trap!

Every must be followed by a noun or a pronoun.

'I recommend that you read all the stories on the website:

every story
every one   is interesting in its own way.'
~~every~~

BUT We <u>can</u> say 'Each is interesting in its own way.'

➤ **Check it out** page 158

8 **CD3.19** Replace the <u>underlined</u> words or phrases with quantifiers that have similar meanings. Sometimes more than one answer is possible. Then listen to Alastair and compare.

1 <u>More than a few</u> of the people seem to appreciate the chance to talk to someone from outside the family.
2 <u>Nearly all</u> interviews with famous people are easy to write about, in my experience.
3 We watched <u>a large number</u> of people leaving their homes by boat.
4 A <u>small number of</u> lucky ones had rides on helicopters.
5 The best thing is that for a <u>large amount</u> of the time it can be exciting.
6 Like <u>every</u> job there are times when the work is quite routine.
7 It sometimes feels like there is <u>not any</u> time to say things exactly the way you want.
8 <u>Almost none</u> of them get their faces on the screen!

9 Complete the sentences with the correct quantifiers from the box.

> very few a few very little none every
> whole a number quite a few most

1 This newspaper's full of photographs and advertising: there's _____ real news.

2 I'd really like to be a photographer and spend the _____ day taking photographs!

3 Only _____ of our features are written by our journalists: we get _____ of them from freelance writers.

4 There are _____ mistakes in this TV guide: I've found one on _____ page so far.

5 I'm afraid we can't use your article: _____ of our readers are interested in ferrets.

6 The photographer gave me _____ of photos to use with this story, but _____ of them is quite right.

10 Circle the correct answers.

When it comes to writing a news story, there are ¹___ important rules which ²___ journalists are taught. Firstly, they learn to use an upside down pyramid: this 'inverted' pyramid represents the news story. In this structure ³___ the most newsworthy information comes first, then as the story goes on, the details are explained. The first paragraph, or 'lead', should contain enough information to give the reader a good overview of ⁴___ story. This means that if the editor cuts the last paragraph because of space limitations, the reader will still have a summary of the story and ⁵___ additional details.

Another 'key' thing reporters learn is to make sure they ask the five 'W' questions: what, who, where, when, why. ⁶___ good news story provides answers to ⁷___ of these questions. If it doesn't, the writer can be sure that it will come back to them for ⁸___ revision. Finally, they learn to keep their sentences and paragraphs short, and not to use ⁹___ heavily descriptive language. When a story is finished, they go through it and try to remove ¹⁰___ words which aren't necessary.

1 a few **b** several **c** a lot **d** little

2 a most **b** all of **c** no **d** any

3 a every **b** quite a few of **c** all **d** a lot

4 a all **b** every **c** a lot **d** the whole

5 a no **b** a few **c** few **d** very few

6 a Most **b** All **c** A great deal of **d** Any

7 a each **b** the whole **c** every **d** several

8 a any **b** little **c** a little **d** a few

9 a lots of **b** a lot **c** a number of **d** no

10 a each **b** most of **c** every **d** any

128

Tsunami commemoration ceremony in Thailand

SPEAKING AND LISTENING

1 Look at the examples of photojournalism: which concept from the box does each one represent for you? Discuss your ideas in pairs, giving reasons.

> happiness peace human achievement
> courage harmony hope

2 [CD3.20] Listen and choose the photos and the concepts that the two people are talking about.

Ana photo ___ concept _____
Ivan photo ___ concept _____

3 [CD3.20] Listen again and write Ana (A) or Ivan (I) next to the phrases in Speak Out, according to which person uses them.

SPEAK OUT | Presentation skills: Emphasis

auxiliary *do*
I **do** remember … ☐   it **does** have … ☐

adverbs
really amazing ☐
the people **really** look as if … ☐
incredibly brave ☐
absolutely stunning ☐
they **even** went on travelling … ☐
we'll **never ever** have … ☐

so* and *such
They seemed **so** strong, and **so** resilient. ☐
It was **such** a tragic end to the year. ☐

patterns with *what* … and *it* …
What I remember most clearly **is** … ☐
What's particularly striking about it **is** … ☐
It's this sense of infinity **that** makes …. ☐
It was this courage of theirs **that** made … ☐

Maria Sharapova at Wimbledon

Stonehenge in England

Anti-war protest at Big Ben in London

The Olympic opening ceremony in Athens

The London bombings

4 CD3.21 **Add the correct word from the brackets in a suitable place in the sentence. Change the verbs if necessary. Then listen, check and repeat.**

1 I've heard so many people cheering and clapping. (even/never ever)
2 Some people queued all night to get tickets. (even/do)
3 They had a difficult task ahead of them. (so/did)
4 The idea was brilliant. (absolutely/very)
5 It makes you think. (does/did)
6 His words were moving. (absolutely/incredibly)

5 Finish the sentences so that they mean the same as the original sentences.

1 There was such a big crowd that we couldn't see the stage.
The crowd _____ .
2 The rain was so heavy that they had to stop the match.
There was _____ .
3 The costumes that they were wearing were so beautiful.
They were wearing _____ .
4 The lack of music was such a disappointment for me.
I was _____ .

6 Rewrite each sentence beginning with the word in capital letters.

1 I love the combination of colours.   WHAT
2 The light in the photograph first strikes you.   IT
3 The people's enthusiasm impressed me.   IT
4 We have to remember how difficult it was.   WHAT
5 I'll never forget the expression on her face. IT
6 The photographer has managed to capture a feeling of excitement.   WHAT

7 Choose a photo from the remaining four photos and prepare a short presentation. Use Speak Out to help you give emphasis.

- Say why you chose the photo and what concept it represents for you.
- Explain any personal significance that the photo has for you.
- Describe the interesting/impressive features of the photo itself.

8 Give your presentation to the class. While you listen to the other presentations, answer the questions giving reasons.

Which presentation ...
- was the most interesting and why?
- made the best use of emphasis?
- was the most surprising and why?

129

a Thanks to their brilliant performance in the second half, the <u>team</u> have secured their place in the final …

b OUR <u>CONGRATULATIONS</u> go to Paris Hamilton and Rowan Lawton, who were recently spotted wearing engagement rings at 'Hip', London's newest nightclub.

c Is <u>Maths</u> giving you a headache? Help is at hand with our online Mathematics tutor, available from …

d <u>Peugeot-Citroën</u> announced last week that it was shutting one of its main British factories …

e <u>Crowd</u> of 20,000 wait outside Windsor Castle to cheer Queen on birthday.

f If your <u>surroundings</u> are beginning to seem all too familiar, now is a good time for a change: take a holiday or even think about a new job …

g While it is true that the Prime Minister made some mistakes, I feel that the <u>media</u> have blown them out of proportion …

h The <u>orchestra</u>, which was conducted by Sir Leonard Williams, played superbly, and the <u>audience</u> were quick to show their appreciation with thunderous applause.

VOCABULARY

1 Why would you look at each of sections 1–8 of a newspaper? Discuss in pairs. Then match extracts a–h to the sections.

1 gossip column ☐
2 sports pages ☐
3 letters to the editor ☐
4 classified ads ☐
5 horoscope ☐
6 business news ☐
7 national news ☐
8 entertainment section ☐

2 Add the <u>underlined</u> nouns in the extracts to Train Your Brain.

TRAIN YOUR BRAIN | Nouns

Nouns which are always plural:

acoustics, belongings, clothes, earnings, premises, refreshments, thanks, [1] _____ , [2] _____

Nouns which end in -s but have a singular verb:

• subjects of study: *economics, linguistics, politics,* [3] _____
• sports and games: *aerobics, billiards, gymnastics*
• other: *news*

Nouns which can be singular or plural (group nouns):

• names of institutions, companies and teams: *the United Nations, Manchester United,* [4] _____
• other: *class, crew, family, government, group, press, public, staff,* [5] _____ , [6] _____ , [7] _____ , [8] _____ , [9] _____

The choice of a singular or plural verb depends on how you 'see' the noun.
• as a single unit: *My singing <u>group is</u> quite small.*
• as a number of individuals: *The <u>group have</u> all got very good voices.*

Mind the trap!

Make sure that you use the correct pronouns and possessives with group nouns:

The management **have** increased **their** pay offer. (as individuals)
The management **has** increased **its** pay offer. (as a unit)

The crew **who** looked after us on the flight **were** excellent. (as individuals)
The crew **which** looked after us on the flight **was** excellent. (as a unit)

3 Complete the sentences with the correct forms of the verbs from the box. Which of the extracts does NOT come from a newspaper?

start   lose   be   criticise   cost   appeal   move   produce

1 The family of a five million-pound lottery winner _____ to the media to respect their privacy.
2 Bath _____ 7–12 to Cardiff and their dreams of repeating their 2005 victory have been shattered.
3 Members please note that aerobics _____ at 8a.m. on Mondays, not 7.30.
4 The company _____ recently _____ to new premises outside London, which _____ much less to rent than its office space in the city.
5 The BBC, which usually _____ high-quality TV programmes, _____ for launching a lifestyle magazine aimed at girls as young as five.
6 According to a survey, one in five teenagers thinks that billiards _____ more fun than football.

READING AND VOCABULARY

1 Which of the words and phrases in the box are NOT used to talk about films? Use a dictionary to help you.

director   crew   remake   continuity   shot
close-up   footage   to shoot   backstage
back projection   shot   scene
dress rehearsal   on location

2 In pairs, look at the film posters on pages 132–133 and discuss these questions.

1 Which of the films have you seen? What did you think of them? What scene(s) do you remember in particular?
2 What do you know about the others? Which of them would you like to see and why?
3 Some people think that remakes are never as good as the original. What's your opinion?
4 Who are the best film directors of all time? Why?

3 **CD ROM** Read the article on pages 132–133 quickly and answer the questions.

1 How many mistakes are described in the article?
2 Which do you remember seeing? How 'serious' are they?
3 What is the author's opinion of the mistakes? Choose from a–d.
   a There are too many of them.
   b They are often intentional.
   c They are a sign of poor directing.
   d They add to the 'magic' of the film.

4 Match the films with the statements.

PC – *Pirates of the Caribbean*
T – *Titanic*
R – *Raiders of the Lost Ark*
P – *Psycho*
D – *Die Another Day*
K – *King Kong*
C – *Citizen Kane*

1 A mode of transport is involved. ☐☐☐☐
2 Film crew or equipment used in making the film is visible. ☐☐
3 The hero or heroine is in a dangerous situation. ☐☐☐
4 The film contains things that belong to a different time. ☐☐
5 There are mistakes in the continuity. ☐☐☐☐
6 Authenticity is sacrificed for the sake of the heroine's appearance. ☐☐
7 An object is used wrongly or seems to behave strangely. ☐☐☐

5 Vocabulary Find words or phrases in the article that match the definitions.

1 very good at noticing things (para. B)
2 tending to make a lot of mistakes (para. C)
3 very obvious (para. D)
4 able to make mistakes or be wrong (para. E)
5 someone who has different ideas and ways of behaving from other people (para. E)
6 someone who insists on every detail being right (para. E)
7 someone who is interested in films and knows a lot about them (para. F)
8 a sudden feeling that you want to do or have something, especially when there is no particular reason (para. F)

6 In pairs, discuss the following. Then compare your ideas with other pairs.

Think of a film or TV character who
1 is a music buff.
2 is accident-prone.
3 is a maverick.
4 is a stickler for rules.
5 often acts on a whim.
6 thinks they are infallible.

7 Underline sentences in the article that mean the same as sentences 1–3. Why is their form different?

1 As soon as he has shot himself in one scene, he is seen trying to untie one of the lifeboats in another. (para. B)
2 She shows no discomfort and she also climbs a metal ladder. (para. D)
3 He seldom started shooting a film that wasn't already completely planned in his head. (para. E)

8 Rewrite the sentences using the inversion patterns that you underlined in the text. Which two sentences could also be written using the pattern *Hardly … when …*?

1 There are a lot of mistakes in *Titanic* and some of them are also very obvious.
2 As soon as I had seen the first scene of the film, I realised it was a remake.
3 You rarely see Hitchcock's films on TV nowadays.
4 I had just got to the front of the queue when they told me the film was sold out.
5 Orson Welles directed *Citizen Kane* and he also starred in it.
6 I never realised that Spielberg made so many mistakes.

9 Why do *you* think films are released when they contain so many mistakes? Discuss in pairs.

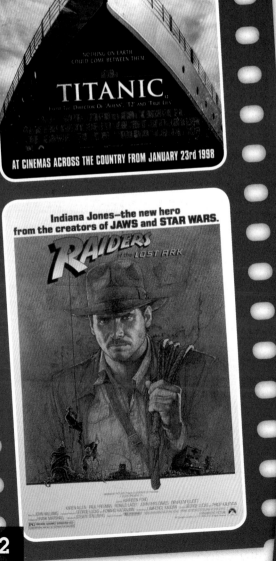

How did that make the final cut?

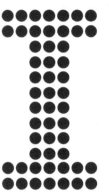

A **I**n the final scene of *Pirates of the Caribbean: The Curse of the Black Pearl*, Jack Sparrow (Johnny Depp) calls his crew back onto the ship with a polite 'On deck, you scabrous dogs', and over his shoulder, to the left of the 5 screen, is a man in a white T-shirt, tan hat and sunglasses, standing looking out to sea. Oops! It's a member of the film crew! This is just one of several mistakes in the film where crew or equipment are visible: there are many 10 others which are factual. For example, Port Royal in Jamaica is built on a low spit of sand that is not more than ten feet above sea level: in the film set it's built on top of hundred-foot cliffs. And the way the heroine's maid uses a bed warmer would 15 have been positively dangerous: by placing it at her mistress's feet, full of red-hot coals, she would have barbecued her toes. Bed warmers held warm coals and were removed before the sleeper got into bed!

B Another famous film with a seafaring theme does no 20 better. *Titanic* is reputed to contain more than 180 mistakes, a number of which are anachronisms. Given that the Titanic sank in 1912, it's very unlikely that Captain Smith would be wearing contact lenses, as we see in one close-up. Also, Rose would not have been able to 25 admire Monet's 'The Nymphs', which he painted in 1915, and it's impossible for Jack to have gone ice fishing on Lake Wissota, as he claims, since it wasn't created until 1918. But perhaps only the eagle-eyed historians in the audience would notice these blunders. The majority of us 30 are more likely to notice continuity mistakes like the one involving First Officer William Murdoch. No sooner has he shot himself in one scene than he is seen trying to untie one of the lifeboats in another. We could also be forgiven for getting confused when the ship's orchestra 35 seems to alternate between having four and five players in different shots.

C Or are we? Maybe we're too busy concentrating on the action to pick up on details. For example, in *Raiders of the Lost Ark* when Indiana Jones is confronted by a cobra in the Well of Souls, did you see the reflection of the snake in the safety glass between it and Harrison Ford? Incidentally, the director of this film, Steven Spielberg, tops the list of mistake-prone directors, with a grand total of 1,148! You begin to wonder if some of them are deliberate – put there to see how willing we are to believe everything we see in the escapist world of the movies. This might explain some of the more obvious goofs in *Die Another Day*, like the one where Bond's Aston Martin flips over during a chase on the ice, and part of the left wing mirror breaks off. When the car flips back over, the wing mirror is intact. We also see Jinx (Halle Berry) being cut across her stomach in the final fight scene. Yet, moments later, she and 007 are pouring diamonds over each other and her stomach is unblemished.

D Of course, we wouldn't want our heroine's beauty to be spoilt, would we? This unwritten rule must be the cause of a lot of glaring mistakes. A good example is in the 2005 remake of *King Kong*. The scenes in New York take place in winter, on a day cold enough for the lake in Central Park to freeze and hold Kong's weight. Yet Anne Darrow shows no hint of cold, even though she's wearing a sleeveless gown. Kong takes her to the top of the Empire State Building, where it's even colder. Not only does she show no discomfort, but she also climbs a metal ladder, holding on with her bare hands.

E But are all directors fallible? What about maverick director Alfred Hitchcock, who was known for being a stickler for detail? Seldom did he start shooting a film that wasn't already completely planned in his head, so surely his films are error free? Well – no. Take his acclaimed horror film, *Psycho*: when the heroine, Marion, is leaving town after stealing from her boss, she keeps checking the speedometer of her car, and you can clearly see that the gear stick is in 'park'. Later, when she stops at the Bates' motel and shares some food with the owner, she tears the same piece of bread down the middle in three different shots.

F And even *Citizen Kane*, regarded by many film buffs as one of the best films ever made because of its innovative filmmaking techniques, contains twelve mistakes. One of these features a jigsaw puzzle: in the first shot of Kane's wife doing the puzzle, it's nearly complete, but in a subsequent close-up it seems to have undone itself, and is in pieces again. Another is in an outdoor picnic scene: director Orson Welles did not have enough money to film on location, so he had to shoot the scene in the studio, using back projection. The footage he used was from *King Kong*, and four pterodactyls can clearly be seen flying by. The studio told Welles to take the pterodactyls out of the shot, but he liked them and decided to keep them.
This begs the question: how many other gaffes were left in a film at the whim of its director?

G So, when is a mistake not really a mistake? Next time you watch *Harry Potter and the Philosopher's Stone*, look out for the start of term feast. Harry sits down on the right side of the table, next to Ron. When the food appears, Harry is on the other side of the table, next to Hermione. A mistake, or just Harry showing off his magic powers? I'll leave you to decide: after all, in the world of the movies, everything is magical.

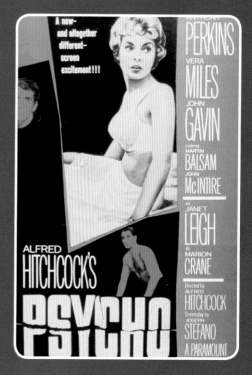

133

LISTENING

1　Why are some people so interested in celebrities? Discuss in pairs.

2　**CD3.22** Listen to the first part of a lecture about celebrity. Are the statements true (T) or false (F)?

　1 To be a celebrity, you have to do something else apart from being famous. ☐
　2 Richard Branson was not famous until he tried to go round the world in a balloon. ☐
　3 Shakira was famous before her songs were translated into English. ☐
　4 Kings and queens do not qualify for celebrity status. ☐
　5 The first modern celebrities were film actors. ☐
　6 The Hollywood film industry grew during the Great Depression. ☐

3　Look at the notes that Beth and Leo made during the lecture. Why are Beth's notes easier to follow?

4　Read Train Your Brain and check your answers to Exercise 3.

TRAIN YOUR BRAIN | Listening skills

Taking notes

To organise your notes:
• Give the notes a main heading in capital letters.
• Give each new topic a sub-heading and underline it.
• Put each fact or piece of information on a new line, beginning with a bullet point (•).
• Put inverted commas (' ') round any quotes or titles.

To save time:
• Don't try to write everything you hear.
• If you can't catch a particular word or phrase, try to guess the meaning and write something similar.
• Leave out unnecessary words such as articles, pronouns and auxiliary verbs.
• Use abbreviations and symbols such as:
　eg　ie　&　C20th　→　vs　approx

5　Rewrite Leo's notes using Train Your Brain.

6　**CD3.23** Listen to the rest of the lecture and make your own notes. Then swap notes with a partner and compare the techniques you have used.

7　In groups, discuss what you would do or say if you could be famous for just fifteen minutes.

Beth

CELEBRITY

What is a celebrity?
· Definition: 'person widely recognised in society who commands public & media attention'
· Not always enough to be famous
· Need something to start media interest, eg public figure like Branson going round world in balloon

National vs. global celebrities
· Each nation has own celebrity system → may be unknown abroad
· Most global celebrities: actors, musicians, religious & political figures
· Can cross over national → global, eg Shakira: well-known in Spanish-speaking world before internationally famous

---

Leo

How and when were the first celebrities created? Before the twentieth century Celebrity status was (strict?) to biblical mythical figures and royalty
For example fer of Egypt.
The film industry invented the modern personality, and the first global celebrity was Charlie Chaplin
He was an entertainer - famous in Hollywood in the 1920s and '30s. The mass media made celebrity culture a national pass (past time?) in the United States.
During the Great Depression of the 1930s, Hollywood (?), approximately 80 million people a week went to the cinema.

Media Habits

Introduction

The purpose of this report is to present the findings of a survey into media habits. The information was collected from a group of twenty-five students aged 18–20 at Portsmouth College of Further Education.

Television

As expected, television is by far the most popular medium. Most of ¹_____ people we interviewed said they prefer to get the news from the television, and about ²_____ thirds of them estimated that they watch at least four hours of TV on a typical day. As far as favourite programmes are concerned, a large number of people mentioned films and chat shows, while ³_____ a few favoured documentaries. In contrast, ⁴_____ few respondents put soap operas in their top three.

Newspapers

⁵_____ is in this area, the print media, that the group vary the most in ⁶_____ answers. A quarter of the people we asked admitted to never reading a newspaper, and about thirty percent said they only look at the ⁷_____ page headlines and photographs. Of the rest, about half read the sports pages, and several regularly read the horoscopes and the gossip ⁸_____ . It was not really surprising to find that hardly ⁹_____ of our interviewees read the ¹⁰_____ newspaper from cover to cover.

Radio

Although radio is a less popular medium than television, there were some unexpected answers in this section. ¹¹_____ was most surprising was the number of people who still listen to music on the radio: about sixty percent usually have the radio on in the car or in the background while studying. On the other hand, only a small minority felt that the radio news ¹²_____ worth listening to.

Conclusion

¹³_____ conclusion, it appears that television plays a large part in ¹⁴_____ people's lives. However, our survey also showed that not ¹⁵_____ their media habits are predictable.

WRITING

1. Look at the title of the report and discuss the questions in pairs.

   - What is included in the term 'media'?
   - How are your media habits similar to or different from other people in your family?

2. Read the report and write six questions that the people in the survey were asked.

3. Complete each gap in the report with one suitable word.

4. Read the report again and follow the instructions.

   1 Complete the table with words and phrases from the report.

Quantifier	Noun	Verb
Most (of)	the people we interviewed	said ...
Two ¹_____ (of)	them	estimated ...
A large number (of)	people	⁴_____ ...
Quite a few (of)	³_____	favoured ...
²_____ any (of)	interviewees	⁵_____ ...
A small minority (of)		felt ...

   2 Underline the following useful phrases:
   - two phrases to introduce the report
   - four words or phrases to show a contrast
   - two phrases to conclude the report

5. In pairs, prepare six questions to ask other students about films and cinema-going habits. Use some of the prompts to help you.

   How often ...?
   prefer/cinema/DVD?
   read/reviews?

   What/make/good/film?

   What kind of ...?
   favourite director?
   best cinema/your city?
   best/ever/see?

6. Interview the other students, then write a report on your survey.

   - Make sure that your report has an introduction and a conclusion.
   - Divide the body of the report into sections for different topics.
   - Use the 'report' language from Exercise 4.
   - Give the report a title and give each section a heading.

VOCABULARY AND GRAMMAR

1 Complete the sentences. Make new words from the words in capital letters.

1 A free ads paper contains lots of
_____ ads.   CLASSIFY
2 They often accuse Jan of being
critical and _____ .   JUDGE
3 Just work on the _____ that
most of them have never touched
a computer.   ASSUME
4 Dave sat daydreaming and was
_____ to everything around him. OBLIVION
5 I've come to the _____ that it's
not worth renting a DVD player.   CONCLUDE
6 Just out of _____ , are you
really planning to marry Nick?   CURIOUS
7 The head teacher has made
some _____ as to what clothes
the students can wear.   CONCEDE

2 Complete the sentences with the correct forms of the verbs in brackets.

1 In recent years, politics _____ (become)
an increasingly popular subject to study.
2 On several occasions the staff _____
(voice) their concern regarding longer
working hours.
3 Over the next few years, the EU _____
(plan) to set tough standards for nuclear
safety in all its member states.
4 By the time the news _____ (start) I'll be
fast asleep.
5 At the end of the play the audience often
_____ (show) their appreciation by giving
the cast a standing ovation.

3 Complete the text with one word in each gap.

Escaped prisoner still free

The bank robber who escaped from prison last
week has still not been caught. It [1]_____
thought that he might [2]_____ left the country.
At the moment, very [3]_____ information has
been given to us by the police but [4]_____ is
now known is that he escaped through a tunnel, not
over the wall as was first thought.

A police spokesman said yesterday, 'We're keeping
an open [5]_____ about the escape. There have
been quite a [6]_____ people who have
telephoned with information and the news
[7]_____ positive, although I can't give too many
details yet. The [8]_____ incident is very worrying
but some of the reports of security failures in our
prisons have been wildly inaccurate. A number
[9]_____ people have been putting two and two
[10]_____ and making five, and it is these people
who are making life difficult for those investigating
the case.'

4 Complete the sentences so that they mean the same as the original sentences.

1 I'm almost certain they invited Dan to the
dress rehearsal.
Dan _____ .
2 Scientists now believe that the Red Planet
was once water-rich.
The Red Planet _____ .
3 It is said that the *The Echo* is publishing
further details of the story next week.
The Echo _____ .
4 It wasn't necessary for me to do a creative
writing course because I knew it all already.
I _____ .
5 As soon as *Celebrity Big Brother*'s finished,
Craig starts rehearsals for a new comedy.
No sooner _____ .
6 Music critics expect that her new album will
be released in the early spring.
Her new album _____ .
7 I'm almost sure she didn't believe it was just
a coincidence.
She _____ .
8 The article gives plenty of facts and casts a
new light on the issue of home-schooling.
Not only _____ .

5 Read the text and choose the correct answers a–d.

I never thought that I would end up believing in
ghosts. But in my family strange things have
happened, and quite [1]___ of us have similar
stories to tell. [2]___ I remember most clearly is a
story about my great-grandfather, who heard
strange voices after the sudden death of his wife.
[3]___ family thought this was just a symptom of
depression but my great-grandfather was
convinced it had been his wife speaking to him.
He is said [4]___ back to her every night until he
died himself. To be honest, I never really [5]___
the possibility that he had actually heard his
wife's voice. That is, until my mother, my
cousin and my sister told me their stories. [6]___
was strange in its own way and [7]___ could be
explained in any rational way. I bet you [8]___ to
hear at least one of them. OK, here we go …

1 **a** a little   **b** a few   **c** few   **d** little
2 **a** Thing   **b** Which   **c** What   **d** This
3 **a** All   **b** Every   **c** A lot   **d** The whole
4 **a** to have talked   **c** that he talked
  b to talk   **d** to be talking
5 **a** thought   **c** entertained
  b had   **d** felt
6 **a** Every   **b** All   **c** Any   **d** Each
7 **a** no   **c** none of them
  b any of them   **d** all
8 **a** are dead right   **c** nearly died
  b are dying   **d** wouldn't be seen dead

PRONUNCIATION

1 ⬚ CD3.24 Listen to the following statements and underline the stressed words.

1 I will never ever watch this film again.
2 I do remember reading about it.
3 They were so hospitable to visitors.
4 War correspondents there were incredibly brave.
5 What I really like about Julia Roberts is her smile.

2 ⬚ CD3.24 Listen again and repeat.

READING SKILLS

1 Read the texts and match the people to questions 1–8. Write N for Nigel, B for Barbara, J for John, P for Paul and S for Susan.

1 Who implies that she/he would never want to become a journalist?
2 Who thinks that criticism of contemporary journalism is not always legitimate?
3 Who feels that journalists' duties extend beyond getting information and reporting it accurately?
4 Who implies he/she is a journalist himself/herself?
5 Who points out the difficulty in precisely defining the field of journalism?
6 Who holds the view that journalists are fallible?
7 Who appears to be the most critical of journalism among the interviewed people?
8 Who points to the similarity between journalism and many other professions?

SPEAKING SKILLS

1 You and your friends are discussing starting a school newspaper. Use the words in brackets and write what you can say if …

1 You know there are some problems with other people's suggestions. (pitfalls)
2 You're sure something is not a good idea. (work)
3 You want to refer to something one of your friends said before. (point)
4 You want to discuss the next issue. (move)
5 You're sure you and your friends will solve a problem in one way or another. (round)

2 Choose one of the topics and prepare a three-minute presentation.

1 'Every country has the media it deserves.' Do you agree with this statement? Why?/Why not?
2 Some people believe that doing crossword puzzles and riddles develops your mind while others consider them to be just time wasters. What are your views? Justify your opinion.

It's often claimed that without good journalism, we wouldn't have an informed public. But the question arises as to what makes good journalism today, when the public is increasingly 'informed' through more immediate, visual media, such as the Internet, satellite and cable twenty-four-hour news channels. We asked several people of different ages to tell us what their attitude towards journalism and journalists is. Here is what they had to say.

Nigel (46)

Recent events have put journalism in the spotlight and there are lessons to be learned from this. It's obvious that journalists have not been doing a very good job of educating the public about what they do and why they do it the way they do. We spend too much time talking amongst ourselves, just assuming that our motives and methodology will be generally understood and appreciated.

Barbara (20)

I think there are bad journalists, just like there are bad hair stylists and bad architects and bad funeral directors; but the overwhelming majority of journalists are out to do a good job because they believe that what they are doing is important – getting good information, reporting accurately and fairly, telling the truth. Of course, journalists make mistakes like any other professionals whose jobs entail making dozens of judgement calls and decisions every day. But the key thing is that good journalists acknowledge their mistakes and correct them.

John (17)

Last year at school I learned that journalism was the key to understanding the media and it should always show the facts in an unbiased way. I think now, with the commercialisation of television media, most journalism has been reduced to the standard of the tabloids. And journalists? You should consider a profession that you will not need to apologise for being a member of.

Paul (23)

Most of us tend to be highly critical of journalism today, especially given that the past couple of years have not been a good time for journalism ethics. There have been far too many examples of flawed reporting and bad judgement. That's all true, but we must remember one simple fact: people are always anxious to seek out the media when doing so works to their advantage, but quick to find fault when the press covers something they don't want to talk about.

Susan (35)

It's really easy to say what makes a good journalist. But there are grey areas when it comes to what is a journalistic situation. For example, talk show hosts of almost all kinds are not generally journalists and that is not a problem as long as they are clear about it. When some talk show hosts try to 'borrow' the credentials of journalism to make their statements carry the weight earned by years of honest reporting by real journalists, I have a problem with that.

CULTURE SHOCK 1

THE BRITISH FASHION SCENE

Glossary mascara blusher piercings safety pins studs to dress down
innovative anarchic scruffy

1960s

1

2

1970s

3

4

5

1980s

6

7

1990s

8

2000s

9

10

11

12

1 Match the clothing and accessories in the photos to the words in the box.
Use a dictionary to help you.

flared jeans ☐ fishnet tights ☐ a cropped top ☐ Ugg boots ☐
bouffant hairstyles ☐ Doc Martens ☐ low-rise jeans ☐ a peaked cap ☐
a flannel shirt ☐ platforms ☐ frills ☐ spiky hairstyles ☐

FACTFILE: the British fashion scene

1960s

The 'swinging sixties' was a decade of social and political change, with an attitude of 'anything goes'. In London this was reflected in a fashion revolution which produced bold and innovative designs. One of the defining fashions of the 60s was the mini skirt, which was worn about 20cm above the knee, and was seen as a tool of social rebellion and freedom for young women. It was made popular by British designer Mary Quant, who named it after her favourite car! The Hippie movement later in the decade had a strong influence on the style of jeans: very flared or 'bell bottom' legs were popular, as were hipsters, which sat below the waist, on the hips.

1970s

Punk was the name given to an aggressive and anarchic movement in fashion and music which started in London in the mid-1970s. Punks' clothes and hair were designed to attract attention and shock people. Clothes from charity shops were cut up and reconstructed using safety pins and chains, jeans and leather trousers were deliberately torn, Doc Martens boots were worn with skirts and fishnet tights. Hair was spiked as high as possible by using soap, hair spray and even glue! Punks also put pins and studs in their noses, eyebrows and lips.

1980s

New romanticism appeared in the British music scene in the early 80s as a direct reaction against the harshness of the punk movement. Where punk protested about life in Britain's council estates, the New Romantics celebrated glamour. They created a colourful and dramatic look using frills and luxurious fabrics associated with historical periods. Men wore make-up, particularly blusher and mascara, and had large, bouffant hairstyles. Vivienne Westwood, one of Britain's most influential designers and involved in creating the punk style, went on to develop the 'pirate look' worn by New Romantic bands such as Adam & the Ants and Spandau Ballet.

1990s

The 90s will probably be remembered as the decade of 'anti-fashion'. People tended to dress down and wear casual, comfortable clothing, such as baggy jeans and sportswear. The tendency can be seen clearly in grunge fashion, popularised by fans of grunge music. The look was scruffy and featured worn-out jeans, flannel shirts and Converse sneakers or Doc Martens. Long straight hair was favoured after the extravagant styles of the 70s and 80s. Body decoration was also a significant trend of the decade, with people of all ages getting tattoos and piercings if they wanted to look 'cool'.

2000s

A decade of nostalgia? The fashion conscious look back to previous decades for inspiration as pirate styles and fabrics from the 80s make a comeback, and designers create looks from a mixture of old and new. Low-rise jeans are in vogue again and are often teamed with a cropped top. Another popular look is 'boho-chic', which features long 'peasant' style skirts, cowboy boots and Ugg boots. An important designer of the period is Alexander McQueen, whose career started in the 90s, and whose controversial styles earned him the title 'the hooligan of British fashion'.

---

2 In pairs, look at the photos and discuss the questions.

1 What do you think of the 'look' in each case?
2 Which would or wouldn't you wear and why? Use words and phrases from the box.

- X looks really dated/funky/childish/cool/weird/drab/original/over the top/retro …
- I could imagine wearing X to …
- I wouldn't be seen dead in X …
- X is in fashion again/is all the rage now.
- You'd have to be skinny/confident/mad/daring to wear X …

3 Read the factfile and match the statements to the decades.

1 The pirate look was in fashion. ____
2 The fashion was closely associated with a style of music. ____
3 Comfort was more important than fashion. ____
4 Extravagant hairstyles were a key part of the 'look'. ____
5 The clothes were a form of protest. ____
6 Piercings and Doc Martens were popular. ____

4 CD4.1 Listen to three interviews and answer the questions.

1 a Which item of clothing was he most proud of?
  b Why did it take his girlfriend a long time to get ready to go out?
2 a What does she think is lacking in British fashion nowadays?
  b How did she use to make her hair straight?
3 a What does she think is different about British fashion now?
  b Why does she think it's easy to find clothes that will suit you?

5 Crossing Cultures In groups, discuss the questions.

1 Which designers from your country do you like and why?
2 How far do *you* express your personality through your clothes? Give examples.
3 Is fashion given too much importance nowadays? Do you know any 'fashion victims'?

139

CULTURESHOCK2

BRITISH FOOD

Glossary yeast gravy peel to pickle raisins layer pastry spices spread to mince to bake
savoury batter currants to sprinkle leftover bun to mash

1 In pairs, look at the photos of the dishes and discuss the questions.

- Which products/dishes do you think are sweet and which are savoury?
- Which seem to have a misleading name?

shortbread

marmalade

rock cakes

crumpets

black pudding

toad-in-the-hole

shepherd's pie

bubble and squeak

bread and butter pudding

pickled eggs

Factfile: British Food

1 _____ : a sausage made from pig's blood, cereal, spices and fat. Sometimes eaten as part of a 'full English' breakfast, with bacon, eggs, baked beans and fried bread.

2 _____ : a dessert consisting of layers of buttered bread and raisins, baked in a mixture of eggs and milk.

3 _____ : a dish made from leftover cooked vegetables from a roast dinner. The vegetables are mixed with mashed potato, then fried on both sides.

4 _____ : a thick pastry case with a filling of beef, potato and onion. Traditionally eaten by Cornish tin miners; it is an important symbol of Cornwall.

5 _____ : a small round cake made from flour or potato and yeast. It has a distinctive flat top covered in holes. Usually toasted and served with butter.

6 _____ : a sweet spiced bun containing currants, with a cross on top, which is symbolic of the Christian cross. Eaten at Easter.

7 _____ : a jam made from citrus fruit, most commonly oranges. Usually also contains the peel of the fruit, which gives it a bitter taste. Eaten on toast at breakfast.

8 _____ : a dark brown savoury spread made from yeast extract. It is usually served on toast or bread, but should be spread thinly because of its powerful, concentrated taste. People either love it or hate it!

9 _____ : hard boiled eggs which are pickled in vinegar. Usually found in fish and chip shops and pubs.

10 _____ : small, fruity cakes which are sprinkled with sugar before baking to make them go hard on the outside. Usually eaten at teatime.

11 _____ : a savoury dish consisting of a layer of minced lamb in gravy, which is covered with a topping of mashed potato and baked.
NB If made with beef, it is called a 'cottage pie'.

12 _____ : a type of biscuit made with a lot of butter and baked at a low temperature so that it remains pale in colour. Usually associated with Scotland.

13 _____ : sausages baked in a batter made from milk, eggs and flour. Served with vegetables and gravy.

14 _____ : a savoury dish made from a batter of milk, eggs and flour, and baked in a very hot oven. Traditionally served with roast beef for Sunday lunch.

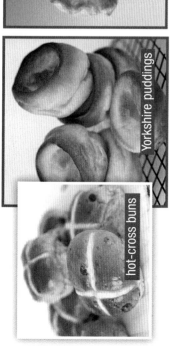

hot-cross buns

Yorkshire puddings

Cornish pasties

marmite

2 **Complete the factfile with the names of the food products and dishes, and check your answers to Exercise 1.**

3 **Which food would and which wouldn't you like to try and why? Use the adjectives from the box and a dictionary to help you.**

spicy   light   heavy   greasy   rich   sticky   crumbly   moist   soggy   filling   sickly
bitter   salty   fattening   appetising   buttery

4 **CD4.2** **Listen to Part 1 of the radio programme. Are the statements true (T) or false (F)?**

1 British food deserves its bad reputation.
2 You should accept an invitation to Sunday lunch at a British person's house.
3 In Australia, the 'toad' in a 'toad-in-the-hole' is an egg.
4 Tracy expected marmite to be salty.
5 Shane liked pickled eggs as soon as he tried them.
6 You can only get hot-cross buns at Easter.

☐☐☐☐☐☐

5 **CD4.3** **How do you think the following got their names? Listen to Part 2 and check.**

1 rock cakes   3 shortbread   5 marmite
2 Yorkshire pudding   4 bubble and squeak

6 **Match 1–6 with a–f to make phrases from the radio programme.**

1 get a bad   ☐   a beat
2 hard to   ☐   b tooth
3 an acquired   ☐   c a guess
4 have a sweet   ☐   d down
5 wash it   ☐   e press
6 hazard   ☐   f taste

7 **Crossing Cultures In groups, discuss the questions.**

1 What are the two most important food products or dishes that a visitor to your country should try?
2 What food products or dishes in your country might a visitor find strange? Why?
3 How have eating habits in your country changed in recent years?

CULTURE SHOCK 3

SUMMER – MAGIC AND MADNESS

Glossary risk life and limb   steep slope   date back to   sprained ankle   venue   launch   flyer   be renowned for   overwhelming   fire up   cracked rib   scrapes and bruises   live up to   put sb off   stick to   all walks of life   get caught up in the buzz

Cheese Rolling

Full title: The Cooper's Hill Cheese Rolling and Wake

What: One of the strangest and most spectacular of all Britain's weird and wonderful traditions. People risk life and limb in a 200-yard race down a steep slope, trying to catch a seven-pound, round Double Gloucester cheese!

When: every year on Spring Bank Holiday Monday

Where: on Cooper's Hill near Gloucester

Origins: The tradition is at least 200 years old but may date back to an ancient pagan ritual at the return of Spring.

Key facts:
- there are five downhill and four uphill races
- from 3–4000 spectators from far and wide attend the event
- competitors rarely catch the cheese since it reaches speeds of up to 70mph
- paramedics attend the event since there are usually a number of injuries, ranging from sprained ankles to broken bones

IN A NUTSHELL:
'It was madness. Cheese was won, shoes were lost, people were knocked out – but no deaths. What more could you want?!'

Follow that cheese!

Double Gloucester Cheese Winner!

The Fringe

Full title: Edinburgh Festival Fringe

What: In 1996, *The Guinness Book of Records* named the Fringe as the largest festival in the world.

When: every year in the month of August

Where: anywhere there's a space to perform in Edinburgh

Origins: When the Edinburgh International Festival was launched in 1947, its main focus was on classical music. Eight British theatre companies decided to put on their own, more alternative work. The Fringe was born.

Key facts:
- attendance figures: hundreds of thousands!
- over 1.5 million tickets worth over £10m sold
- Fringe 2006 presented 28,014 performances of over 1800 shows in 261 venues with 16,990 performers
- renowned for staging shows in unusual venues, such as a Ford Escort, a public toilet or a lift
- many popular entertainers like Hugh Grant and Jude Law launched their careers there

IN A NUTSHELL:
'If you wanted to see every performance, one after the other, it would take over four years!'

Fringe street performers

The Fringe hits the Royal Mile, Edinburgh

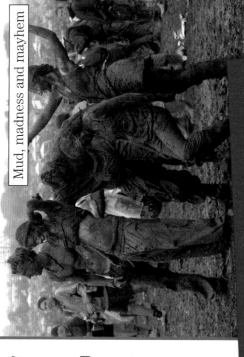

Mud, madness and mayhem

The Pyramid stage at Glastonbury

Glastonbury

Full title: The Glastonbury Festival for Contemporary Performing Arts

What: The largest outdoor performing arts festival in the UK, legendary for its 17 stages, mud, sea of tents and mass of humanity in search of an 'alternative' experience.

When: a three-day event at the end of June

Where: on Michael Eavis's farm in Somerset

Origins: First held in 1970 in reaction to other over-commercialised music festivals.

Key facts:
In 2005
- 153,00 people attended
- £125 for three-day ticket; sold out in under three hours
- over 300 bands, including the White Stripes and Coldplay
- £1,350,000 raised for charities
- Glastonbury came top in a Ben and Jerry survey on what people most associated with British summer – and an entirely new ice cream was created: *Glastonberry*

IN A NUTSHELL:
'Come rain or shine, Glastonbury is undoubtedly the place to spend the best time of your life!'

1 **In pairs, look at the map and photos and answer the questions.**

1 What do you know about these events? What happens there?
2 What sort of people might
- perform or take part in each event?
- attend as spectators?

2 **Read the factfiles. Which event would you most and which least like to go to?**

3 CD4.4 **Listen to extracts 1–3 and match them to the correct event. What sounds, words and phrases helped you decide?**

The Fringe ☐   Glastonbury ☐   The cheese rolling race ☐

4 **Look at the phrases in the box. At which event(s) might you experience these things? Discuss in pairs.**

win a prize   perform in the streets   get very muddy
launch your career   get knocked out   queue up for the loo
sprain your ankle   put up a tent   need a paramedic

5 CD4.5 **Listen to three interviews. Are these statements true (T) or false (F)?**

1 A complete stranger did something James did not expect. ☐
2 He advises the first-timers to play an active part. ☐
3 Rachel was disappointed that she hadn't won the race. ☐
4 She advises people not to take part without the right clothing. ☐
5 Harriet plays one of the three witches in a production of *Macbeth*. ☐
6 The street performers wear weird costumes to attract people to their shows. ☐

6 Crossing Cultures **Discuss the questions in small groups.**

- What unusual or popular festivals and events are there is your country? Describe them. (what/when/what happens/what sort of people attend them/your own experience of attending or participating in them)
- Which do you think are the most interesting? Why?
- What advice would you give people who go there?

143

CULTURESHOCK 4

THINGS YOU'VE ALWAYS WANTED TO KNOW ...

Glossary to instate   in (their) own right   anglicised   to imply   to date from   to merge with   respectively   be broke
to derive from   stout   to commission   to inscribe   copper button   to trace back to   Auld Lang Syne
dock builders   to rhyme with   be broke   be puzzled   mixer taps   plumbing   knights   sword   prohibitive

WHY ...?

1 do the British drive on the left?
2 are the Yeoman Warders at the Tower of London usually known as Beefeaters?
3 is British currency called the 'pound sterling'?
4 is the famous London landmark called Big Ben?
5 is the British flag known as the Union Jack?
6 are New Year celebrations in Scotland called Hogmanay?
7 is the day after Christmas known as Boxing Day?
8 do the British use the slang word 'bread' for money?
9 are policemen known as 'cops'?
10 do many British bathrooms have separate hot and cold taps instead of one mixer tap?

Factbox

A The Yeomen Warders, popularly known as **Beefeaters**, were instated by King Henry VII as his bodyguards in 1485. Nowadays they act as tour guides at the Tower of London, where they are a tourist attraction in their own right.
The word *Beefeater* is probably an anglicised version of *buffetier*, the French term for the guard of the king's food in the Middle Ages – which might imply that Yeoman Warders ate very well!

B The **Union Jack** dates from 1800, when Ireland was merged with Great Britain to form the United Kingdom of Great Britain and Ireland (now only Northern Ireland). The original flag combined the red cross of Saint George for England and Wales with the Saint Andrew white diagonal cross on a blue background for Scotland. The new design added the red diagonal cross of St Patrick. The name Union Jack dates from the early 1700s and is probably derived from its use as a 'jack' flag at the front of British ships.

C The name **Big Ben** refers to the bell in the tower at the Houses of Parliament, not to the tower or large clock itself. There are two theories about its name. The first is that it was taken from the nickname of a champion heavyweight boxer of the time, Ben Caunt.
The second, and more probable, explanation is that it was named after the rather stout Welshman, Sir Benjamin Hall, who commissioned the bell and whose name was inscribed on it.

D The term *cop* could refer to the copper buttons on the uniforms of the first policemen in London or it might be an acronym for 'Constable on Patrol'. However, the most likely explanation is that around the year 1700, the slang verb cop entered the English language, meaning 'catch or capture'. By the mid 19th century, the *-er* suffix had been added and a policeman became a *copper*, a man who catches criminals.

E The word *pound* as a unit of English money was first recorded around 975 when the value of coins was calculated by their weight. The term **pound sterling** can be traced back to the time of King Henry II in the 12th century. The derivation of the word *sterling* is almost certainly from Easterling Silver, which was used to make coins at the time, and came from Easterling in Germany.

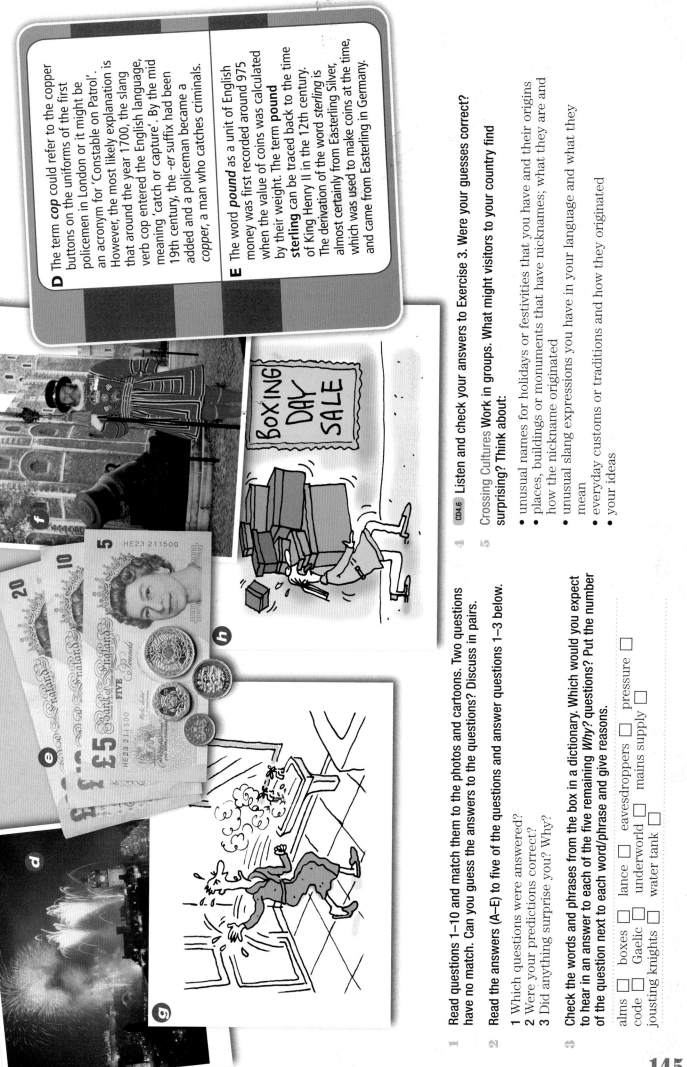

1 Read questions 1–10 and match them to the photos and cartoons. Two questions have no match. Can you guess the answers to the questions? Discuss in pairs.

2 Read the answers (A–E) to five of the questions and answer questions 1–3 below.

1 Which questions were answered?
2 Were your predictions correct?
3 Did anything surprise you? Why?

3 Check the words and phrases from the box in a dictionary. Which would you expect to hear in an answer to each of the five remaining *Why?* questions? Put the number of the question next to each word/phrase and give reasons.

alms ☐   boxes ☐   lance ☐   eavesdroppers ☐   pressure ☐
code ☐   Gaelic ☐   underworld ☐   mains supply ☐
jousting knights ☐   water tank ☐

4 [CD4.6] Listen and check your answers to Exercise 3. Were your guesses correct?

5 Crossing Cultures Work in groups. What might visitors to your country find surprising? Think about:

• unusual names for holidays or festivities that you have and their origins
• places, buildings or monuments that have nicknames; what they are and how the nickname originated
• unusual slang expressions you have in your language and what they mean
• everyday customs or traditions and how they originated
• your ideas

145

Student Activities

Unit 1, Reading and Listening, Exercise 6, page 9.

1 EMI – Electrical & Music Industries, a recording company
2 CAA – Civil Aviation Authority, the British aviation association
3 MI5 – Military Intelligence, section five, a government intelligence agency

Unit 1, Writing, Exercise 10, page 15.

Summer / Seasonal Jobs Overseas

We are one of Europe's leading tour operators and the market leader in self-drive, self-catering family holidays, offering a wide range of positions to suit all our overseas employees.

Operating in 10 countries throughout Europe on over 230 holiday parks and campsites, we employ around 2,000 campsite staff every year.

We have requirements for a wide range of skills, whether you have experience with working with children, coordinating activities, leading a team or you're just committed to working hard and enjoy helping people make the most of their holiday experience.

All employees are provided with:

Accommodation
Uniform
Subsidised insurance
Training
Travel to resort

If you think you have the qualities to provide our customers with the 'perfect family holiday' we want to hear from you.

Ref No

104344-NETSU001

Unit 2, Reading, Exercise 8, page 22.

In pairs, think of a situation where you

- would want to come across in a good light.
- might give away a secret.
- would try to hold back a sneeze.
- would have to take on extra work.
- would not want to strike up a conversation.

Compare your ideas with another pair.

Unit 3, Grammar, Exercise 8, page 35.

CD1.25 **Song:** *El Condor Pasa* (If I Could) – Simon and Garfunkel

I [1]_____ be a sparrow than a snail
Yes I would, if I could, I surely would
I [2]_____ be a hammer than a [3]_____
Yes I would, if I only could, I surely would

Away, I [4]_____ sail away
like a [5]_____ that's here and gone
a man gets tied up to the [6]_____

he gives the world its saddest sound
its saddest [7]_____

I [8]_____ be a forest than a [9]_____
Yes I would, if I could, I surely would
I [10]_____ feel the [11]_____ beneath my feet
Yes I would, if I only could, I surely would

Unit 4, Vocabulary, Exercise 3, page 43.

Multiple intelligences scoring sheet
Circle the numbers of the statements you ticked to find your strongest and weakest intelligences.

Linguistic	4	8	15	20
Logical – mathematical	7	9	16	17
Visual – spatial	1	3	10	23
Musical	5	14	18	22
Bodily – kinaesthetic	6	11	13	21
Interpersonal	2	12	19	24

Unit 5, Speaking and Listening, Exercise 6, page 53.

In pairs, think what questions you could ask about this material. Then Student A, look at page 147. Student B, look at page 149.

Massive levels of workplace stress revealed

Stress is the biggest health concern for British workers, according to a study published today.

Yoga voted top alternative therapy

A new study has shown that yoga is Britain's favourite alternative therapy.

People all over the country now claim it has helped relieve health complaints from back problems and stress to asthma and digestive disorders.

Unit 8, Speaking and Listening, Exercise 5, page 85.

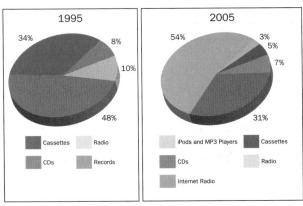

Teenagers preferred ways of listening to music

Unit 8, Vocabulary, Exercise 1, page 89.

Answers to quiz: 1b, 2c, 3a, 4a, 5c, 6 a, b, c, d

Unit 10, Reading and Vocabulary, Exercise 8, page 109.

CD3.3 Listen to the song and answer questions 1–4.

Song: *She's Leaving Home* – The Beatles

Wednesday morning at five o'clock as the day begins
Silently closing her bedroom door
Leaving the note that she hoped would say more
She goes downstairs to the kitchen clutching her
    handkerchief
Quietly turning the backdoor key
Stepping outside she is free

She (We gave her most of our lives)
Is leaving (Sacrificed most of our lives)
Home (We gave her everything money could buy)
She's leaving home after living alone
For so many years (Bye bye)

Father snores as his wife gets into her dressing gown
Picks up the letter that's lying there
Standing alone at the top of the stairs
She breaks down and cries to her husband 'Daddy
    our baby's gone
Why would she treat us so thoughtlessly?
How could she do this to me?'

She (We never thought of ourselves)
Is leaving (Never a thought for ourselves)
Home (We struggled hard all our lives to get by)
She's leaving home after living alone
For so many years (Bye bye)

Friday morning at nine o'clock she is far away
Waiting to keep the appointment she made
Meeting a man from the motor trade

She (What did we do that was wrong?)
Is having (We didn't know it was wrong)
Fun (Fun is the one thing that money can't buy)
Something inside that was always denied
For so many years (Bye bye)

She's leaving home
Bye bye

1 Why is the girl leaving home?
2 How do the parents feel?
3 Who do you feel more sympathy for? Why?
4 What do you think will happen next?

Unit 11, Grammar and Listening, Exercise 12, page 117.

Riddle 1: Students A and C
Discuss possible explanations for riddle 1. You can
ask Student B for help using questions with *Yes/No*
answers, but will lose one point, from a total of 10, for
each question.

Riddle 3: Students B and C
Discuss possible explanations for riddle 3. You can
ask Student A for help using questions with *Yes/No*
answers, but the same rules as before apply.

Student A Activities

Unit 2, Speaking and Listening, Exercise 5, page 24.

Notes:

- ID: identification: a bank card or passport
- proof of address: an official letter with your name
  and address on it, eg a phone/gas/electricity bill
- overdue DVDs will incur a fine: you have to pay 50p
  if you return the DVD late
- at the discretion of the library staff: the library staff
  can decide to end your membership

Unit 3, Grammar and Vocabulary, Exercise 10, page 30.

Student A
Look at the picture of Chris and follow the instructions.

Chris lived next door to you when you were thirteen
and you went to school together. What was she like?
Make notes about:

- her appearance
- her hobbies
- her habits
- her likes and dislikes
- your relationship with her

You know that Student B shares a flat with Chris
now. Talk to Student B and find out if Chris has
changed.

Unit 5, Speaking and Listening, Exercise 6, page 53.

Student A
Ask Student B these questions.

1 What alternative therapies do the photos show?
2 Why do people do alternative therapies?
3 Which alternative therapy would you like to try,
    and why?

Unit 7, Grammar, Exercise 9, page 79.

Student A
Tell Student B the story using suitable reporting verbs.

Frederick Forsyth sent the manuscript of *The Day of
the Jackal* to publishers, WH Allen. Two months later
it was returned with a note saying, 'We can't publish
this. It has no reader interest.' After several more
rejections, Hutchinson's said they would publish it.
The book became an international bestseller and was
made into a film.

Unit 7, Speaking and Listening, Exercise 7, page 80.

Student A, roleplay a conversation with Student B.

You think there should be stricter control of the press in terms of people's privacy. Newspapers should *not* be allowed to print stories about the private lives of public figures and famous celebrities because:

- damaging: psychologically to friends and family
- dangerous: running away from paparazzi/ encourages spying
- unfair: can't move around freely in public
- your ideas

Unit 8, Grammar and Listening, Exercise 12, page 84.

Student A
Complete eight clues about a familiar household object and read them to your partner. How quickly can he/she guess what the object is? Then write eight clues of your own for another object and test your partner again!

1 The first one _____ (invent) in 1827.
2 500 billion of them _____ (use) every year.
3 Their inventor died without _____ (recognise) for his invention.
4 They _____ usually _____ (sell) in a book or a box.
5 People who collect them _____ (call) phillumenists.
6 The early ones _____ (know) as 'lucifers'.
7 They should not _____ (give) to children to play with.
8 They can _____ (use) as toothpicks.

Answer: matches

Unit 9, Vocabulary, Exercise 6, page 97.

Student A
On a piece of paper, write down the name of someone you know who:

- is saving up for something at the moment
- finds it easy to save money
- is always in debt
- has recently blown a lot of money on something

Close your book. Show the names to Student B and explain why you wrote them.

Unit 10, Speaking and Listening, Exercise 6, page 111.

Student A

Situation One
You've been sharing a flat with Student B for a couple of months. Although you get on very well, you're very neat and tidy, and he/she isn't, so you end up doing most of the housework. You don't want to hurt Student B's feelings but need to make some suggestions about sharing the chores. Talk to Student B, using the prompts below, and your own ideas.

- take it in turns to clean the bathroom
- have a rota for doing the washing up
- hoover the carpet once a week at least
- put dirty clothes in the basket in the bathroom
- help take the bed linen and towels to the launderette
- do the shopping together every Saturday morning

Situation Two
Although Student B isn't very helpful in the flat, neither is he/she the party animal you thought he/she was. He/she is beginning to get bad-tempered and irritable, but you haven't asked what's wrong yet. Respond to Student B's suggestions by agreeing, apologising or making excuses.

Unit 11, Grammar and Listening, Exercise 12, page 117.

Riddle 3
Student A
Read riddle 3 and the solution below. Students B and C will try to solve the riddle. They can ask you for help using questions with *Yes/No* answers, but the same rules as before apply.

Solution: The poison was in the ice cubes in the punch. When the woman drank it, the ice was completely frozen. When the ice melted it poisoned the punch, killing the people who were still there.

Unit 11, Speaking and Listening, Exercise 5, page 124.

Student A

Socrates
Socrates, the Ancient Greek philosopher, was famous for responding to one question by asking another. He was strong willed and courageous about his beliefs, and was not afraid to say what he thought, or criticise those he thought were wrong. It is said that he let his hair grow long, and walked around barefoot and unwashed.

Bono
Lead singer and songwriter of U2, Bono is charming, clever and enthusiastic but also outspoken and argumentative. He has now gained a name for himself as a well-informed social activist and defender of the developing world. He mixes with Presidents, Prime Ministers and other influential people, campaigning for movements like Make Poverty History.

Jane Austen
She is one of Britain's greatest novelists and lived at the time of Napoleon and the Battle of Trafalgar. Although she led a quiet country life, she had a good education and was a great conversationalist. She was witty and an astute observer of human nature, which is reflected in novels like *Pride and Prejudice*.

Queen Elizabeth I
Britain's most famous queen is legendary for her courageous defence of England against Spain in the 16th century. She was very well educated and could speak Latin, French and German. However, she was short tempered and intolerant of foolish people. She was also very astute, creating a glamorous and powerful public image to inspire her people.

Student B Activities

Unit 1, Speaking and Listening, Exercise 6, page 13.

Student B

1 You work for a package holiday company and advertised for representatives in Greece. Answer Student A's questions using the prompts below.

- contract: June 1st – September 31st
- location: on Corfu, a Greek island
- working hours: mornings/evenings/six days a week
- interview date: April 14th

2 You saw an ad for a trainee manger in a department store. Phone the recruitment manager and ask for the information below.

- interview and start dates
- working hours/days off
- length of training
- salary/holidays

Unit 2, Speaking and Listening, Exercise 5, page 24.

Student B
Roleplay the situations with Student A. First, think about what you are going to say.

1 You work at the theatre box office. Be prepared to answer Student A's questions, using the following information:
The only seats you have for the day Student A wants are in the Upper Circle and have a partially obscured view. They are not reduced in price. Otherwise you may have some standby tickets or returns available on the day.

Notes:
- the Upper Circle: the top level of seats, quite high above the stage
- a partially obscured view: there is a pillar in front of the seats and you cannot see the left side of the stage
- standby tickets: tickets that are sold a short time before the performance, usually at a lower price
- returns: tickets that people bring back because they cannot use them

2 You want to join a video library. Talk to Student A, who works there. Ask how to join and what the rules of membership are. Ask for clarification of anything that you are not sure of in Student A's answers.

Unit 3, Grammar and Vocabulary, Exercise 10, page 30.

Student B
Look at the picture of Chris and follow the instructions.

You share a flat with Chris now. What is she like? Make notes about:

- her appearance
- her hobbies
- her habits
- her likes and dislikes
- your relationship with her

You know that Student A lived next door to Chris and went to school with her when they were thirteen. Talk to Student A and find out if Chris has changed.

Unit 3, Vocabulary, Exercise 3, page 34.

Student B
On a piece of paper, write down the name of:

- a sportsperson who is conceited,
- a singer who is infantile in their behaviour,
- an intriguing television programme.

Close your book. Show the names to Student A and explain why you wrote them.

Unit 5, Speaking and Listening, Exercise 6, page 53.

Student B
Ask Student A these questions.

1 What information can you get from the cartoon and the newspaper extracts?
2 Why do so many people suffer from stress nowadays?
3 What do you do to relax?

Unit 5, Grammar and Listening, Exercise 7, page 57.

Student B
Think of:

- something you'll stop doing and something you'll always remember doing when you leave school.
- two things you can try doing if you can't sleep.
- something you should try not to do and something you should remember to do at a job interview.
- something you sometimes stop to do and something you often forget to do on your way home from school

Tell your partner the two things, but not the situation. Can they guess the situation?

Unit 7, Grammar, Exercise 9, page 79.

Student B
Tell Student A the story using suitable reporting verbs.

After seeing the first showing of *The Wizard of Oz* in 1939, some studio bosses at MGM had doubts about it. When asked what he thought about it, one producer said, 'Judy Garland is too old for Dorothy. And that 'rainbow' song is no good. It slows the movie down.' Eventually, the film came out and became one of the most popular films ever made.

Unit 7, Speaking and Listening, Exercise 7, page 80.

Student B, roleplay a conversation with Student A.

You think there should be less control of the press in terms of people's privacy. Newspapers should be allowed to print stories about the private lives of public figures and famous celebrities because:

- role models: need to set good example
- justice: should not be treated differently to anybody else
- the price of fame!
- your ideas

Unit 8, Grammar and Listening, Exercise 12, page 84.

Student B
Complete eight clues about a familiar household object and read them to your partner. How quickly can he/she guess what the object is? Then write eight clues of your own for another object and test your partner again!

1 They _____ first _____ (produce) in the 1890s.
2 They _____ usually _____ (make) of metal or plastic.
3 Their basic design _____ never _____ (improve).
4 They _____ (wear) by Norwegians in World War II as a symbol of unity.
5 They _____ (know) as 'gems' in Swedish.
6 Only 1 in 10 _____ (use) for its intended purpose.
7 They can _____ (unfold) and _____ (use) to reset computerised devices.
8 They are supposed _____ (use) to hold papers together.

Answer: paper clips

Unit 9, Grammar, Exercise 9, page 95.

Student B, read the notes and think of answers to the questions. Then listen 'actively' to Student A's situation (ask questions, show sympathy, etc). Afterwards, tell Student A about your situation.

A friend of yours is not happy with his/her university course (why?), but he/she doesn't want to talk to anyone about it. You don't know what to do to help him/her.
What do you wish your friend would do or you could do?
What do you think your friend should(n't) have done/could've done before he/she started the course?

Unit 9, Vocabulary, Exercise 6, page 97.

Student B
On a piece of paper, write down the name of someone who:

- used to be well-off but isn't any more
- donates a lot of money to charity
- inherited a lot of money from a relative
- is worth at least £1 million

Close your book. Show the names to Student A and explain why you wrote them.

Unit 10, Speaking and Listening, Exercise 6, page 111.

Student A

Situation One
You've been sharing a flat with Student A for a couple of months. Although you get on very well, you think he/she's too neat and tidy. You hate doing housework and as he/she seems happy to do it, you let him/her. Respond to Student A's suggestions by either agreeing, apologising or making excuses.

Situation Two
Although Student A is neat and tidy, he/she is also a party lover. You're finding it difficult to study and his/her behaviour has begun to irritate you. You don't like confrontation but need to make some suggestions for changes, otherwise you'll have to move out. Talk to Student B, using the prompts below, and your own ideas.

- turn the music down after midnight
- clean up after parties
- don't invite gangs of friends round every night
- ask before borrowing my clothes
- don't eat all my food in the fridge
- put back CDs/books you borrow

Unit 11, Grammar and Listening, Exercise 12, page 117.

Riddle 1
Student B
Read riddle 1, and the solution below. Students A and C will try to solve the riddle. They can ask you for help using questions with *Yes/No* answers. They lose one point for each question, from a total of 10.

Solution: Romeo and Juliet were goldfish. Their bowl was knocked over and broken by a clumsy dog, and they died.

Unit 11, Speaking and Listening, Exercise 5, page 124.

Student B

Bill Gates
Founder of Microsoft, he is one of the richest men in world and an ambitious, innovative businessman who likes reading, playing bridge and golf. Since 1995, he has become one of the world's top philanthropists, donating over $7bn to good causes. His long-term vision is to improve the lives of millions of people across the globe.

Napoleon
Napoleon was a self-made, charismatic man whose strength of character and military genius made history. He had an impressive intellect and was a charming conversationalist. He was also arrogant, manipulative and authoritarian. He believed in the rights of man, but this did not extend to women: he thought their main purpose in life was to marry.

Madonna
Madonna is famous for being able to endlessly recreate herself and her image. She's also known to be tough and inscrutable, so it is difficult to know what she is really thinking. She is said to have an IQ of 140. She is also a great supporter of charities and human rights, especially those of women.

Check it out

Unit 1 Page 7

Present and past tenses

Present tenses
We use the Present Simple to talk about:
a habits and routines.
   He always **wears** suits.
b permanent situations around the present time.
   He now **shares** a flat with a friend.
c states (verbs not usually used in the continuous form),
   for example, *love*, *like*, *believe*, *think* (opinion), *know*,
   look (appearance).
   He still **loves** his leather jacket. He **looks** very fit.

Some verbs change their meaning and can be used in the
continuous form, For example, *think of/about*, *see* (go out
with), *look at*.

We use the Present Continuous to talk about:
a actions in progress at the time of speaking.
   He **is talking** on his mobile.
b temporary actions in progress around now.
   He**'s thinking** of buying his own flat.
c changes and developments.
   The effects **are** already **beginning** to show.

Perfect tenses
Present Perfect tenses link the past and the present. We
use the Present Perfect Simple to talk about:
a actions or
b states that began in the past and continue up to now.
   Mark**'s worked** for a large company for three months.
   [action]
   I**'ve known** him for five years. [state]
c completed past actions that happened at an
   unspecified time.
   He **has bought** some smart clothes.
d recent actions with a present relevance/result.
   He**'s changed** dramatically. (He looks very different now.)

We use the Present Perfect Continuous to emphasise the
continuity of actions that began in the past and continue
to the present. The Present Perfect could often be used in
examples like this.
He**'s been working out** since July.
He**'s worked out** since July.

Past tenses
We use the Past Simple to talk about actions or events
completed at a specific time in the past.
He **sold** his motorbike two months ago.
We use the Past Continuous to talk about actions that
were:
a in progress at a specific time in the past (this often
   provides background to other past events)
   Last May, Mark **was studying** business administration.
b interrupted by a shorter past action.
   I **was having** a coffee when he walked in.

We use the Past Perfect to make it clear which was the
first of two past actions.
Before Colin changed, he **hadn't been** to the hairdresser's
for two years.

Unit 1 Page 11

Articles – indefinite, definite and zero article – ø (no article)

The indefinite article – *a/an*
We use *a/an* with a singular countable noun when we
don't know what it refers to, or it doesn't matter which
one. This is because:
a it is one of many of the same class.
   I am **a** descendant of an Irish family.
b we mention a person or thing for the first time.
   Mum was working in **a** local restaurant.

We also use *a/an* with phrases to talk about frequency.
158,000 people **a** day/month/year

The definite article – *the*
We use *the* (with any noun) when both speakers know
what they are talking about. This might be because the
thing or person:
a was mentioned before.
   She's working in a restaurant. **The** restaurant belonged
   to her family.
b is unique. There is only one.
   Half of **the** population live in **the** capital, Buenos Aires.
c is defined specifically by the words that follow.
   My grandmother is still **the** head of **the** family.

We also use *the* with:
superlatives
The largest Japanese population in the world outside
Japan is in São Paulo.
ordinal numbers
The second largest Oktoberfest in the world takes place
in Blumenau.
decades, centuries
in **the** 1950s; in **the** eighteenth century

Ø (no article)
We use no article with plural and uncountable nouns when
we make general statements about people and things.
But we still observe **Polish customs** at home.
Life was very hard and over one million people left Ireland.

We also use ø with:
most **place names**, for example, countries, continents,
cities, towns, states.
Australia, North America, New York, Blumenau, California.
Exceptions: the USA, the UK, the Czech Republic.
months, years
in **August**; in **1849**

Unit 2 Page 17

Future forms

We use *will*:
a to make predictions based on our opinions or
   expectations. We often use *will* with phrases like *I think*,
   I'm sure, *I expect*, or adverbs like *probably*, *definitely*.
   I**'ll probably** have to go to the park with him.
   I**'m sure** Professor Evans won't notice.
b to express a decision made at the moment of speaking.
   I think I**'ll** give it a miss.
We use *going to*:
a to talk about plans or intentions for the future.
   I**'m going** to look at that flat for rent.
b to make a prediction based on evidence you have now.
   You **are going** to have a busy weekend!
   (I know all the things my friend has to do at the weekend.)

We use the Present Continuous to talk about a future arrangement:
Are you **doing** anything on Saturday afternoon?
My aunt and uncle **are coming** to lunch on Sunday.

NB The Present Continuous is not used for general plans and intentions.
NOT I'm losing weight. I'm going to lose weight before the summer.

We use the Present Simple:
a to talk about a future event which is part of a timetable.
  The lecture **starts** in ten minutes.
b in a subordinate clause after words like *when, as soon as, before, after, until*. The main clause contains a future form.
  I'll give you a ring **as soon as** my aunt and uncle leave.

We use the Future Continuous (*will* + *be* + Present Participle):
a to talk about an action that will be in progress at a particular time in the future.
  By the time we're sixty, more people **will be speaking** Hinglish than 'standard' English.
  Will you **be working** on it at five thirty?
b to talk about events that will happen as part of the normal course of events, or routine.
  They**'ll be bringing** my little cousin. (They always do.)

As with other continuous tenses, we do not use state verbs (*be, believe, forget, like, want,* ...) with the Future Continuous.

We use the Future Perfect (*will* + *have* + Past Participle) to talk about an action that will be completed before a particular time in the future.
In 100 years' time half the world's languages **will have disappeared**.
Will you **have finished** it by then?

The Future Continuous and the Future Perfect are often used with *by* (*2050, next year, then, the time* ...) and *in* (*ten years, two months*).

Unit 3 Page 29

Present and past habits

Present/Past Continuous
We use the Present or Past Continuous + *always, constantly, forever* to talk about a habit which is repeated more than usual, which the speaker finds unexpected or annoying.
She**'s constantly** telling Ben that he spends too much time on the computer.
She **was always going** into my room and taking things without asking.

will/would + infinitive
We use *will/would* + infinitive without *to* to talk about behaviour which is typical or characteristic of the person. They can describe both pleasant and annoying habits.
She**'ll turn up** at eleven and act as if nothing's wrong.
We**'d watch** TV and eat takeaway pizza together.

used to + infinitive
We use *used to* + infinitive to talk about a past state or repeated past actions.
I **used to feel** more like a father than an older brother.
She **used to go** on peace marches and campaign to ban the bomb.

used to and *would*
Would is not used to talk about past states. (NOT I'd feel more like a father than an older brother.)
We can introduce new topics with *used to* and we do not need to specify a time.
I **used to** eat a lot of chips and burgers, but now I eat healthy food. (NOT I'd eat ...)

We use *would* when the topic has been established and we usually specify the time.
My dad used to work nights. He**'d** come home at six in the morning and we**'d** have breakfast together, then he used to take me to school.

Present or Past Simple
The Present or Past Simple can be used for talking about habits and states.
He **doesn't** speak much English.
He **tells** her to be home by ten.
She **was** fit and healthy because she **played** outside all day.
She never **understood** the concept of privacy.

Most texts describing habits contain a mixture of forms, for variety.

Unit 3 Page 35

would prefer/would rather

We use *would prefer* and *would rather* to talk about present and future preferences.

We use *would prefer/would rather* to:

a refer to what we (the subject of the sentence) want to do.

  would prefer + (not) + infinitive
  She **would** ('d) prefer to marry someone 'more like her'.
  I **would** ('d) prefer not to eat leaves.

  would rather + (not) + infinitive without *to*
  I **would** ('d) rather eat pizzas.
  'I **would** ('d) rather not marry you, Ted.'

b refer to what the subject (of the first clause) wants someone else to do.

  would prefer + object + infinitive
  He would ('d) prefer **us to go** to a cricket match.
  She would ('d) prefer **us not to have** fish and chips.

  would rather + Past Simple clause
  I would ('d) rather **we tried** something different.
  He would ('d) rather **we didn't go** to my mother's for lunch.

Unit 4 Page 39

Past Perfect Simple and Continuous

Past Perfect Simple
subject + *had* (not) + Past Participle

We use the Past Perfect Simple to talk about:
a actions that happened before a specific point in the past.
  By the age of six, he **had played** before the Austrian empress.
b states before a specific point in the past.
  When she made her crossing, she **had been paralysed** for four years.

Past Perfect Continuous
had (not) + *been* + Past Participle

We use it to emphasise longer actions or events over a period of time up to, or shortly before, a specific point in the past.
Just before his death, he**'d been composing** the *Requiem.*
When the train finally **arrived**, we**'d been waiting** for two hours.

We often use linking words or time phrases with the Past Perfect tenses, for example, *when, after, because, as, before, by, by the time.*
By the age of six, **he had played** before the Austrian empress.
When she made her crossing, she **had been** paralysed for four years.

Unit 4 Page 40

Participle clauses

verb + *-ing* vs *having* + Past Participle

In Present Participle clauses, we use the Present Participle: verb + *-ing.*
Using only her breathing …,

We use a Present Participle clause when both actions in a sentence happen at the same time, or one after the other.
He worked all over Europe during the next seventeen years, finally **settling** (and finally settled) in Vienna.

In Past Participle clauses, we use *having* + Past Participle.
Having arrived in France, …

We use a Past Participle clause when one action in a sentence happened at an earlier time.
Having arrived (after she had arrived) in France, Mrs Lester said, 'I'm just thrilled!'

We use participle clauses to join two clauses instead of using linking words like *and, after, because, so, while.*

Participle and main clauses must have the same subject.
Driving through the park, **he** was struck by another bolt of lightning.
When **he** was driving through the park, **he** was struck by another bolt of lightning.
NOT ~~Driving through the park, a bolt of lightning struck him.~~

Unit 5 Page 51

Infinitives and gerunds

Infinitives
We use an infinitive with *to*:

a to explain the purpose of an action.
  Some redheads dye their hair **to avoid** jokes about 'carrot tops'.
  It has been used **to treat** blindness.

b after certain verbs.
  So you **tend to feel** tired.
  They still **refuse to give up** their high heels!

Other verbs like this are: *agree, allow, appear, attempt, encourage, expect, force, help*, persuade, plan, promise.*
**help can also be followed by the infinitive without *to*

c after certain adjectives.
  It is **dangerous to wake** a sleepwalker.
  You're **likely to get** distracted and overeat.

Other examples: *difficult, easy, helpful*

Infinitive without *to*
We use an infinitive without *to*:

after *let* and *make*.
They may not **let** you **touch** them!
… that **makes** you **lose** or **gain** weight.

Gerunds
We use a gerund (*-ing* form) in the same way as a noun:

a as the subject of the sentence.
  Sleeping more than usual disrupts your sleep cycle.
  Perhaps **being** tougher than the rest gave famous redheads …
  Taking aspirin reduces your chances of having a heart attack.

b after certain verbs.
  If you **fancy having** a snack before bedtime …
  Most doctors **suggest leading** the person gently back to bed.

Other examples: *avoid, can't stand, consider, don't mind, enjoy, imagine, involve, risk*

c after prepositions.
  Compared with **walking** barefoot, …
  Next time you feel like **taking** a dose of vitamin C, …

Infinitive or gerund
The following verbs can be followed by the infinitive with *to* or the gerund, with no difference in meaning: *begin, continue, hate, love, prefer, start.*

be used to and *get used to*
I'm **used to wearing** glasses. (The situation is familiar to me, I am comfortable with it.)
I'm **getting used to wearing** glasses. (The situation is becoming more familiar, but I am not comfortable with it yet.)

Unit 5 Page 57

-ing/to

Verbs followed by an infinitive or a gerund, with a difference in meaning.

remember + infinitive
To remember something, then do it.
I **remembered to get** your favourite cheesecake.

remember + gerund
To do something and remember it later.
Do you **remember saying** that you wouldn't do any more fad diets?

forget + infinitive
To forget about something, so you don't do it.
I **forgot to tell** you.

forget + gerund
To do something and (not) forget it later.
I'll never (I won't) **forget going** shopping with you when you were on that Beverly Hills diet.

forget + gerund is usually used in the negative.

try + infinitive
To make an effort to do something difficult.
I've been **trying to lose** weight for ages.

try + gerund
To do something and see what happens.
Have you **tried turning** it on?

try + gerund is often used for giving advice.

stop + infinitive
To stop something in order to do something else.
They went hunting all day and **stopped to eat** one big meal in the evening.

stop + gerund
To no longer do something.
I haven't **stopped eating** cheesecake.

like + infinitive
To do something because it is a good idea.
I always **like to clear up** straight after a meal.

like + gerund
To enjoy something.
It even sounds as if you **like doing** it.

Unit 6 Page 61

Modal and related verbs

Modal auxiliary verbs are widely used but we can't use them in all tenses. We use other verbs to express the same meanings in other tenses. They have no -s form and do not change their form in other ways. NOT ~~musted~~

Obligation and necessity
We use *must* to talk about what is right or necessary. There is no choice.
A good spy **must** be an excellent driver.

Have to means the same as *must*. As it is not a full modal verb, it can be used in all tenses.
A pigeon **had to** wear a camera around its neck.

NB *Have to/have got to* are often used to indicate that the obligation is external, while *must* is used to show it comes from the speaker.

We rarely use the modal auxiliary verb *need*. In this example, it is used as a main verb (not an auxiliary).

He **needs** to be extremely courageous.

Related verbs
We use verbs like *be required to/obliged to* in all tenses to refer to an 'outside authority' that gives permission.
Another pigeon **was required** to wear a camera around its neck.
The rats **are obliged to** run around a specified area.

Duty and advice
We use *should, shouldn't, ought to* and *oughtn't to* to give our opinion or advice. They are also sometimes used for rules and instructions. The meaning is weaker than *must*.
Animals **shouldn't** suffer like this.
He **ought to** be an expert dancer.

Related verbs
We use *be supposed to* to talk about what should/shouldn't happen according to rules/what is generally expected. It is not used in continuous tenses.
They're **supposed to** be free.
Animals are **not supposed to** suffer like this.

No obligation
We use *don't have to* and *needn't* to mean 'It isn't necessary'.
He **doesn't have to** be glamorous.

Needn't is a modal verb and has the same meaning as *don't need to*. The modal auxiliary *need* has no past tense form.
Human divers **don't need to/needn't** do this.

Related verbs
Human divers are **not required to** do the job.
Secret agents are **not obliged to** be glamorous.

Ability
We use *can/can't* and *could/couldn't* to describe ability, or lack of ability.
Sea lions **can** see and hear extremely well underwater.
Pigeons **could** fly at great speed.

To describe the completion of a specific action in the past we use *be able to*, not *could* in affirmative sentences. In negative sentences both *be able to* and *could* are possible.
Unfortunately, he wasn't **able to/couldn't** fly very far with it, but he **was able to** ~~NOT could~~ return on foot two days later.

Related verbs
The rats **managed to** find nine mines in one day.
The pigeon **succeeded in** returning on foot two days later.

Permission
We use *can/could* to ask for and give permission.
Can/Could I ask you a question?
You **can** stay out late tonight./I **couldn't** stay out late when I was younger.

Related verbs
Why **has** cruelty to animals **been allowed** in this country?
Scientists **are permitted to** treat animals badly.

Prohibition
We use *mustn't, can't* and *couldn't* to say that something is not permitted.
Ordinary people **can't** treat animals badly.

Related verbs
Ordinary people are not allowed to treat animals badly.
UK citizens **were forbidden** to shoot pigeons.

Possibility
We use:
a *can* to talk about things which are generally possible.
  It's very hot here in summer but it **can** rain heavily in winter.
b *could/might* to say that a specific thing is possibly true.
  There **could/might** be life on other planets.
c *can/could* to suggest a possible future action, not that it is likely to happen.
  If we finish early tonight, we **can/could** go for a meal.
d *might* to talk about an uncertain future intention.
  If we finish work early tonight, we **might** go for a meal.

Related verbs
The Navy is **likely to** (might) start using other marine animals for this work.
They **are bound to** (are sure to) get better at it in future.

Reported speech

Basic rules

When we report what people said we usually:

- move the original verb 'one tense back' except for the Past Perfect and modal verbs (see below).

- change pronouns as necessary.
  'I've found you a husband.'
  He said/told me (that) he had found me a husband.

- use *say* (*that*) or *tell* + obj (*that*) to report statements.

- use *ask* + (obj) + *if/whether* for questions.
  The word order of the question becomes a statement.
  He asked (me) if/whether I could write.

- use *tell* + obj + (*not*) + inf to report commands.
  He told me to meet him there that night.

- use *ask* + obj + (*not*) + inf to report requests.
  He asked me to take the fish finger out of the soup.

We use reporting verbs like: *say, tell, ask, reply, answer, enquire, announce, order.*

References to time, place and *this/that*

- **place:** *here* → there

- **time:** *now* → then; *tomorrow/next week* → the following day/week or the next day/week; *yesterday/last week* → the day/week before; *tonight/today/this evening* → that night/day/evening

- *this* → that

- *this/that* → the

Modal verbs

- *can/may* → could/might

- *must* → must or had to

Other modal verbs (*could, would, should, might*) do not change.
'You should pack your things. We must go to Hong Kong tomorrow.'
He said I should pack my things because we must/had to go to Hong Kong the following day.

No change

It is not necessary to change the verb tenses in reported speech when:

- we use a Present Simple/Present Perfect reporting verb.
  He says/has said he'll be back next week.

- the statement is reported soon after it was said so the situation is still relevant.
  He said he'll be back next week. (It's the same week.)

- the reporter believes that the fact/opinion is still true.
  Dad said that secrets always come out in the end.

Reporting verbs and their patterns

We use a great variety of verbs to summarise what people say. Some of them have more than one pattern.

A

1 Verb + [*that*]
He explained (that) four-member groups were out.
She admitted (that) she had given Norma Jean the wrong advice.
Others: *agree, complain, deny, insist, promise, recommend, regret*

2 Verb + object + [*that*]
He warned him (that) he was wasting his time.
Others: *persuade, tell, advise, promise, remind*

3 Verb + [*not*] infinitive
He offered to pay them $130 for the rights.
The publishers promised to look at her book again.
Others: *agree, decide, threaten, refuse*

4 Verb + object + [*not*] infinitive
She advised her not to become a model.
The executive recommended him to give up.
Others: *ask, encourage, invite, order, persuade, remind, tell, warn*

5 Verb + [*not*] gerund
She suggested getting a job as a secretary.
The boys regretted not making a better deal.
Others: *admit, advise, deny, recommend*

6 Verb + preposition + [*not*] gerund
They apologised for rejecting her book.
Others: *insist on, object to*

7 Verb + object + preposition + [*not*] gerund
Publishers criticised her book for being too long.
Others: *accuse sby of, blame sby/something for, congratulate sby on, praise sby for, suspect sby of*

More than one pattern is possible with these verbs:
admit, advise, agree, deny, insist, promise, recommend, regret, remind, suggest, warn.

B

We use *that* + *should* clause to provide information about the object. We use it with verbs that express the idea that an action is necessary, for example, *recommend, suggest, insist, propose, demand.*
The woman suggested that Norma Jean should get married.
They recommended that she should make the book shorter.

We can also use these verbs with *that* + Present/Past Simple clause.
He insisted that they take/took the money.
She proposed that she learn/learnt secretarial work.

The Passive

Present Simple	A transmitter is worn on the body and digital messages are sent via the body's electrical field.
Present Continuous	According to a spokeswoman, the invention is being welcomed by coffee-lovers and couch potatoes everywhere.
Past Simple	'Fresh Brew' was created by British coffee company 'Beans R Us'.
Past Continuous	When we last heard, the 'mirror' was still being developed in a lab in France.
Present Perfect	Once a profile of your lifestyle has been built up …
Past Perfect	When Lois realised she had been followed to her front door, she quickly activated her bag.
Modal verbs in passive	The computer shows you how your the appearance will be affected in five years' time. It can be switched on by text message. Music and games could be downloaded in seconds via your right arm. It should not be used as protection from wild animals.
Going to	It is going to be shown at the 'New Investors' show next month.
The passive infinitive	There's one drawback: it needs to be filled with coffee and water first. The company expects Body Download to be launched next year.
The passive gerund	It's a 'must have' if you are worried about being attacked. Nobody likes being told about their bad habits, especially by a computer!

Form
The passive is made with a form of *be* and a Past Participle.

The agent
If we mention the agent, we use *by*.
'Fresh Brew' was created by British coffee company 'Beans R Us'.
In the above example, we mention the agent (Beans R Us) because it is new information.

We don't mention the agent if it is obvious,
A transmitter is worn on the body. (We know it is worn by a person.)

or unknown,
Lois realised she had been followed. (We do not know who followed her.)

or unimportant,
It will be shown at the 'New Inventors' show. (Who will show it is not important.)

Contexts for the passive
We usually avoid the passive in informal language.
We can use *you* or *they* to refer to people in general.
'Look! You can switch it on by text message.'
'They expect to launch Body Download next year.'

The passive is common in newspaper reports and academic writing because it makes the style more impersonal and objective.

The passive with two objects
Some verbs can have two objects, and either object can become the subject in the passive: it depends where the writer wants to put the focus.

It will show people the consequences of an unhealthy lifestyle.
People will be shown the consequences of an unhealthy lifestyle.
The consequences of an unhealthy lifestyle will be shown to people.

It gives anyone who touches it an electric shock.
Anyone who touches it is given an electric shock.
An electric shock is given to anyone who touches it.

Other verbs like this are: *send, promise, teach, hand, offer, pay.*

Expressing dissatisfaction and regret

wish/if only
We use *I wish/If only* + past to talk about present regrets.
If only I had a knife.

We use *I wish/If only* + Past Perfect to talk about past regrets.
I wish I'd gone first.
If only I'd done some market research.

We use *I wish/If only* + *would(n't)* + infinitive when we want something to happen, or a situation to change.
I wish he'd sing something different.
NB We cannot use *would* for an impossible change.
I wish he'd be older.

should
We use *I should(n't)* + infinitive when we are unhappy about a present situation.
I should be selling umbrellas. (I'm not selling umbrellas, and I'm unhappy about this.)

We use *I should(n't) have* + perfect infinitive when we are unhappy about a past action.
I should have bought her some jewellery. (I didn't buy her jewellery, and I'm unhappy about this.)

could have
We use *I could have* + perfect infinitive when something was possible, but didn't happen.
I could've been a taxi driver. (It was possible for me to be a taxi driver, but it didn't happen: I'm a lorry driver now.)

had better
We use *I'd better (not)* + infinitive when we think something is the best thing to do/not to do in the situation.
I'd better turn off the TV.

Conditionals

Zero conditional

If + present, + present to talk about situations which are always true.
If I **meet** someone in a situation like that, I **get** very nervous.
If you **get** proper financial advice, it **can** be a good investment.

First conditional

If + present, + *will/won't/might/could* + infinitive to talk about a possible situation in the future.
I**'ll lend** you the money, provided that you **pay** it back by the end of the month.
I**'ll never** know what it's like unless I **try** it. (unless = *if not*)

Second conditional

If + past, + *would/might/could* + infinitive to talk about an unlikely or imaginary situation in the present or future.
I **wouldn't do** it if you **paid** me!
I**'d go** as long as I **could take** a friend with me.

Third conditional

If + Past Perfect + *would/might/could have* + perfect infinitive to talk about an imaginary situation in the past.
If I**'d been able** to afford it, I**'d have gone** with them.
Companies like Google and eBay **might** never **have existed** if those people **hadn't taken** the risk.

Mixed conditionals combine clauses from the second and third conditional types.

1 We use this pattern to talk about the effects of an imaginary present situation/state on the past:
If + Past Simple, *would(n't) have* + perfect infinitive
If I **didn't get** seasick, I**'d have gone** too.
(I get seasick. → I didn't go.)
If I **had** a really great voice, I**'d have done** the same. (I don't have a really great voice. → I didn't do the same.)

2 We use this pattern to talk about the consequences in the present of an imaginary past situation:
If + Past Perfect, *would(n't)* + infinitive
If I**'d had** more time to prepare myself for it, I**'d go**.
(I didn't have time. → I'm not going.)
I**'d lend** you the money if you**'d paid** off some of your other debts. (You didn't pay off your other debts. → I don't lend you the money.)

Relative clauses

We use *who(m)*, *which*, *that*, *whose*, *where*, *when* in relative clauses. They are like adjectives, and we use them after nouns, or noun phrases, to describe or give information about a person, thing, possessions, places and time.
There are two kinds of relative clauses: **defining** and **non-defining**.

A Defining clauses are necessary to give **essential** information about exactly which person/thing is being talked about in the sentence. Commas are never used.

1 We can use *that* instead of *who/which* in defining clauses.
It's an area **which/that all** Fleming's friends loved visiting because of its secluded beaches.

2 When the relative pronoun is the **object** of the relative clause, you can omit *who/which/that*.
It's an area (**which/that**) all Fleming's friends loved visiting because of its secluded beaches.
(All Fleming's friends loved visiting the area.)

3 When the relative pronoun is the subject of the relative clause, you cannot omit *who/which/that*.
It was the man **who/that** later killed him, Mark Chapman.

B There are two kinds of **non-defining** clauses.

a To give **extra**, **non-essential** information about the person or thing being talked about in the sentence.
He had just arrived home with his wife, **who had been recording a new single that afternoon**.
The building, **which many considered ugly at first**, is today a UNESCO World Heritage site.

b To add a comment about the first part of the sentence.
People from all over the world now visit the Dakota, **which shows how deeply admired John still is**.
Defining clauses **always** need commas: on either side if it's in the middle of the sentence, or before if it's at the end.
We never use *that* in non-defining clauses.

C Prepositions in relative clauses

Prepositions usually go at the end of the clause in conversational English. In more formal written and spoken contexts, they can go at the beginning, but must be followed by *which* (for things) or *whom* (for people).
The master bedroom still contains the desk (which/that) he wrote **at**.
= The master bedroom still contains the desk **at which** he wrote.
John had earlier signed a copy of it for a fan (who/that) he'd shaken hands **with**.
= John had earlier signed a copy of it for a fan **with whom** he'd shaken hands.

Past modals: Speculating about the past

We use past modals of probability to speculate and make guesses based on our knowledge of the situation, or the evidence available.

must/can't/couldn't

We use *must* + perfect infinitive (*have* + Past Participle) when it seems certain that something happened.
We use *can't/couldn't* + perfect infinitive when it seems certain that something *didn't* happen.
The man **must have been** thirsty.
The barman **can't/couldn't have** liked the look of the man.

1

might/may/could

We use *might/may/could* + perfect infinitive when we think it is logically possible that something happened/ didn't happen.
The barman could've been scared.
He might've just walked across the desert.
The barman may have recognised him from the newspapers.

NB The negative form is used with *may/might not*, but not *couldn't*.
He may/might not have known his photo was in the papers.

The passive form is *must/can't/couldn't/might/could/may* + passive perfect infinitive (*have been* + Past Participle).
The barman might've been insulted by the man in some way.

The continuous form is *must/can't/couldn't/might/could/ may* + continuous perfect infinitive (*have been* + Present Participle).
The barman could've been playing a joke on him.

might vs could

1 The man could've helped him – but he refused.
  Here *could've* means it was possible for something to happen, but it didn't. (ie, it was possible for the man to help him, but he didn't.)

2 The barman could/might/may have wanted just to frighten him.
  Here, *could*, *may* and *might* can be used to say we think it is logically possible that something happened.

Unit 11 Page 122

Impersonal report structures

We use *it* + passive to report what people generally believe or say is true, and when it is not important to mention who the people are. We use this structure with verbs like *say*, *think*, *believe*, *know*, *claim*, *expect*.
It is thought that famous brand names are increasingly using DNA technology to protect their products from unauthorised copying.

We can also start the sentence with the person/thing that is being talked about and use subject + passive + infinitive.
The **infinitive** is used to report an event that happened in the same time frame.
The hairs were thought to be from a cat.

We use subject + passive + perfect infinitive to make it clear that an event happened before the time it is reported.
He was said to have died in prison during the French Revolution.

We use *is expected* + infinitive to report future events.
The new technology is expected to ensure the authenticity of sports items for years to come.

We can also use the passive and continuous forms of the infinitives in these structures.
Louis XVII was claimed to have been rescued and replaced by an impostor.
Famous brand names are increasingly thought to be using DNA technology to protect their products from unauthorised copying.

Unit 12 Page 127

Quantifiers

very few, hardly any, few, a few, quite a few (+ countable nouns)
We use *quite a few* and *a few* in positive sentences, and we use *few*, *very few* and *hardly any* in negative sentences. *Quite* emphasises the positive and *very* emphasises the negative.

very little, little, a little (+ uncountable nouns)
We use *a little* in positive sentences. NB we cannot say *quite a little*.
We use *little* and *very little* in negative sentences. *Very* emphasises the negative.

no (+ countable and uncountable nouns)
no means 'not any'.
There's no water left.
No tourists were allowed into the castle.

We cannot use *no* without a noun, so we use *none* instead.
I had some biscuits, but there are none left.
NOT there are no left

A lot of, lots of, quite a lot of, a great deal of (+ countable and uncountable nouns)
A lot of and *lots of* mean the same.
Quite a lot of is similar in meaning to *quite a few*.
We use *a great deal of* in more formal contexts.

whole (+ singular noun)
whole means 'all of'.
I had a terrible cold and spent the whole/all weekend in bed.

several, a number of (+ countable nouns)
several and *a number of* mean 'more than a few, but not a lot'.
Several/A number of people clapped before the orchestra had stopped playing.

each, every (+ singular noun)
We use *each* and *every* to talk about all the members of a group. We can use *each* to talk about two or more things: *every* refers to three or more.
The girl had three earrings in each ear.
Every/Each time I hear that song, I think of summer.

In many contexts we can use either word, although there is a difference in meaning: *every time* means 'all the times' and implies a large number; *each time* means we are thinking of the times separately, one by one.
We cannot use *every* without a noun or pronoun.
Every one/Each of these rings is valuable.
NOT Every of these rings is valuable.

any (+ countable and uncountable nouns)
We can use *any* to mean 'all, it doesn't matter which'.
You can borrow any of these books – I've read them all.
Any student will tell you they hate studying for exams.

most (+ countable and uncountable nouns)
We can use *most* to make a generalisation.
Most cafés serve cappuccino nowadays.

To talk about a more specific group, we use *most of the*.
Most of the cafés round here are very expensive.

Irregular verbs

Verb	Past Simple	Past Participle		Verb	Past Simple	Past Participle
arise	arose	arisen		lean	leaned/leant	leaned/leant
be	was/were	been		learn	learned/learnt	learned/learnt
bear	bore	borne		leave	left	left
beat	beat	beaten		lend	lent	lent
become	became	become		let	let	let
begin	began	begun		lie	lay	lain
bend	bent	bent		lose	lost	lost
bet	bet	bet		make	made	made
bind	bound	bound		mean	meant	meant
bite	bit	bitten		meet	met	met
blow	blew	blown		pay	paid	paid
break	broke	broken		put	put	put
bring	brought	brought		read	read	read
broadcast	broadcast	broadcast		ride	rode	ridden
build	built	built		ring	rang	rung
burn	burnt/burned	burnt/burned		rise	rose	risen
burst	burst	burst		run	ran	run
buy	bought	bought		say	said	said
can	could	been able to		see	saw	seen
cast	cast	cast		seek	sought	sought
catch	caught	caught		sell	sold	sold
choose	chose	chosen		send	sent	sent
come	came	come		set	set	set
cost	cost	cost		shake	shook	shaken
cut	cut	cut		shine	shone	shone
deal	dealt	dealt		shoot	shot	shot
do	did	done		show	showed	shown
draw	drew	drawn		shut	shut	shut
drink	drank	drunk		sing	sang	sung
drive	drove	driven		sit	sat	sat
eat	ate	eaten		sleep	slept	slept
fall	fell	fallen		smell	smelled/smelt	smelled/smelt
feed	fed	fed		speak	spoke	spoken
feel	felt	felt		speed	sped	sped
fight	fought	fought		spell	spelt/spelled	spelt/spelled
find	found	found		spend	spent	spent
fling	flung	flung		spill	spilt	spilt
fly	flew	flown		split	split	split
forbid	forbade	forbidden		spoil	spoilt	spoilt
forecast	forecast	forecast		spring	sprang	sprung
forget	forgot	forgotten		stand	stood	stood
forgive	forgave	forgiven		steal	stole	stolen
freeze	froze	frozen		stick	stuck	stuck
get	got	got		strike	struck	struck
give	gave	given		swim	swam	swum
go	went	gone		take	took	taken
grind	ground	ground		teach	taught	taught
grow	grew	grown		tell	told	told
have	had	had		think	thought	thought
hang	hung	hung		throw	threw	thrown
hear	heard	heard		understand	understood	understood
hide	hid	hidden		wake	woke	woken
hit	hit	hit		wear	wore	worn
hold	held	held		weave	wove	woven
keep	kept	kept		win	won	won
know	knew	known		withdraw	withdrew	withdrawn
lay	laid	laid		write	wrote	written
lead	led	led				

Pronunciation table

CONSONANTS

Symbol	Key word	Other common spellings
/p/	**p**ark	ha**pp**y
/b/	**b**ath	ru**bb**ish
/t/	**t**ie	bu**tt**er walk**ed**
/d/	**d**ie	te**dd**y bear
/k/	**c**at	**k**ey s**ch**ool che**ck**
/g/	**g**ive	**gh**ost bi**gg**er
/tʃ/	**ch**air	ma**tch** na**t**ural
/dʒ/	**j**eans	a**g**e ga**dg**et sol**di**er
/f/	**f**ace	co**ff**ee **ph**one lau**gh**
/v/	**v**isit	o**f**
/θ/	**th**row	
/ð/	**th**ey	
/s/	**s**ell	**c**inema li**s**ten **ps**ychology **sc**enery me**ss**age
/z/	**z**oo	no**s**e bu**zz**
/ʃ/	**sh**op	**s**ure ambi**ti**on
/ʒ/	mea**s**ure	revi**si**on
/h/	**h**ot	**wh**o
/m/	**m**ap	su**mm**er
/n/	**n**ot	**kn**ow su**nn**y
/ŋ/	si**ng**	thi**n**k
/l/	**l**ot	ba**ll**
/r/	**r**oad	so**rr**y **wr**ite
/j/	**y**ellow	**u**sually **Eu**rope b**eau**tiful n**ew**
/w/	**w**arm	**o**ne **wh**ale q**u**ick

VOWELS

Symbol	Key word	Other common spellings
Long and short vowels		
/iː/	f**ee**t	n**ie**ce r**ea**d th**e**se k**ey** rec**ei**pt pol**i**ce
/ɪ/	f**i**t	g**y**m g**u**itar pr**e**tty
/i/	happ**y**	spaghett**i** marri**ed**
/e/	b**e**d	**a**ny br**ea**d fr**ie**nd
/æ/	b**a**d	
/ɑː/	b**a**th	**ar**t h**al**f **au**nt h**ear**t
/ɒ/	b**o**ttle	w**a**tch
/ɔː/	b**ou**ght	sp**or**t y**our** d**au**ghter sm**al**l dr**aw** w**ar** fl**oor**
/ʊ/	p**u**t	b**oo**k c**oul**d
/uː/	b**oo**t	r**u**de bl**ue** fr**ui**t m**o**ve sh**oe** gr**ou**p fl**ew**
/ʌ/	b**u**t	s**o**me c**ou**sin
/ɜː/	b**ir**d	s**er**ve **ear**ly t**ur**n
/ə/	broth**er**	th**e** **a**bout act**or** col**our**
Diphthongs (two vowel sounds pronounced as one)		
/eɪ/	gr**ey**	l**a**ke w**ai**t pl**ay** **eigh**t br**ea**k
/əʊ/	g**o**ld	sh**ow** c**oa**t
/aɪ/	b**y**	l**i**ke d**ie** h**igh** h**eigh**t **eye**s b**uy**
/aʊ/	br**ow**n	ab**ou**t
/ɔɪ/	b**oy**	n**oi**sy
/ɪə/	h**ear**	h**ere** b**ee**r
/eə/	h**air**	th**ere** th**eir** squ**are** teddy b**ear**
/ʊə/	s**ure**	p**oor** t**our**
Triphthongs (three vowel sounds pronounced as one)		
/eɪə/	pl**ayer**	
/əʊə/	l**ower**	
/aɪə/	t**ire**d	
/aʊə/	fl**ower**	